SIXTY FEET, SIX INCHES

SIXTY FEET, SIX INCHES

A Hall of Fame Pitcher & a Hall of Fame Hitter
Talk about How the Game Is Played

Bob Gibson & Reggie Jackson

with Lonnie Wheeler

Doubleday
New York London Toronto
Sydney Auckland

ᴰᴰ

DOUBLEDAY

www.doubleday.com

DOUBLEDAY and the DD colophon are registered trademarks
of Random House, Inc.

Book design by Michael Collica

Library of Congress Cataloging-in-Publication Data
Gibson, Bob, 1935–
Sixty feet, six inches : a Hall of Fame pitcher & a Hall of Fame hitter talk about
how the game is played / by Bob Gibson and Reggie Jackson, with Lonnie
Wheeler.—1st ed.
p. cm.
1. Batting (Baseball)—Anecdotes. 2. Pitching (Baseball)—Anecdotes.
3. Gibson, Bob, 1935—Anecdotes. 4. Jackson, Reggie—Anecdotes. I. Jackson,
Reggie. II. Wheeler, Lonnie. III. Title.
GV869.G53 2006
796.357—dc22   2009010573

ISBN 978-0-385-52869-6

PRINTED IN THE UNITED STATES OF AMERICA

1 3 5 7 9 10 8 6 4 2

First Edition

*To Kimberly Jackson, who never saw me play: Some words
about the past, and what great fun it was—RJ*

To Wendy, who has been my life after baseball—BG

CONTENTS

SIXTY FEET, SIX INCHES

INTRODUCTION

There was a time when Bob Gibson was loath to talk baseball—to talk *anything*—with a fellow from another team. It was part of his mystique, which translated into the game's deadliest competitive edge, with which—along with a pretty fair slider and fastball—he blew away more than three thousand big-league batters, won seven consecutive World Series games (completing every one), and dominated his own league so absurdly (there was that unimaginable 1.12 earned run average in 1968) that baseball officials, throwing up a backhanded salute to him and his near-peers, were compelled to tamp down the mound and squeeze the strike zone to give the failing, flailing hitters a more sporting chance.

These days, ol' number 45 is more generous with his conversation, and in fact, for the purposes of this book, set out in search of a fraternal Hall of Famer—one possessed of conspicuous oratorical and hitting skills—with whom to banter about the dynamics and mechanics, the complexities and perplexities, the ins, the outs, and the inevitable betweens of the game they both mastered. When he flipped through the pages of leading suspects, every one of them had Reggie Jackson's mug shot on it.

The game has no better talker than the tailor's son from

Philly, and no thinker more thorough. Nor has the World Series ever produced a greater batsman. Gibson being the Classic's foremost starting pitcher, there's a sacred place in October where only the two of them have been. There's a language, in turn, that only they can speak. And they do it here.

Their book is kick-back, nitty-gritty dialogue between leaders of the rival pitchers and hitters lobbies, an epic matchup of right vs. left and the hottest hard stuff against the wickedest rip. It's a give-and-take compressed from sixty-feet-six to facing chairs, a volley of views about sliders on the corner and fastballs in the back; about playing under pressure, through pain, and over the decades; about frank recollections and Frank Robinson; about full counts, full swings, full bases, and conventional wisdom that's simply full of it. It's about the ways the various parts of the plate are regarded by the guy with the ball, the guy with the bat, and don't forget the gentleman with the little whisk broom. It's about pitches that can't be hit and those that can, and how, in the case of the latter, one man's eleven o'clock highlight can ruin another's week, or year, even career. It's about what Jackson sees in Derek Jeter that he once observed in Roberto Clemente, and in Greg Maddux that so impressed him about Tom Seaver. It's not about life stories or stories of any sort, for that matter, unless they illustrate what occurs when, say, a Dick Allen, in Gibson's experience—could be Manny Ramirez, same thing—is presented with the loitering curveball that he happens to be on the lookout for.

Gibson and Jackson also share a characteristic candor that has not always contributed to their respective popularity but gussies up the printed page. I was, of course, more familiar with Gibson's legendary demeanor, having collaborated on his autobiography (*Stranger to the Game*) some years back. Because of that, folks ask all the time what the man is *really* like, because, well, there was that mystique, if you will. In deference to my favorite pitcher, I won't entirely blow his cover, other than to say that Bob Gibson was a genius of gamesmanship, a ballplayer to whom winning was a lifestyle (and to say, also, that he has apparently reached a lengthy period of accommodation and congeniality). If he seemed inordinately serious—and believe me, he's *not*, in the grander scheme— it's because seriously is how he took the game. The former Harlem Globetrotter bit off baseball by the chunk. And after half a century of chewing on it, he was ready to write his review.

His is a voice that still silences the room. In the matter of Gibson, it's more than mere personality that has captivated so many people. They remain fascinated by the searing, uncompromised competitiveness he flaunted in his seventeen-year career with the Cardinals. In the decades since, Gibson has simmered into a living symbol of that very thing. It's particularly telling that the folks most infatuated by his flaming ferocity are cap-tipping fans of the old Yankees, Red Sox, and Tigers, the teams against which he proved his champion's mettle.

The last of those World Series seasons happened to be 1968, the year that changed everything. The following summer was Jackson's third in the big leagues, and his most prolific in terms of both home runs and RBIs. It was also the year in which the national media learned that, if they could just find Oakland, they could back up their trucks to the young slugger's locker and load them with precious quotes and priceless color, the likes of which had never before been culled from a baseball clubhouse. In 1974, the year after he had been named MVP of both the American League and the World Series, Jackson was pronounced the world's first "superduperstar" by *Sports Illustrated*. Three years later, the Yankees made him the richest player, as well. They were rewarded with daily headlines—never mind the details—and another World Series MVP performance, this time featuring home runs on four consecutive swings. When his new signature nickname was affixed, Mr. October glittered with such stunning effulgence that sporting celebrity had attained a new dimension.

If, as the generations turn, Gibson remains the standard for the old-school baseball ethic, Jackson occupies a similar station in terms of elocution and showmanship. He was a visionary in cultivating the advantages of media-friendliness, an unapologetic pioneer in the areas of style and self-marketing. The heavy cosmetics, however, obscured his studied dedication to the finer points of the game, which he applied with a surpassing intellect. For that matter, they obscured his emotional dedication to the game itself.

The chapters ahead reveal Jackson as the more ardent traditionalist of the two Cooperstowners, his sentimentality unchecked by the strain of pragmatism that tempers Gibson's. Now employed by the Yankees, the erstwhile "straw that stirs the drink" has carried forward his constant cogitation on ballplaying, all the while couching his impressions in the context of what hooked him as a dazzled youngster smitten by stars and influenced by idols. Among the idolized was a no-fooling fireballer for St. Louis.

Jackson memorized every move of the men he so admired, and put it all into practice. The game was in his head, and by the time he was finished, 563 home runs were on his résumé. Ultimately, Reggie's gift of perception was the principal reason that Gibson pitched him this project. Served it right up into the big guy's wheelhouse.

That, for the record, would make Jackson the first left-handed power hitter that Gibson ever served something up to.

CHAPTER ONE

THE PITCHED BATTLE

Any Little Edge

Reggie Jackson

When I stepped into the box, I felt the at-bat belonged to *me.* Everybody else was there for my convenience. The pitcher was there to throw me a ball to hit. The catcher was there to throw it back to him if he didn't give me what I wanted the first time. And the umpire was lucky that he was close enough to watch.

Gibson was the same way. That's why people thought he was mean. And that's the attitude you've got to have. When I hit, I felt I was in control of the home-plate area, and it was important that I felt that way. If I let the pitcher control it, it would give *him* an advantage.

There are at least three kinds of advantages that the pitcher and batter contest. There's the physical advantage, the strategic advantage, and also the psychological advantage. I didn't want two out of three. I wanted them all.

The pitcher has the ball, and nothing happens until he lets go of it. So, as the batter, I felt I had to fight for any bit of control I could get. I expected the umpire, the catcher, and the pitcher to wait on *me.* I wanted to get ready on *my* time. I'd call time or pause or do something that wasn't *too* annoying but at least would get the pitcher off his pace. If I could disrupt his rhythm a little bit, just for a second or two, the advantage swung to me. But I didn't want to create an ire, some kind of anger to make him bear down harder. I didn't want a guy to step back and grit his teeth. Being a jerk about it just doesn't work. There's a fine line between annoying somebody just a little bit and angering him to the point where you may get drilled in the back.

Bob Gibson

Him backing out of there all the time, that *is* annoying, because I liked to pitch in a hurry. But I never let it annoy me to the point that it distracted me. You don't knock guys down for that kind of stuff. They give you plenty of other reasons to knock them down.

Reggie Jackson

Against the great pitchers, in particular, I'd try to break that rhythm. They're going to try to pitch a fast game, under two hours if possible—although that hardly ever happens anymore. They want to get a flow going, throw strikes, get ahead, keep you off balance and on the defensive. They want you to get in the batter's box, because they're ready to pitch. If a pitcher stays in his groove, he's going to be comfortable. He's going to be on his game plan. So you have to get him out of that comfort zone any way you can. If I could do a little something to break that rhythm—make him say to the umpire, "Come on, get him in there, let's go, let's go!"—I might get a ball one. You want him thinking about something other than where he's putting this first pitch. So you might step out, adjust your helmet, tie your shoe or something; but you want to be careful. You don't want to get hit.

Bob Gibson

I got a chuckle out of the comment that a pitcher wants to keep the game under two hours. After I'd get through warming up in the bullpen and was sitting waiting to go out there, I'd always say to the guys, "Okay, an hour and fifty-seven minutes, let's go!" They play better behind you if you're working quickly.

Reggie Jackson

Ken Holtzman could pitch a game in ninety minutes. Wouldn't throw a breaking ball. And he had a *great* breaking ball.

Bob Gibson

I did that once. Went a whole game without throwing a breaking ball—or threw two or three at the most. Got beat 2–1.

Reggie Jackson

It's not just stepping out of the box or slowing things down. It's any little edge you can get. When I went to home plate in a game-tied situation or with a chance to do something and help the ball club win one, I'd try to make eye contact with the pitcher.

Now, you didn't do that with Hoot—that's what a lot of us like to call Gibson, after the old Hollywood cowboy—or a Mickey Lolich or a Jim Palmer or a Catfish Hunter. You weren't going to stare down those guys. But if a guy was a young player, I would wait to get into the box because I wanted him to *look* at me. If he wouldn't look at me, I felt I had him beat. If a guy did make eye contact, you could find out if you could intimidate him. Later in my career, when I had the weight of a reputation behind me, I did that a lot.

Bob Gibson

Heck, I couldn't see if a guy was looking at me or not. I had enough trouble trying to see the signs back there.

Tell you what I did, though. I used to look in and shake off signs just to mess with the hitters. Did that all the time. Tim McCarver would give me a sign and then give me another one that meant shake me off. The thing was, I didn't have that many pitches to shake off to. So I'm out there shaking my head, and the batter's thinking, "What the hell?"

Reggie Jackson

When I was with the Yankees in 1978, we were playing Baltimore at Yankee Stadium and the score was 3–3 going into the bottom of the ninth inning. I led off against Tippy Martinez— a little left-hander who always gave me trouble—and the count went to three-and-oh. I had the green light in that situation, but instead of digging into the box I stepped out and looked down to the third-base coach for a sign. Then I glared over there like I was ticked off and shot a look into the dugout at our manager, Dick Howser, pretending that I was angry about getting a take sign. After all that, I stepped into the box, the pitch came floating right down the middle, and I hit a game-winning home run. In fact, that was the only home run I ever hit against Tippy Martinez.

Bob Gibson

I got a lot of mileage out of looking angry. Sometimes it wasn't intentional—like when I was squinting in for the signs and the batters thought I was glowering at them—but the fact is, I was deliberately unfriendly to the opposition. I wouldn't even say hello to hitters on the other teams.

I didn't want them knowing me. I didn't want them knowing what I was like or what I was thinking. It was important to me that I retain an air of mystery. I never let the coaches put any kind of clock or gun on my pitches, because I didn't want that information to get out. I wouldn't talk to the team psychologist, because I didn't want anybody figuring me out. I even asked our manager, Red Schoendienst, to keep me out of spring training games against National League teams, if at all possible. In spring training, you're just working on stuff, not trying to get batters out all the time, and I thought that if they got up there and whacked me around a little bit it would only give them confidence. I didn't want them confident. I wanted them wary of me. Uncertain. Intimidated.

The Pirates had a young outfielder named Gene Clines who came up to me before a game with a baseball and asked me to sign it. I took the ball and tossed it over my shoulder into left field.

War Games

Reggie Jackson

Everybody in the league knew I had trouble with the inside pitch. I got away with it only because the great majority of pitchers were afraid of making a mistake in that spot. The threat of power is one of the best weapons you have in the batter's box. They were also concerned that if they missed inside, they'd hit me, put me on base. Now, for a guy like Gibson, that was okay. His attitude was, if I'm gonna miss, I'm gonna miss *at* you.

Bob Gibson

What pitchers are really afraid of is their own control. They don't truly believe that they can get a pitch in there exactly where they want it—especially against a hitter as powerful as Reggie, who can put his team on the board at any moment. They know that if they miss in the wrong place, a power hitter will knock the crap out of it. But you can't go out there with the attitude that you're going to miss your spot. You can't go out there afraid of the hitter or afraid of yourself. You've got to *respect* the hitter, though—some more than others, of course—and you've got to respect yourself.

Contrary to what people thought, I didn't make my living on the inside corner. My idea was to pitch away, pitch away, pitch away, come in, pitch away. I mostly worked the outside part of the plate; but you can't be scared to come in when the time or the hitter calls for it. The thing is, if I'm pitching a guy inside, I'm going to make sure I get it *way* in there. If you put the ball in the *strike zone* inside—especially against a guy who can hit the ball out of the ballpark—that's horrible. Left-handed or right-handed batter, it doesn't matter. Don't do that.

Reggie Jackson

But see, I was a little different. If you got the ball away from me, I could actually hit it to right field. Not down the line. I never tried to hit the ball down the line. I never tried much to pull the ball at all, for that matter; but I could get it into right center, at least, if it was on the outside part of the plate.

If it was up and away, it didn't matter to me whose fastball it was; I could handle it. But the ball on the inside part of the plate, I couldn't hit with power. I don't know if it was because I was big through the arms and chest and got tied up when the pitch was in on me, or what; but if I swung at it, I was going to be in a slump. I'd even try backing up in the box so that I could extend my arms to hit the inside strike. When I did that, I was dead. I'd get a hard slider away, and I couldn't even move. If you could pitch me inside and throw hard, I'd have to tip my cap to you and wait for you to make a mistake. But if you came inside and missed, *I* wasn't going to miss.

Bob Gibson

It sounds like Reggie was a little like Eddie Mathews when it came to the inside pitch. Mathews was the only great hitter I ever pitched against who had what you might call a hole in his swing. And I found out about it by mistake. I kept pitching him away, pitching him away, and he kept hitting the ball through the right side. Most left-handers would try to go the other way with that pitch, but he'd just knock it through the hole between first and second. He got enough hits off me early in my career that he still batted over .300 against me overall. But one day I happened to throw a fastball, and it had pretty good hair on it, but, accidentally, it was right there on the inside part of the plate, belt high, just about the worst place you could throw a fastball to a power hitter. I went, "Oh no . . ." And he went, whoosh! Swung and missed it. Hmmm. *Really?*

I couldn't quite get that. Other great hitters might struggle with curveballs, or something in the dirt, but not a pitch right on the plate like that. Mind you, this was *my* fastball, and it might have been a different story with a pitcher who didn't throw with the velocity or movement that I had. But I never had any more trouble with Eddie Mathews after that. I just pitched him inside at the belt. And believe me, that was a major discovery, because it meant that I didn't have to worry about Hank Aaron. I'd just let him go and get Mathews out.

Anyway, that's probably how I'd go about it with Reggie, although I wouldn't throw him too many fastballs. Even with the knowledge that he has trouble with the inside pitch, if I go inside and throw him a strike it's going to be right on the corner. But I'd rather go off the corner. I'm thinking *way* inside. That's what the slider's for.

Reggie Jackson

A left-handed hitter has a hard time hitting that pitch. It crawls up the label. That's what Mariano Rivera does. It looks good and you just can't lay off it. But you can't hit it, either.

I don't know how I'd do against Mariano, but after I matured a little bit I learned to lay off the inside pitches. I wanted the ball away from me, and I wanted to keep it out toward left center. I tried to make my foul line where the second baseman stood, so I didn't pull off the ball trying to hit it down the line to right. Since I didn't handle the ball inside anyway, I resisted the temptation to be a pull hitter. It wasn't always easy. Yankee Stadium is built for left-handed power hitters. When we played in Detroit, where there was a small porch in right field and a small porch in left, I didn't want to think right field because it would hurt my swing. If I could be in a ballpark where they wanted to keep the ball away from me, that was to my advantage. Yankee Stadium fit that description, because it was so big in left field and left center.

In the World Series, especially, it seemed like I always got a lot of balls away from me. You know, I was the World Series MVP in 1977, against the Dodgers, but I thought I hit the ball just about as well against the Dodgers in 1978. I batted .391 with a couple homers and broke some records of Lou Gehrig's for extra-base hits and consecutive games with an RBI . . .

Bob Gibson

Wait a minute. After a guy wins a World Series with three straight home runs in the final game, I can't believe the same team would allow him to hit .391 in the *next* World Series. Didn't they figure it out?

Reggie Jackson

They *wanted* to pitch me in, I think. But I backed off the plate about four inches more than usual and leaned forward, so it wouldn't look like I'd moved. I faked it to make it appear normal. That way, they'd go ahead and bring the ball in, but I was actually far enough from the plate that I could handle that pitch. It was the only time in my life I ever did that. I baited them into giving me inside strikes. Then, as soon as they started throwing the ball, I would just raise up . . .

Bob Gibson

I would have seen that.

Reggie Jackson

Easy to say now!

Anyway, I'd just raise up and pray that the guy would throw the ball in, where he wanted to throw it; throw a strike. I didn't want to get the count to two-and-two, or something like that. I figured that if I was up there long enough, they'd see me moving around. But they just kept throwing strikes. Every time. I got 'em. If they'd thrown me some balls and seen me moving, it would have been all over. But I just got in the batter's box, faked my stance, and said please throw me a strike; and they did. Boom! Boom! Boom, boom, boom!

Bob Gibson

Orlando Cepeda tried that all the time, but I could see him move. He'd start off on top of the plate and I'd just pound him inside. And every time he came to bat, he'd creep off a little bit more. By the end of the game, he'd be in the back of the box and

I'd be throwing him sliders way out there. When he got traded to the Cardinals, I said, "Charlie, you're always creeping back away from the plate."

And he said, "Did you *see* me?"

"*Of course* I saw you. What do you think I was watching?"

He said, "I wondered why at the end of the game you always pitched me away."

"Because you were way the hell in the back of the box by that time." He couldn't reach that pitch with a flagpole. And he thought he was tricking me.

Now, I said I would have seen Reggie doing that, but in a World Series you wouldn't notice all the things that you'd notice during the regular season. A guy like Cepeda, I saw him all year. In the Series, you're pitching against guys you might be seeing for the first time. I think that's a big part of the reason why I struck out so many guys in the World Series. I had a reputation for throwing heat, and in the World Series they were all looking for it. I guess they didn't know I threw a lot of sliders.

Reggie Jackson

That snapdragon.

Bob Gibson

War games, that's all. That's what it is.

The Learning Curve

Reggie Jackson

Let me ask Bob: How would you describe the art of pitching?

Bob Gibson

It's making the hitter do pretty much what I want him to do. Being in control of the situation. That's something that comes with knowledge and maturity.

When you're an amateur, even a minor-leaguer, a pitcher can

be in control by virtue of his stuff alone: If you have a ninety-five-mile-an-hour fastball, or you can break off a Sandy Koufax curveball, you have an advantage going in because you can simply overmatch most of the hitters. Once they're overmatched, they're pretty much at your mercy. The battle is yours to lose by making a mistake that there's really no excuse for. But the further you go up the ladder, the bigger the window for mistakes and the higher the price you pay for them. And the more you have to learn and *think* the game.

After a couple years in the big leagues, I learned the strike zone a little better. I learned the hitters. I learned that ninety-five miles an hour is good, but you've got to throw it somewhere in particular. When I was young I thought you could just throw it by people, but in the major leagues they turn that stuff around if it's in the hitting zone.

I learned about myself. And I learned how to pitch in certain ballparks. For instance, at old Busch Stadium in St. Louis—where we played until we moved downtown, by the Arch, in 1966—at first I wouldn't pitch any left-handers inside because I didn't want them hitting the ball onto that roof that was sitting out there, way too close, in right field. So I was working the ball away from the left-handers a little bit, out over the plate, and they were hitting it on the roof anyway. In 1965 I gave up thirty-four home runs, and I'll bet you twenty of them were onto that roof. That was before I really learned to pitch. I was the World Series MVP in 1964, and that was because I had good stuff and I wasn't afraid and I could rise to the occasion; but it didn't mean that I knew how to pitch. Eventually, I learned how to keep the hitters away from short porches like that. I learned that just because the pitch is inside doesn't mean it's going onto the roof. Some players would prefer a ball out over the plate to pull toward a short porch. I didn't know that when I was young.

Here's another thing I learned: Hitters who stand practically on top of the plate and don't like the ball inside will still *swing* at a ball inside. Then they might back away a little bit for the next pitch, to give themselves some hitting room, and if you bring the ball a little further inside they'll *still* swing at it because it looks the same to them as the last pitch. They don't realize that they're standing in a different spot. Their body didn't get the memo from their brain. Now the plate's a whole lot wider than it was, and there's no way in the world that guy's going to do anything with a good pitch on the outside corner, even if he's looking for it. He'll pop it up or pull it foul.

You've just got to know who you can do what to. That's what pitching is.

Reggie Jackson

As a hitter, what I had to learn, mostly, was what I could do and what I *couldn't* do. A good pitcher may have an advantage with a big fastball or breaking ball, but I had an advantage, too; a major advantage: I could hit a fly ball and get it out of the ballpark. If I could get the barrel on the baseball, I could put us on the scoreboard.

The pitchers knew that, and because of it they'd be careful not to give me anything I could put the fat part of the bat on. But *that* could work to my advantage, too, if I was patient. That could put me ahead in the count and lead to a situation where a pitcher *had* to come at me with a strike. Patience is a hard thing for a hitter to learn. There's patience involved in waiting for the pitch you can square-up, and there's also patience involved within the act of hitting a pitch that you can't turn on and pull out of the park. If the pitch is away from you, sometimes the best course is to be patient, keep your weight back, and deliver the ball to the opposite field. I was a better hitter after I learned to do that. Maturity makes you better. Confidence makes you better.

It took a while, but eventually I came to realize that there was something else in my favor: My weakness—my inability to handle the ball inside—was one that most pitchers were reluctant or afraid to expose.

It would have been a different story if I hadn't been a home-run hitter; but my power was the reason a lot of pitchers wouldn't throw me inside. It's the same thing Bob was talking about. Most pitchers, especially young pitchers and pitchers who lack knowledge and confidence, assume that a power hitter is going to jump all over a pitch on the inside part of the plate. So as my reputation as a power hitter developed, some pitchers became less inclined to bring the ball into the area that was actually my weakness. And when they did, I learned to let it go.

If I'd have learned that earlier, I might not have had so much difficulty with a guy like Gary Peters. He was a veteran left-hander for the White Sox, and he wasn't the type who was shy about bringing the ball inside against me. He went right to my weakness and kept his fastball on my hands. I hated facing Gary Peters. As a young player, I really didn't know enough to be able to succeed against him. I didn't know enough to lay off the inside fastball.

Instead, I tried to hit that pitch out of the ballpark and it created a lot of bad habits. My first four years, I led the league in strikeouts every year. It really wasn't until I was about thirty that I fully acknowledged the problem and learned to lay off the inside pitch. After that, I still struck out a lot, but I got the number down a little bit by understanding what I couldn't do. And along with that understanding, I came to realize that my inability to hit the inside pitch wasn't really such a terrible problem to have. I made it to the Hall of Fame without being able to hit the inside pitch.

It's all a learning process. I learned concentration and discipline at the plate. I learned how to make contact when contact was all I needed to bring in a run. I learned how to go up to the plate and not try to do too much with the ball. I learned how to hit with men on base. I would talk to good hitters—guys like Thurman Munson, Sal Bando, Joe Rudi, Don Baylor, Frank Robinson, Dick Allen, Willie Mays, Willie McCovey, and Billy Williams; guys who knew what they were doing.

I learned that if you stay within the limits of your ability and play the game the way it should be played, good things will happen. Little things win ballgames.

The Count

Bob Gibson

For the hitter, it's all about getting a pitch to hit. For the pitcher, it's all about not *giving* the hitter a pitch to hit. Pretty simple. And what it usually boils down to, for both of us, is getting ahead in the count.

Reggie Jackson

That's why I would swing at the first pitch if it was something I liked.

That's an important "if." What I mean is, I wouldn't deliberately *not swing* at the first pitch, like a lot of batters do. I wouldn't just let the pitcher get the upper hand in the count. If he makes a perfect pitch on the corner with plenty on it, fine. Congratulations, and we'll go from there. But I'm not *giving* him anything.

Bob Gibson

I'd love to pitch today, because you hear a lot of these guys talk about getting deep into the count. I think I would eat 'em alive.

Reggie Jackson

Because it's going to be oh-and-two.

Bob Gibson

One, two, buckle your shoe, and off you go. If I get oh-and-two on a guy, it seems like ninety-nine percent of the time I'm going to get him out. I know that studies show the numbers aren't that drastic, but they also show that oh-and-two gives the pitcher an overwhelming advantage, which is obvious to begin with. For that matter, the same goes for one-and-two. At any rate, I'm not talking from numbers because, for one, decimal points don't do anything for your fastball, and two, there are so many extenuating circumstances that go into statistics like that. I'm talking from experience, from what my eyes and gut tell me, and from the standpoint of strategy.

When these hitters today put so much stock in getting deep into the count, that means they're going to be purposely taking some pitches. If you take the first pitch against me, you might have a problem, because I didn't pitch like these guys do today. I wasn't pitching *away* from contact; I was pitching *to* contact. I was trying to *make* the guy hit the ball. I didn't want to throw any cripples in there—I'd throw pretty good stuff, and it helps to bring it in there at ninety-five miles an hour with a little life—but I *wanted* the batter to hit it. Hit it right away, by all means.

But you're hitting *my* pitch, not yours. And when you let me get ahead in the count, all my options are wide open. Thank you very much.

Reggie Jackson

There's a real lesson in Hoot's conversation. Once he gets ahead of you in the count, he's got two or three chances to put a ball in the area where you can't get the barrel on it squarely. So it's not only that he wants you to hit the ball and put it in play; he's going to *make* you hit it, and hit it on his terms.

I'm not suggesting that you just go up there hacking. If you swing at a first pitch you can't really deal with, you're just making the pitcher's job that much easier. If you get something nasty on the corner, or some breaking ball you weren't anticipating, let it go and hope for a better pitch next time. That's why you get three strikes. If the pitcher can get ahead that way, then he has earned his way ahead. But for goodness' sake, don't allow him to get ahead by just laying one down the middle. Make him pay for that. Instill in him the fear of doing that. Make him *work*. The harder you make him work, the better chance you have of getting ahead.

Bob Gibson

Getting ahead is the most important part of getting a hitter out. When you're ahead, you're not backed into a corner where you have to throw a certain pitch to get a strike. When you throw ball one and especially ball two—the second pitch in the sequence might be even more significant than the first—there's a pretty good chance that you're going to have to come with the fastball in one of the next two pitches. Now the hitter knows what to expect and he's up there licking his chops. Those guys love it when you *have* to throw a fastball. When I got behind in the count, the batter was going to get something to hit.

There are always exceptions, depending on the situation and the batter. For example, I'd avoid throwing Hank Aaron a fastball over the plate if there was any possible way I could get around it. But in the great majority of cases, I'm going to give the batter a pitch to hit rather than walk him. If it's two-and-oh or three-and-one, he's probably going to get a fastball up in the strike zone, because the high fastball was my best pitch. But if you get ahead in the count, it's a whole different game with a whole different set of possibilities. Now you might throw anything.

That's why a first-pitch strike is so critical, and that's where confidence comes in. Because I had confidence in my stuff, I was a believer that, if I made a mistake on the first pitch and drifted a fastball over the middle of the plate, most of the time the batter was going to foul it back. I had faith that there was enough speed and movement on the ball that he would still have a hard time getting good wood on it. Believe me, I was a pitcher who liked to minimize the risk; but there was greater risk in falling behind in the count than in giving the batter a chance to hit the first pitch. When you pitch from behind, you're asking for disaster. Don't throw balls.

Reggie Jackson

As a hitter, once you get strike one against a guy like Bob Gibson, it's in your best interest to hit the next strike he shows you. You don't want to face him with two strikes. As important as strike one is, strike two is right there with it.

It's a race to see who can get to two first—two balls or two strikes. The second strike puts you on the defensive, without the luxury of being able to let a strike go by or the option of waiting for a particular pitch. Not with that slider on top of that fastball. The bottom line is, you don't want to get behind in the count.

Since I have a position with the Yankees, it's important for me to understand pitching. So I've started asking around about this whenever I'm in the company of a great pitcher. When we played golf a while back, I asked Bob what was the most important part of pitching and he said, "Strike one." So did Greg Maddux, so did Tom Seaver, and so did anyone I asked—Juan Marichal, Steve Carlton, all of them. So I took that to the bank, and I use it as information if I'm talking to our pitchers or if I'm talking to our hitters.

It's good to hear it from the pitchers' side, but really, what those guys were telling me was nothing I didn't know from twenty-one years in the big leagues. And it didn't take that long to figure it out. I wasn't about to get on the wrong side of the count by standing there with the bat on my shoulder watching strike one come right into my breadbasket. And if the guy is a strike-one pitcher, like Maddux, Seaver, Gibson, and most of the great pitchers are, all the more reason to go up there ripping—as long as it's a pitch you can handle, or a pitch that's as good as any you're likely to get.

Those guys trust their stuff. They're not afraid to give you a ball to hit. When they do, be ready. Go to work.

Bob Gibson

At the very least, the hitter has to let you know that he *might* swing at the first pitch, or probably *will* if you throw the ball out over the plate. Most hitters have a pattern, just like most pitchers have a pattern.

Reggie Jackson

There are statistics now about how many pitches a batter sees each particular time at the plate. And there are players who are hell-bent on going deep into the count. Bobby Abreu sees more pitches than any player in baseball, about four and a half per time at bat. Well, I don't understand that statistic.

You go to home plate to swing the bat. Obviously, early in the count you don't want to swing at pitches out of the strike zone that you can't do anything with, or pitches *in* the strike zone that you can't do anything with. That only plays into the pitcher's hands and gets you into trouble with the count. And yes, it's a good thing to make the pitcher work hard. Maybe you can get him out of the game earlier. But to me, the best way to get him out of the game is to *knock* him out of the game. Swing the bat. If you see a good pitch to hit from a good pitcher, it may be the *only* one you'll see. It may be the first inning, but if that guy gets in a groove, you're in for a long day. So bear down. Don't let opportunity pass you by. Swing the bat.

If it's a bad pitcher, or even a good pitcher on a bad day, you've got a chance to get him out of there quickly if you swing the bat. And it doesn't take long to tell if a pitcher doesn't have it. Sometimes, in the first inning, I'd look at Bucky Dent, who was hitting ninth, and say, "Man, you ain't gonna see this guy. I've got a chance to get fat today. And I'm gonna get something early, because he may not be there the next time I come up." Sometimes you say that and screw around, and before you know it it's the seventh inning and you're losing. You've got to take care of your business when you have the chance. Swing the bat.

I always had a plan in mind when I came up to bat, and it always involved hitting the ball before the pitcher got two strikes on me. With two strikes, I had to chuck the plan and fight for my life. At that point, you've got to resort to staying alive and getting the bat on the ball, trying to become a baserunner any way you can. That's why the count makes such a profound difference.

I'd get all messed up if I didn't keep the count in my head. It was sort of my bookmark to tell me where I was in this at-bat. If I didn't keep track of the balls and strikes, I'd lose my place and my purpose. One-and-two is so, so far from two-and-one. Two-and-two and one-and-two are very similar for me. It's still two strikes, do or die. But if I'm one-and-oh, two-and-oh, two-and-one, three-and-one . . . now I've got a count I can work with.

It might sound strange, but I'd actually rather be two-and-one than three-and-one. I'd rather be two-and-oh than three-and-oh. I just like it better. I'm more apt to get something to hit, because the pitcher thinks he's still in the at-bat. There's still a contest going on. Three-and-oh, I'm not going to get a ball to hit. That's too much of a freebie, and he's not going to give me that. He might give that to a singles hitter, but not to someone who can really hurt him.

Bob Gibson

On three-and-oh or three-and-one, depending on the situation, I might be looking over Reggie's shoulder and not caring whether he gets a strike or not. Who's the next hitter?

A Pitch to Hit

Bob Gibson

Unfortunately, as much as I hated to do it—believe me, there's not much that I hated more—there were situations when I'd *have* to give the batter a pitch to hit because I couldn't afford another ball. But at the same time, I'd know who was capable of swinging at a bad pitch when he should be holding out for a good one. Thankfully, there are guys who will swing at a ball in the dirt at two-and-oh. You need to know who's capable of doing that and who's not capable of doing it.

Fortunately for me, when you throw hard, a lot of guys are capable of swinging at bad pitches. They're too eager. They over-commit.

Reggie Jackson

One of Ted Williams's principles of hitting was that an average hitter swinging at a good pitch to hit is better than a great hitter swinging at a bad pitch to hit. I go along with that. And I honestly felt that when I went to home plate, eighty-five to ninety percent of the time I was going to get a ball to put in play hard. Even facing a guy like Gibson, or any of the great ones. It may not be exactly what you want, and it may be tougher to handle than you hoped for, but you're going to get something hittable.

Bob Gibson

That's true, but there are degrees of hittable. I might give a batter something over the plate on the first pitch, and that would be hittable. It would be ninety-five miles an hour and it would be moving one way or another, but comparatively speaking it would be hittable. If the count is three-and-something and it's late in a close game and there's no place to put you, you're going to get something hittable.

All of that is in the flow of the game, me against you and let's see what you can do. But then there's another level. Those are the mistakes. That's when I hang a curveball or leave a fastball out over the plate when I'm ahead in the count and don't have to.

Even the good pitchers make bad pitches, and plenty of them. I couldn't count how many bad pitches I'd make in the course of a game. I'd guess maybe twenty, twenty-five a game, and that's not counting the ones that are so wild and far out of the strike zone that nobody can get the bat on them anyway.

Now, of those twenty-five, it's really hard to say how many will actually get hit hard. Some you get away with, some you don't. It depends on who you're missing to. The bad hitters, the guys who hit .250, are the ones who come in and say, "Aw, man, I just missed that!" It was a *bad pitch* and he missed it. He was given a better chance than he had any reason to believe he'd get, and he comes in complaining that he missed it, like he almost had me. He'll get a ball that he's supposed to hit 400 feet and he'll hit it 320, nice and easy, right to the left fielder, and come back to the dugout and make a little scene and swear he just missed it. He'll do that *a lot.*

Reggie Jackson

Most of the time, home runs come on balls that were not in good spots. They were out over the plate. But there are occasions when the pitcher might throw a pitch that he considers to be a mistake—a breaking ball that doesn't break or a fastball that doesn't go where he wants it to—and it's actually a good pitch if the hitter happens to be looking for something else.

And sometimes, a hitter puts the bat on plain good pitches. I've hit home runs, gone back to the dugout, and somebody has asked me what I hit, and I've said, "I don't know. I just saw the ball and hit it." That usually comes from hitting a good pitch. I'd bet I had fifty home runs like that, where I didn't know what I hit.

There are very few games when you simply don't ever get a pitch to hit. Chances are decent that you'll get one every time you come to the plate, even against the best pitchers on their best days.

In my career, one memorable exception was when I was with the A's, 1973 World Series, Tom Seaver. It was about thirty-eight degrees, and he was sweating and had a big ol' mud spot where he dragged that right knee. After he finished his motion, it was like he jumped forward. I never got a ball to hit that day. I got balls that were in the strike zone, but I never got a ball that I could handle. It was so unusual that, in my twenty-one-year career, it stands out.

The other thing that stands out was that we won the game anyway, 3–2 in eleven innings. Sometimes it just works out like that.

Bob Gibson

It's rare that a pitcher can make it through a game without mistakes. Even on the days when you've got really, really good stuff, you're going to make some bad pitches. When I was on a roll in 1968, even when I threw forty-seven straight scoreless innings and had like an 0.19 ERA over a stretch of close to a hundred innings—when it seemed like every pitch went exactly where I wanted it to go—there were mistakes. I probably got away with more mistakes than usual, because I was making more good pitches and getting ahead in the count and keeping the hitters on their heels. But there were bad pitches, and most of the time good hitters don't miss bad pitches. Those other guys go "Damn it!" and foul it back. Those good hitters go "Whack!" and they've got *you* saying "Damn it!"

Guys like Mays don't miss mistakes. On the whole, Mays didn't hurt me as much as Aaron, and I found him easier to pitch to, but Willie was an example of a guy who just did not miss a mistake. If you threw him a breaking ball and missed with it, home run. At the best, a double. Willie didn't hit singles off hanging breaking balls.

Reggie Jackson

The counterpart for that is a pitcher who refuses to make a mistake. I didn't see Seaver enough to know if that was his standard operating procedure—I suspect it was—but I can say from experience that Ferguson Jenkins was that way.

Fergie Jenkins was a big guy who threw hard and didn't look like it. He had an effortless motion. Fergie threw a changeup and his back foot never left the rubber. He kept the ball away from me, which I should have liked because it played into my style of hitting, but he would never quite put it where I could get to it. In that respect, Jenkins was very similar to Jim Palmer. He didn't throw as hard as Palmer, but he was always in command of the situation. He was an easygoing guy who had a way of looking at you and laughing, like he was saying, "You ain't gonna beat me because I ain't gonna pitch to you. I'm gonna give you a ball and you're gonna maybe hit it to the second baseman or sky one in the air. You're gonna have a good swing on me. You're never gonna look bad. But you ain't gonna beat me."

That's how Fergie treated me, anyway. He just went away from the barrel and got me out. I was very comfortable facing him. I couldn't wait to get to the plate. But I never got the barrel square on the ball. Ferguson Jenkins could control you with his control. He was a great and very underrated pitcher. The man was a twenty-game winner seven times.

Bob Gibson

For a pitcher, it's not just avoiding mistakes. More important is that you avoid mistakes *at the wrong time.*

When the game is on the line, you don't want to leave it up to chance. I was in a hotel lounge watching a game the other night when the Cardinals' closer, a young pitcher named Chris Perez, gave up a home run in the ninth inning that tied the game. After the inning, a guy who was sitting there said, "Too bad, he made one mistake." In the paper the next morning, Perez was saying, "I made one mistake." That's not true. He threw two or three pitches right where they should have been driven, but he throws hard enough that he gets away with it most of the time. Not all mistakes get clobbered. But some do, and a really, really good pitcher won't make mistakes when they can beat him that way.

When Hank Aaron comes up in the ninth inning, you don't make a mistake. If you walk him, you walk him, but if there's any way around it you don't make a mistake to Hank Aaron in a situation where he can beat you. Period. That's how you lose a ballgame.

Guessing

Bob Gibson

I swear, I really don't know what hitters think—especially after I see them swing sometimes.

If they think that pitchers are a superior breed, I'm not going to argue; but I have to say that a lot of times they give us too much credit and make it too hard on themselves by overthinking. Or *not* thinking, whichever way you want to look at it. I've seen where a pitcher might throw ten fastballs in a row and the hitter will still be looking for a breaking ball. He's just guessing, and guessing against the percentages. Dumb, dumb, dumb.

It works the other way, too. A while back I was watching somebody pitch to one of the Cardinals' outfielders, and he threw two straight breaking balls that the guy missed by a foot both times. Then he threw a fastball and the batter hit a double. Had two guys in scoring position. I don't know why you'd do that. I don't have a clue.

It could be, I suppose, that they're plotting out the whole sequence before the batter even steps in. I never did that, and I would never recommend it. You can't plan three or four pitches ahead, because it seldom goes exactly the way you script it. You have to pay attention and respond to what's happening, how it's developing. I always based the next pitch on the last pitch.

There really wasn't much reason for hitters to be up there guessing against me. They pretty much knew what I was going to throw. Fastball, slider. Hard stuff. *Hard.*

Reggie Jackson

There are some guys who just go up there trying to outguess the pitcher. They're not good hitters. But there are times when you can say, yeah, I'm looking for a high fastball away against Bob Gibson because he likes to throw the ball out there. Sooner or later, I'm going to cut my strike zone in half and just wait for that fastball up and away. If he throws me a ball down and in, I'm not going to hit it. It's going to be strike three. But I want to make sure I get on the high fastball away because I'm pretty sure it's coming—it always does—and I want to tie this game up. I'm going to look for that fastball, and I know he's going to throw me *two* of them. If I get it, I'm going to get the barrel on it. I might not hit it out, but I'm going to hit it hard.

Am I guessing? I suppose you could say that. But if I've become familiar with a pitcher over the years, I think I know—I think I *ought* to know—what I'm going to get from him. I call it "calculated anticipation."

Bob Gibson

Guessing.

Reggie Jackson

Okay, maybe it's guessing, if you want to call it that; but there's a *reason* for it. That's why I don't consider it guessing.

If you don't have a history with a pitcher and haven't studied his stuff and his tendencies, you're probably up there looking for a certain pitch in a certain situation. That's what I'd call guessing. And that's not what I mean when I talk about calculated anticipation. I'm talking about tapping into your precedents, utilizing the knowledge you've acquired over a period of time, and using all of *that* to inform you and set your strategy.

Joe Garagiola made fun of me once for that term, calculated anticipation. But it's nothing more than the practical result of what you know. There are guys who just go to home plate and say, I'm looking for a curveball. Why? What leads you to that decision? You can't defend a decision like that unless you have an understanding of what a pitcher may do in that particular scenario. If it's an intelligent, veteran pitcher, especially, there's a certain way he wants to pitch you. It's your job to know what it is. You have to watch, study, figure it out.

It's an ongoing process. If I'm hitting a guy pretty well and taking something away from him, he's not coming back with that same pitch. He might *show* it to me—say, a fastball high and outside—but unless he makes a mistake it's not going to be a ball I can handle. So I can limit the possibilities through the process of elimination and get an idea of what I might see that's hittable. On the other hand, if a pitcher starts beating *me* with a certain pitch in a certain area, I can be assured that, sooner or later—probably sooner—I'll get it again. And that has to become a part of my plan. I have to decide whether I'm going to make an adjustment to handle that pitch or let it go in the "calculated anticipation" of something else.

If I have reason to believe that a pitcher's going to work me inside and I don't handle the ball inside, most of the time I'm not walking up to the plate hoping to get a cut, right off the bat, at a pitch inside. *My* plan is just as important as *his* plan. I'm a professional: I've got to stay on my plan and not deviate from it until I get two strikes, at which point the plan is pretty much worthless. Now, if I'm convinced that the guy is absolutely determined to work me inside and nowhere else, that may allow me to cheat a bit and back up in the box. But that's an unusual circumstance. More often, at least until two strikes, I'll still be looking for a ball away that I can square.

It becomes cat and mouse. The pitcher may say to himself, "He's got to be looking inside. Let me try to sneak one past him outside." If he's smart and he's done his homework, he won't say that; but it happens, thankfully.

There are so many permutations to all of this. I may have hit his fastball hard three times that day. It's a close ballgame and I've lined to shortstop, I've hit a sharp ground ball to second base, and I've just missed a good fastball and skied it to center field. He's gotten me out with the fastball, but he's probably thinking he's running out of luck. Now I can go to home plate figuring that I'm going to see a breaking ball and wait for it. I'm trying to think with him.

Bob Gibson

But a batter can't do that pitch by pitch by pitch. It's more of a general plan. He's got something in mind that he's looking for and he'll look for it three out of four pitches or what have you. But he can't get into a situation where he'll be going pitch by pitch, guessing each one. Unless you really get lucky, that's not going to work.

There would be a better chance of a lucky guess against me, though, than against a pitcher like Juan Marichal, who throws four or five pitches at different speeds from different arm angles. With me, the batter can pretty much count on a fastball or slider. With Marichal, he can only count on getting something he's not counting on.

Reggie Jackson

Against a guy like Marichal, you just go up there to hit what you see.

Marichal threw about ninety-two, ninety-three miles an hour. He could make the ball run this way, make it run that way; he had a curve, a screwball, a changeup; he'd throw from over the top, from the side, with a big leg kick, with no leg kick at all. He'd be a classic see-the-ball-and-hit-it guy. But even with all that stuff and deception, the key thing was that he could put a good fastball where he wanted it. If I were to try to anticipate anything against Marichal, I'd look for a fastball away.

The opposite of Marichal would be a pitcher who specializes in a particular pitch. When I was with the A's in 1974, the Royals had a veteran, Lindy McDaniel, who gave us all kinds of problems with his good forkball. One game he pitched into the tenth inning, and the next time he beat us with a three-hitter. He had some other stuff, but the forkball was his out pitch. Still, every time he threw it we'd act like we were surprised. After that second game, he started against us again a few days later. I pointed out to the other guys that he's got to come with the forkball and it's always the same speed, so wait for it. Take it away from him. That time, we knocked him out in the third inning. Getting a pitch to hit is not an accident. It's a plan.

There was an occasion, again while I was with Oakland, when we were trailing Texas 2–1 with two outs in the eighth, runners on second and third. With two outs, there's no such thing as a sacrifice fly or run-scoring groundout, so I had to make solid contact in that situation. And for that to happen, I had to get a ball I could handle. Steve Hargan was the pitcher, and he kept pouring in tough strikes that I couldn't get the barrel on. I fouled off seven pitches until I got something I could work with. The result was a three-run homer. You could call it a case of stubbornness, I suppose, or maybe *committed* anticipation.

Bob Gibson

There's no way I would have allowed that to happen. Not with first base open. Not unless I was more concerned about the next hitter, which I doubt was the case.

I was rigid on that philosophy: The great hitters were *not* going to beat me. They were not going to get anything to hit, pure and simple. After our careers were over, Willie Mays once told me, "Man, when you pitched, I wasn't worried about hitting you. Curt Simmons is pitching tomorrow, and I'm gonna get *three.*"

That's not to say I didn't make some mistakes to the wrong hitters at the wrong times. But if I did, it was most likely against a guy whom I wasn't too concerned about as far as hitting a home run.

Tommy Davis of the Dodgers fit into that category. He was a terrific hitter, but not really a home-run hitter. At least, I wasn't worried about him hitting a home run. Maybe I should have been. In 1961, at Busch Stadium, I hooked up with Sandy Koufax and it was 0–0 in the seventh inning when Davis came up. On a one-oh count, I threw him a fastball inside, which I always think is a bad pitch, and he hit a line-drive home run off the left-field foul pole. I'd been pitching him away, away, away, and then I came in on him one time and bonk, there it goes. I think he was just waiting for me to bring one inside, and I was still young and dumb enough to oblige him. A year later, in Los Angeles, I was pitching against Koufax again and this time it was 0–0 in the ninth inning when Davis came up. I thought, okay, this is familiar. There's no way he can be looking for another inside fastball because I wouldn't be *that* dumb. Well, I was. I came inside again on oh-and-one, and sure enough, there it went, another line drive off the left-field foul pole. It was a textbook case of overthinking. Dumb, dumb, dumb.

Worse yet, I went against my better judgment. When I started winning big was when I stopped doing stuff like that.

Reggie Jackson

When I was facing a great pitcher late in a ballgame, and the ballgame was close, I'd try to get really focused on doing what *I* do best. That's when it's fun, because the great pitcher is doing the same thing.

If it's the eighth or ninth inning, with the game on the line, and Gibson can throw me three strikes on the inside part of the plate, I'm going to be an out. I would *settle* for that, because at that point in the game I'm holding out for something away. And I'm pretty sure Gibson's going to give it to me, because that's *his* strength, too. In that situation, we both want to go strength against strength. That's the time to bet on what I'm capable of doing, not try to handle something in my weakness. So I'm letting the inside pitch pass and waiting to catch a ball in my power zone.

Bob Gibson

There's a pretty good chance you might get what you're looking for, too.

Here's how it goes. The first time I face a batter in a ballgame, it's not necessarily that I'm trying to set him up or anything; I'm trying to establish my fastball and my control—in both my mind and his—because my fastball is my best pitch. My slider's not much use if I don't make the batter respect my fastball from the outset.

So if Reggie comes up in the first inning and he's batting third and there's nobody on base, that's the time for me to take charge, sort of assert my presence, and establish a foundation for how I want to pitch to him the rest of the game. But even if I do that successfully and he comes up later in the game in a spot where he can hurt me, I might change it up a little bit, because by that time I know what he's looking for and he knows I know what he's looking for. If he cheats or overcompensates or somehow changes his pattern of hitting, that's when you have to adjust your way of pitching to him. Now, I doubt that he'd do that. Most of the home-run hitters will pretty much stick with what they do, because they're looking to put the barrel on the ball with a big swing; at least until they get two strikes. You'll find that the guys who hit singles and doubles are more likely to adjust to the way you pitch them. So you've got to change it up and move it around a little more with them. If a guy like Reggie would alter his approach, I'd feel like I've gained an advantage because I've taken him out of his game and turned him into a contact hitter. I've gotten him out of his comfort zone.

But when it comes down to the key spot in the ballgame, I might just change the way I pitch him regardless of whether he's adjusted or not. Say, for instance, I've decided to work Reggie with a lot of hard sliders in on him because I know he has trouble with those. Even if the inside pitch is his weakness, I don't believe that I'd be throwing him many fastballs to that spot. The reason I'd throw him sliders instead is that with a slider I can make sure the ball gets *in there*. I mean *way* in there, from the corner in. The last thing I want to do is leave it out over to the plate to a guy as strong as Reggie.

So I'm working him all night with sliders in. That's my plan. Well, when we get to that moment of truth in the eighth or ninth inning and I've got nowhere to put him, I might say the hell with that. There's a decent chance that, since I've pitched him inside all night, he might not be looking away. On the other hand, there's also the risk that he's given up on the inside pitch by this time and he's holding out for something on the outside part of the plate that he can get the barrel on, since that's his strength. I'm well aware of the risk, believe me. But at that point, I don't care anymore. I've gotten myself into a spot where I can't *afford* to care. I need a strike so badly that I might just go ahead and throw the ball out there where I know he can crush it if I make a mistake.

The thing I've got going for me is the confidence that I'm *not going* to make a mistake. I think I can get him out that way because I believe in my ability to make a good pitch in a tough spot. I probably wouldn't keep the ball out there *every pitch*—I'm stubborn, not stupid—but I certainly might add that to the discussion. When push comes to shove, you have to do what you do best.

Reggie Jackson

When it comes down to strength against strength, the guessing, if you want to call it that, is out the window. There's not much guesswork anymore.

But I would have one advantage against Hoot. His strength is away, he's confident away, and I *want* the ball away. I'm on the defensive when it's oh-and-two, one-and-two, but if the count gets turned around and there's no place to put me and it's all out there on the line, I'm going to get what he does best. We both know that. Sooner or later, it's going to be me against him, his strength against mine. Now I feel like, come on, let's go.

Bob Gibson

Yep. Here it comes, ready or not. And it's coming out over the plate, just like he likes it. If I have no choice but to throw a strike—and that's the only excuse—I can't be that concerned about location, other than just getting it over. I'm just trying to throw it down the middle, above the belt, with the best stuff I have. When my back is to the wall, it's on.

Here it is, buddy.

CHAPTER TWO

MECHANICS

Raw Materials

Reggie Jackson

When I'm evaluating young players for the Yankees—young hitters—I see them roughly in two types. The first would be in the mold of a kid in our organization named Austin Jackson. He has very, very high motor skills—skills like Derek Jeter—and he'll be a big-leaguer. Jackson had a full ride to Georgia Tech as a point guard, and he's such a good athlete that he's going to figure out how to get the bat on the baseball. With a guy as talented as that, you give him suggestions, counsel him, and then step back and let him adapt because he has the ability to figure it out on his own.

We also had a somewhat younger kid by the name of Jose Tabata, whom we signed when he was sixteen and traded to the Pirates when he was nineteen. To me, Tabata's the other prototype, a classic behind-the-ball hitter in the mold of Roberto Clemente, Tony Perez, Albert Pujols, and Manny Ramirez. I'm talking about the kind of guy who is not looking to pull a pitch into the seats but is always behind the ball, putting it in play. I'd put Jeter in that company, because he stays behind the ball as well as anybody, but he's a little different in that he's not a power hitter in the mold of those other guys. In that sense, he could be a good model for Tabata. Derek simply refuses to get off his plan and try to pull the ball. That's the reason he has been so successful. But it's something he's had to consciously stick with, and that takes a lot of mental effort. In 2002, after hitting well over .300 for four years in a row, Derek was struggling a bit and came to me asking for input. My advice was to quit trying to hit the inside fastball. All he was doing on those was grounding out to third and jerking foul balls down the line. Jeter's game is hitting line drives the other way. Pulling the ball made his swing a little tighter and took away his real strength. He eventually got back to doing what he does best and had another great season.

For Derek, it's all about being a "professional hitter." His approach allows him to stay in the groove longer than most hitters because he does things right. Power hitters create more extension than Derek does, and he could hit for more power if he added extension, but there's a trade-off involved with that. It makes you strike out a little more. Since Jeter doesn't have the natural power that guys like Manny and Pujols have, and since he's a smart hitter, he stays within his God-given gifts, which is hitting line drives—singles and doubles—with an occasional display of power. What he's done better than the next guy is produce in the clutch. That's mental makeup.

When Jose Tabata was sixteen, his first thoughts were to hit the ball to right center. So he's very seldom out in front, he very seldom rolls over the ball and taps a ground ball to shortstop or second base. He just has a natural feel for the game, the innate ability to do things that other players have to be taught and may never pick up. Pitchers look at a guy like that and see a tough out, a tough guy to pitch to, because he's not trying to pull every ball out of the park. He's not creating weaknesses for himself. He does things that I view as gifts, things that tell me this guy has a real chance to be a hitter.

Of course, the great players are the ones who have both the athletic ability and the grasp of the game. Both of those things are gifts. That's what you saw in Mays and Clemente and Aaron, and what you see today in hitters like Jeter, Pujols, Ramirez, and Alex Rodriguez. They combine physical talent with the ol' noggin.

There aren't many of those guys.

Bob Gibson

You could categorize pitchers the same way. The pure athletes would be the hard throwers, and then there are the guys who just have a touch, like Maddux or Tom Glavine or somebody like Jamie Moyer, who seems like he can pitch forever on brains and moxie.

People might argue that finesse pitchers get by without the natural ability of guys like Nolan Ryan or Roger Clemens or Randy Johnson. I'm not sure I'd go along with that. To some extent, control is a natural ability, too. Some pitchers naturally throw better curveballs than other pitchers, or better changeups. The feel for the game is a natural ability. Reggie described it as "innate," and that's a good way to put it. Some guys are athletes and others are just ballplayers. Put the two together and you've really got something.

Reggie Jackson

You can teach somebody to be a *better* hitter, but you can't teach the ability to hit to a guy who can't. He's just not going to hit. Now, a guy who's a good ballplayer but can't hit can end up as a pitcher. That's a lot more common than somebody like Rick Ankiel converting from a pitcher to a hitter. That's rare.

But certainly you need good hand-eye coordination to do either. Hand-eye coordination is perhaps the most critical thing for hitting.

Bob Gibson

Hand strength is very important.

Reggie Jackson

All good hitters have big, thick hands.

Bob Gibson

Pretty much. Mays is not a big guy, but you ought to look at his hands. Big, thick hands.

Reggie Jackson

Johnny Bench is another one.

Bob Gibson

The only real good hitter I can think of with small hands was Stan Musial. Little bitty hands. But you couldn't find a better hitter.

Reggie Jackson

So much of it is timing. Not all power hitters are built like Ryan Howard or Albert Pujols. Ken Griffey Jr. was thin when he was young and hitting home runs. Aaron wasn't a big guy when he was young. A slender player can hit a ball a long way with co-ordination, good timing, and strength in his hands.

You see it better when you watch the golf swing of a skinny person who drives three hundred yards. Michelle Wie is a young, thin girl, but she's six feet tall and has a long arc to her swing. And timing. Tiger Woods is a big person, but it's obvious that with torque, timing, and strength in his hands he gets the maximum out of his body. If Tiger Woods or Michelle Wie were baseball players, they'd be power hitters, because of their timing.

A guy who hits for power just looks different when he swings the bat—different than a guy like Jeter, who has a good swing, an athletic swing, but one with an arc that is clearly not the arc of Manny Ramirez.

Bob Gibson

Studying the golf swing gives you a pretty good idea of how hard it is to hit a baseball. Hitting requires the same kind of timing and rhythm and hand-eye coordination, but then add to that the quick-twitch ability you need to hit a ninety-five-mile-an-hour fastball, and the reactions you need to handle the dramatic changes from pitcher to pitcher and even pitch to pitch, and the mental dexterity you need to process all the strategic considerations that pile up constantly.

Another difference is eyesight. Good vision is extremely important to hitting. Joe Torre's eyes were so strong that he'd be talking about something going on out in center field—a light or a disturbance or whatever—and I'd have no idea what he was seeing out there.

I was a good hitter for a pitcher, and I even pinch-hit a few times, but I wasn't a good *hitter* because I didn't have the eyes to see the rotation on the ball. I'm not sure you *have* to see the rotation to be a good hitter, and I'm not sure all good hitters can— Torre could, and Ted Williams certainly could—but it helps. When the ball comes out of the pitcher's hand, you see two dark lines coming at you, and if they're straight up and down there's a pretty good chance it's a fastball. There's a possibility it could be a breaking ball, but if you see the rotation going sideways you *know* it's a breaking ball. I couldn't pick that up.

I had no idea what my eyesight was, but I've been wearing glasses since I was nineteen. The problem was, I sweated so much when I pitched that I'd have to take a rag out of my pocket to wipe my glasses off, and then they'd smear and I couldn't see at all. So I left them in the clubhouse.

Reggie Jackson

People assume my eyesight was bad because I wore glasses when I played. Actually, it was twenty-twenty with my glasses off, twenty-ten with them on. I needed glasses to correct my astigmatism. I suppose I could have played without them, but I struck out enough with my glasses *on*.

As a hitter, eyesight is not something you can afford to shrug off. In my estimation, there's no such thing as a good hitter who can't read the spin on the ball. You've *got* to be able to read spin. You've got to read it right away, as soon as the ball leaves the pitcher's hand.

Bob Gibson

There are so many things that go into hitting—eyesight, hands, hand-eye coordination, quickness, timing, strength, intelligence, instinct—that you can't stereotype the guys who do it well. There's no way to tell a hitter just by looking at him. There's no prototype body for a baseball player.

What kind of body does a pitcher need to throw hard? Big, strong legs? Hell, mine look like bird legs. I had plenty of spring in my legs—I could easily dunk a basketball back in the day when the coach would take you out of the game for doing that—but it's not something you could tell by looking at me. You've got skinny guys who can throw the ball ninety-five miles an hour and great big guys who throw ninety-five.

Arm speed makes a big difference. But I couldn't tell you exactly what kind of athlete has it, or how to get it.

Reggie Jackson

Arm speed is the thing that jumps out at you with a pitcher like Joba Chamberlain. He's a big guy, thick and strong, but that's not what makes him different. His arm speed is what makes him different.

To some extent, that's a product of strength, which, to an extent, is a product of size. Pitchers like Carlos Zambrano and C. C. Sabathia produce a lot of power on the mound, and their big bodies have a lot to do with it. Tim Lincecum is just the opposite. But they all have arm speed. You look at Joba Chamberlain's arm speed, especially when he wants to crank it up, and there's just more of it than most guys have.

The characteristic that all these guys have in common, for certain, is that they're good athletes.

Bob Gibson

Physically, there wasn't any particular thing that gave me an advantage, although I do have one odd feature. My fingers are symmetrical. My forefinger and little finger are the same length and my two middle fingers are the same length. The only other person I know who has fingers like that is my son, Christopher. That's how I knew he was mine.

My forefinger is a little shorter than normal, and maybe, because of that, the ball came out of my hand in a way that made it sail, like a cut fastball. I didn't have to try to throw a cutter; it just acted that way. But if you went around cutting a quarter of an inch off everybody's forefinger, I don't think you'd create a class of Hall of Fame pitchers. It's just something strange about me.

Reggie Jackson

My distinction was that, physically, I was unusually muscular for a ballplayer. I watch myself on tape and I look stiff. I always thought I'd appear more fluid than I did. But my strength was a big part of who I was as a hitter. I never had to worry about pulling the ball to right field, because I knew that if I put the barrel on it and got it in the air, I could hit it out of any part of the park. Strength is also what helped me generate bat speed at the last instant and catch up with balls that seemed to be past me already—maybe even flick them over the fence. There were plenty of times when I surprised myself and wondered how I hit that pitch. The answer is strength—along with God-given talent.

Of course, this was before steroids and really before ballplayers did much weight training. In baseball, lifting weights had been frowned upon for a long time, because they thought it would make you too tight, that your muscles wouldn't have the elasticity you needed to play the game. There were just a few who believed in it, and I was one.

I always worked out—it was a way of life for me, and still is—but I was also naturally thick through the chest, arms, and thighs. My biceps were seventeen inches, the same as Sonny Liston's. My legs gave me a great power base—you generate power from the ground up—but they were so tight that they gave me a lot of hamstring trouble. Make sure you stretch.

Bob Gibson

I didn't do any weight training, but I got plenty of work on my legs from pushing off the mound the way I did; and my right arm—especially my forearm—got hard and tight from throwing sliders. The inside of my forearm, right below my elbow, was always sore. One time it got so hard in there that I went to see the doctor. He tried to give me a shot to loosen it up and broke the needle.

He said, "That's really hard in there."

I said, "I know, Doc. That's why I'm getting a shot."

Delivery

Bob Gibson

My power came from my motion, and for the most part my motion came from my legs. I'm sure the spring in my legs showed up in my fastball. You build up torque from the waist down. That's probably why all the cartilage in my knees was torn up by the time I was through—and well before. It was all that twisting.

I had a violent delivery. I jumped at the hitter. If they would have let me, I'd have loved to back up and run up over the mound, like jai alai, like Happy Gilmore hitting a drive. I wanted everything to be moving that way when I let go of the ball. Everything. I wanted to be a gathering storm and blow that fastball in there with all the force and fury I could muster up.

Jim Bunning's motion looked as much like mine as anybody I've seen. He used to fly around, too. But other than that, there was really no similarity in the way he threw and the way I threw. His arm angle was lower than mine. For me, dropping the arm angle was a bad habit I had to avoid. When I dropped lower than three-quarters, the ball would tend to shoot up in the strike zone because I didn't get on top of it to drive it down. I liked throwing high fastballs, but those weren't my *best* fastballs. Every once in a while, I'd raise my angle and come from over the top, but I'm not sure that I ever threw a strike that way. It was always high. So I stayed three-quarters.

Reggie Jackson

There aren't many Juan Marichals out there who can throw every pitch from every angle, thank goodness.

These days, there aren't many pitchers who have a lot going on in their windups, either.

Bob Gibson

I have to wonder whether, if I pitched today, they'd try to simplify and quiet down my motion. I'm pretty sure they'd have gotten to me early in my career, when I didn't have much idea of where the ball was going. I can just hear it: "Well, you know, it's no surprise that you were a little wild out there. If you would find your balance point and slow everything down a little bit . . ."

They'd have also told me—and I heard this more than a few times—that I wasn't in any position to field the ball after my delivery because I was falling off the mound and wheeling toward first base. Well, maybe I wasn't, but I was a good fielder because I was quick and had body control; I was a basketball player. Somehow, I won nine straight Gold Gloves being out of position.

In order to end up in perfect position to field the ball, I would have had to take away from my velocity. I'd rather have the velocity and then have to recover afterwards. Getting the hitter out is more important to me than trying to snag a ball coming back up the middle.

Reggie Jackson

Put it this way. As a hitter, I'd have liked it very much if Bob Gibson had slowed down or cut back on his delivery. And it's not just the velocity he gained from it. It's also the motion itself. A hitter tries to get in sync with a pitcher's motion. When *he's* rocking, *I'm* rocking. I'll start getting into my swing before the ball is actually delivered.

If the motion is harder to time, that's an advantage for the pitcher.

Bob Gibson

I like the idea of having a lot going on in your windup, and the hitters trying to figure out where the ball's coming from and when it's coming. Man, with a big windup the hitter sees all this stuff going on in front of him, knees and elbows, the hat flying off, all this crazy whirling motion, the ball's moving from high to low, from side to side, the glove flashes out there, and then boom! Here it comes at ninety-five miles an hour.

For the first half of my career, I was doing all this off a fifteen-inch mound. It was a little different when they lowered it down to ten in 1969. The pitcher shrank by five inches. Now couple that with the fact that, gradually, big windups and motions have almost become a thing of the past, and you can see that a pitcher is not quite the formidable figure he used to be out there.

Dontrelle Willis is one of the few who still uses an elaborate windup, and he was devastating for a while, before he lost some of his stuff. I have a hard time understanding why so few pitchers do that anymore. Somebody started a trend and this is how it ended up.

Now everything's all sedate. The gurus thought that pitchers could have better control if they minimized their motions, and everybody bought into it. Somebody told the pitchers they could throw just as hard without the windup. Maybe some guys can. I'm sure this is the best thing for a lot of guys, but I'm not buying that it's best for practically everybody.

If I were pitching today, I'd still wind up and fly around. Personally, I'd rather have the batter *look* for the ball. If you start with a calm little windup, the hitter sees the ball all the way; or at least he sees the release point where it's coming from.

And that's not the entire issue. The most important thing, to me, is that I felt I threw harder when I wound up. It was more of an effort to throw that hard from the stretch, when you're trying to generate power from a dead standstill. That's got to take a little bit away. Does it take a lot? I don't know. But I know that, if you're trying to maintain velocity, it takes a lot more *out of you,* which can't be good for your control. It's a double-edged deal, because when you're throwing from the stretch, or without much of a windup, you absolutely have to locate the ball better.

It really all depends on what kind of stuff the pitcher has. If you're throwing ninety-five, the velocity is a little more important than the location. But if you're throwing ninety, you'd better put that ball exactly where you want it. So I can see the value of restricting your motion, exchanging velocity for control, if you're not that hard of a thrower. The difference between eighty-eight and ninety-one is not that significant. At that speed, I'd better damn sure have good control. Now, if the windup can increase your fastball from ninety-one to ninety-four or ninety-five, that's a different thing. At ninety-five, my control doesn't have to be quite as fine.

But if you don't feel comfortable, don't do it.

Reggie Jackson

Some pitchers have clean, smooth windups that look really nice, but instead of all the extra business taking place on the mound and creating a distraction, the ball's just coming out right there where the hitter can keep his eye on it.

Think about how they pitch in batting practice. The batting-practice pitcher wants the hitter to get a good look at the ball, so he'll hold it up for the guy to see and just take one step and throw it from right out in front of the batter's face. A lot of the pitchers today do it almost the same way.

Back in the day, Marichal had that big foot sticking in your face, and he'd change his angles and make you look so bad it just took the spirit right out of you. Luis Tiant had all that twisting and turning and looking this way and that—whatever he could come up with to throw you off. El Duque is a throwback with that big ol' funny-looking leg kick of his. Those guys are all classic examples of how a pitcher's motion can have a lot to do with his success.

Bob Gibson

Warren Spahn won 363 games with a big fancy windup that involved a lot of arm and leg action. With the Cardinals, we had a relief pitcher, Bob Humphreys, who might not have made it to the big leagues if he hadn't had a gimmick in his windup, and he lasted nine years. He'd vary the number of times he pumped his arms before every pitch. We called him Double Pump. We could have called him Triple Pump.

Most pitching coaches today tell you that the more gyrations you go through on the mound, the greater your chance for error. I can't argue with that. Sometimes when I leapt at the hitter, I'd leap a little too far and the ball would get away from me. You might kick your leg too high and lose balance. It *is* a matter of balance. Mostly, you've got to balance whether you want that extra control or that extra confusion and velocity.

And you know where I stand on that one. But that's just me.

Reggie Jackson

At least with Bob you could pretty much count on the ball coming from three-quarters. He wasn't going to change much out there from pitch to pitch.

Bob Gibson

Once in a while, against right-handers, just to give a little different look, I'd drop down and throw a slurve—a slower slider or a faster curveball, whichever you wanted to call it. It was really too big to be a regular slider, and not as crisp. And I was careful about keeping it away. But that thing would flash down across the batters' knees and you could almost hear them curse.

I wouldn't do it for Willie Mays, because you have a better chance of making a mistake with a pitch like that. I'd throw it to somebody like Dick Stuart, where if I missed I'd have a better chance of getting away with it. You pick your spots.

Reggie Jackson

When you've got a big-time power pitcher who suddenly throws in the kitchen sink like that, you do a double take and hope it's out of the strike zone.

Bob Gibson

I also tinkered a bit with where I stood on the rubber. You're always looking for an advantage, so you always tinker. I felt the most comfortable standing on the right corner of the rubber, where a right-handed hitter might have to look over his shoulder a little bit instead of straight-on. But once in a while I'd move to the other side if I was pitching to a left-hander. It's not easy for a hitter to make adjustments every time he goes to the plate.

What I really liked, though, was when the *other* pitcher used the left side. That way, my foot wasn't landing in the same hole where his foot was landing. It can throw you off, maybe buckle your ankle, if the other guy makes a hole that's just a few inches from where yours is. That's why you'll occasionally see the grounds crew out there filling in a hole. You can also have that problem next to the rubber if the other pitcher sets up in the general vicinity of where you do and scrapes out a little hill that tilts your foot.

I started with my foot *on* the rubber, and then when I wound up I'd pick it up and turn it sideways against the rubber. If you happen to put your foot down a couple inches in front of the rubber, the umpire's not going to see that. Nobody's actually looking for it, but sometimes somebody in the other dugout will notice it and go "Hey! What'd he just do there?!" Spahn would do that. He'd get two strikes on somebody and want to get the ball up there just a little bit quicker, and he'd step several inches in front of that rubber. We'd holler, and while we're hollering, whoosh, the ball would shoot in there for strike three. The umpire's going to watch for it now, but Spahn wouldn't do it again for a long time, when everybody had forgotten about it.

There's a lot of stuff that goes into 363 wins.

Reggie Jackson

There are also a lot of pitches, and a lot of innings, that go into that. Spahn had almost four hundred complete games. Gaylord Perry had more than three hundred. Gibson had 255. There's no current player in the top *hundred* in that category. Greg Maddux has the most, with just over a hundred.

The emphasis on relief pitchers and pitch counts has quite a bit to do with that, obviously. But it's interesting that all the pitchers who threw the most complete games and the most innings come from the age of bigger windups. Of the top ten all-time in innings pitched, six guys—Phil Niekro, Ryan, Perry, Don Sutton, Spahn, and Carlton—come from my day and Bob's. They were all in the game by the time I got there in 1967; and Spahn was already out of it, thank goodness.

Bob Gibson

It's not just windups. The whole delivery has been stream-lined and homogenized. There's a concerted emphasis these days on protecting the pitcher, and part of that involves fussing over his mechanics.

Mechanics are good. But people come up with all kinds of rea-sons why some pitchers last and others break down, and I don't know that you'll ever be able to pinpoint the reasons why. We're all different. Our bodies are different, they can withstand different things, and in my opinion none of that stuff is worth a crap. If you try to teach one person to do something the way another person does it, you're usually walking down the wrong road.

In the end, we're all fundamentally similar, even if we arrive at our release points by different routes. It's the same with hitting. One guy—remember Dick McAuliffe?—will set up with an open stance and Stan Musial will twist around so he has to peek over his shoulder; a hitter like Richie Hebner will hold his bat flat and down below his waist and Craig Counsell will swirl it up above his helmet, high as he can go; Pete Rose and Jeff Bagwell batted out of a crouch and Eric Davis stood straight up. But when the barrel addresses the ball, they all end up in roughly the same po-sition. Likewise, if you took a picture of every major-league pitcher just as he's letting go of the ball, you'd see that the arm angle might differ but there isn't much variation in body posi-tion. There aren't a lot of different ways to throw ninety-three miles an hour.

The fact is, some of us are going to break down and some aren't, regardless of the mechanics. There's not a recipe for it. Some guys appear to be straining their arms when they throw, and people today will watch and say, well, that's no good, he's going to hurt his arm for sure. Maybe. But let's just see. Don't try to head things off. We don't know. Maybe he's got an unorthodox way of throwing that will last forever. Maybe it would strain *my* arm to throw that way, but unless he's having some problems, why mess with it?

If he starts to have arm trouble, maybe then we can break

down his mechanics and suggest this or that to ease the problem. Is that going to cure it? We don't know. But unless it's broken, don't try to fix it. You just can't predict it.

We're all different.

Swing

Reggie Jackson

Keeping my front side closed is what made me a decent hitter. When I got to the plate I'd remind myself to stay closed in order to keep the right front hip in, in order to keep my shoulders square, in order to have proper plate coverage, in order to keep the barrel of the bat in the pay zone for a long time.

I was a good hitter if I could think to keep the ball to the left-field side of the diamond and concentrate on driving it over the shortstop's head. And I could say one thing to myself—"keep your front side closed"—to make all those other things happen. Or I could say any of the countless variations on the same theme: "stay behind the ball" or "keep your nose behind the ball" or "cover the plate" or "stay square" or "wait for the ball to get on the barrel."

It all works together. If you keep your front side closed, then your body stays behind your legs, your arms stay behind your body, your hands stay back, your bat stays behind your hands, and when you swing, all that momentum, all that torque, all that power, is brought to bear on the baseball. You could call it timing. It's also called rotational force, which I generated a lot of.

Rotational force starts with the transfer of weight from back to front, or back foot to front foot. It's the rhythm of hitting, and that part of it was natural for me. It was my natural coordination, my natural swing. Ted Williams—I wore his number nine when I was with Oakland—once said I was the most natural hitter he'd ever seen. I don't know about that, but I did come into the game with power. To put that power into play, I had to execute the *fundamentals*. Stay behind the ball. Keep my front side closed.

Because I was strong, I could hit the ball out of the park without pulling it and also without lifting it. A lot of home-run hit-ters will uppercut at the ball, but the best *hitters* don't do that. It was a lesson I learned from Dick Allen. We had long conversations about hitting. I wasn't able to duplicate his style, though, because he could keep his hands low and get to the ball with power from that position. My method was to build up force with my rotation. So I held the bat higher. But I still dropped the bat head on the ball, essentially swinging down, like Allen did. Dick's power was based on natural explosiveness. Mine was based on strength and natural mechanics, which combined to make me explosive.

We both generated it with the gifts we were given, and that's what Bob Gibson did on the mound. He didn't have to preoccupy himself with building up a big-time fastball; he *had* one, just like I had the strength to drive the ball out of the park, any park. But as a hitter, you can squander that power with poor fundamentals and an improper approach.

Bob Gibson

Some things are basic to baseball. The same way a hitter loses his power if he flies open too soon in his approach to the ball, a pitcher has to stay back on the rubber and not bring his weight forward prematurely. If a hitter flies open, there's nothing left to hit the ball with. If a pitcher doesn't keep his weight back as he gets into his motion, there's nothing left to *throw* the ball with. Same thing.

Of course, that doesn't make it easy to fix. If a pitcher has to think about mechanics in the heat of a game, he has a problem that particular day.

Reggie Jackson

For a hitter, that's why it's important to simplify things. As I teach today with the Yankees, I try to show them the one thing—keeping the front side closed—that almost always will make everything else fall in line.

As you stand at home plate, clear your mind of everything except what you have to do next. I might tug on the shoulder of my shirt to remind me to keep the shoulder in. I might bang on my hip to remind me to keep the hip in. Find your own little ways to focus. Find one thought that will make four or five things happen.

Bob Gibson

He has time, sitting in the dugout and standing in the on-deck circle, to converse with himself about what he has to do in this next swing or two. A pitcher can't sit back and do that every couple of pitches. We're out there working. We have to get all that stuff straightened out ahead of time.

Reggie Jackson

No matter how much talking to yourself you do, you still have to recognize the ball coming out of the pitcher's hand. But again, if I'm staying back with my front side closed, it keeps my head in and my eyes locked on the baseball so that I'm able to read the spin on it. In other words, when I keep myself square it allows me to stay in a position to hit. It allows me to be able to respond whether the ball's in, up, or down, whether it's off-speed or whatever.

It's a lot easier to fall into a rut, or a slump, if you're constantly looking for a pitch on the inside part of the plate to pull. One of the things that used to mess me up was coming home to Yankee Stadium and wanting to get the ball around to those seats that looked so easy to reach in right field, the ones that Babe Ruth and Mickey Mantle had so much fun with. That kind of temptation led to an eagerness that caused me to start pulling off the ball too early. It created a bad habit. That's why, in batting practice, I'd pick out a sign in right center, draw myself a border that ran right through the second baseman, and make that my foul line. I tried to do the same thing during a game. I'd remind myself, keep your front side in, keep your front side in.

If you're looking for a pitch away, as opposed to an inside pitch to pull, that makes you stay back on the ball longer, makes you more patient. It keeps your eye on the ball. Sometimes you can actually see the ball *too* well—so well that you think you can do anything with it. When that happens, you tend to try to hit it where you want it to go, rather than where it's pitched.

By thinking "hard the other way," you're harnessing the movements of your body. Your swing becomes shorter. The eyes don't travel as far. The bat doesn't travel as far. With the shorter path, there's less chance for error. The natural move, for a left-hander, is to start out with the idea of hitting a line drive in the direction of the shortstop and then let the speed of the pitch—and of course the location—move the ball around from there. Don't let your own predetermination tell you which way to go with the pitch. Let the pitch itself dictate that.

Most of the big home runs I've seen Alex Rodriguez hit—and big ones in the context of the game—have been to center field and right center. He's going to finish with 750 or 800 home runs, and he'd hit even more if he were more interested in staying behind the ball and driving it to right center, his opposite field. A good portion of the time, he does that. His game is hard to right center. But he doesn't stay on his approach to right center the way Manny Ramirez and Albert Pujols do. For that reason, A-Rod is not quite as good a hitter as those guys. Don't get me wrong: Nobody has more ability. He's got great hand-eye coordination and he's a great talent. He's the first player in the history of the game to hit at least thirty-five homers in twelve seasons. Those are the facts. It's also a fact that he gets off his game a little more than Ramirez or Pujols. Think "hard to right center" and let the rest take care of itself. If A-Rod did that more regularly, he'd consistently hit for a higher average and at the same time produce more home runs, the way he did in 2007.

Ryan Howard is another one who hasn't quite learned to stay behind the ball, and consequently is not as good a hitter as Manny or Pujols. Don't misunderstand: He's one of the most productive hitters in the game, and he has the kind of power that can carry a team. All I'm saying is, he's still young and learning. The talent, the power and the swing will take you a long way, but there's more to it than that.

Guys who are high-skill-level hitters, like Hank Aaron and Manny Ramirez, are smart hitters. You have to know who's on the mound, the situation, the score, the count, whether you need the ball in the air or on the ground or to the right side or to the left. Know what your team is trying to do every inning, every day. Learn to think like a manager.

And whatever the count is, or the score, or the situation, stay behind the ball. Keep your front side closed.

Repetition

Bob Gibson

When I was a kid in Omaha, my older brother Josh worked with me a lot on my mechanics. Josh coached our baseball teams and basketball teams, and when we weren't practicing as a team he had me out there by myself all the time, shooting, ballhandling, pitching, hitting, fielding ground balls, whatever. Practice, practice, practice. There was never an excuse to stop practicing.

One time, before a tournament game in Missouri, he hit me a ground ball that bounced up and caught me above the eye and I was bleeding all over the infield. Josh slapped a Band-Aid on it and told me to get back out there. He'd work me so hard he'd have me crying. I told my mom I didn't want to play for him because he was so mean, and she said, "Honey, you don't have to play for him if you don't want to." But I was right back out there.

Josh was huge on fundamentals. How-to stuff. I can't say that he had all the mechanics broken down to a science, but his approach to the game certainly made an impression on me. Josh had strong opinions on how to do things—he knew exactly what he wanted— and he drilled into me that there was always a right way and a wrong way. He also made it clear that you'd never master the right way if you didn't practice, practice, practice. I believe in practice.

Reggie Jackson

Yeah, and I played football for Frank Kush at Arizona State. Talk about a guy who was hell in practice. If you didn't do things the right way for Frank Kush, you'd be sure to regret it. He would put me through so much—mostly, having big linemen pound on me in one-on-one drills, with the whole team watching—that it brought tears to my eyes. One time it made me run off the field and quit until Charley Taylor, the former ASU player who became a great running back and receiver for the Washington Redskins, came after me and convinced me that I didn't want to "let that 'SOB' win." But Coach Kush instilled a toughness in me, mental and physical, that I didn't know I had. He showed me what it took to be a great professional.

Because of that, I'd say he did as much to make me a good baseball player as anybody did—and my baseball coach at ASU was Bobby Winkles. Between those two, I came out of college equipped with the knowledge that any game worth playing is worth playing right.

Bob Gibson

I doubt that there are any big-league pitchers who didn't play a lot of ball as a kid. It's not essential that they were *pitchers* when they were young, but they had to throw the ball a lot.

For the last fifteen years or so, there have been all kinds of theories on why the pitching is so much worse than it used to be. People talk about smaller parks, steroids, the ball being juiced, and all that; and they're probably right. But you also have to consider that kids these days don't grow up playing baseball every day all summer long. In this age, if you come across a neighborhood ballfield on a sunny weekday in July, there's probably nobody on it. It's too hot. There's too much other stuff to do. When I was a kid, that was the place to be.

The upshot is that kids aren't playing as much ball as they used to, which means that they aren't *throwing* the ball as much as they used to. You have to throw a lot to build up your arm, and you have to throw a lot to build the hand-eye coordination that leads to control.

At some point, though, a pitcher has to start pitching. Even in the big leagues, there are guys who were converted to pitcher in the minors because they had great arms, but those guys don't make it to the majors in a month or even a year. Pitching is a muscle-memory thing. You have to develop command, and command comes from repetition. The more you pitch, the better your command—your control—is going to be.

It's the same as shooting a basketball. Shooters have to shoot a lot. You have to develop that feel, that eye, that touch, that coordination, that consistency. You show me a good shooter and I'll show you somebody who has taken a whole lot of shots in his life. That's probably somebody who, as a kid, was on the playground all day shooting the ball, or in the gym at ten o'clock at night shooting the ball. Pitching is no different. You have to put the ball in the pocket, and if you don't do it a lot you're not going to be great at it.

Mechanics are important, of course. There are things you can do with your mechanics and your delivery to sharpen up your control. A control pitcher can lose his control by lapsing into bad mechanics. He can improve on his mechanics and get back to where he used to be. But improving your mechanics doesn't mean a thing if you don't practice that way. That's why, even in the major leagues, guys work out in the bullpen.

In the final analysis, the best way to become a better pitcher is by pitching.

Reggie Jackson

And a hitter has to hit. No hitter is so good that he can't get better by spending time in the cage, or out on the field at three o'clock before a night game, taking swings against a fifty-eight-year-old coach.

That's when you tend to your mechanics, and that's the way you guard against bad habits. Slumps will happen because we're human, but you can sometimes head them off by swinging the bat to stay sharp. The more pitches you see, the better you can tell if a ball is an inch and a half off the plate, or an inch and a half away from your power. There's a feel you want to develop for keeping your shoulder in. There's a certain length of stride that fits you, and you want to stay in that groove.

You want it all to become as familiar and natural as possible, because there will be times when you step into the box and everything's foreign. It's like you've never been there before. Your spikes feel too long, the dirt's too hard, the ball has shrunk, and the pitcher looks like he's standing in your lap. It doesn't happen often, but sometimes you feel like a stranger up there. That's when you have to understand your mechanics.

You want them—you *need* them—to carry you through those times when nothing feels right, or when you're mentally dragging and don't even know it. That's why it's imperative to keep them crisp and sound. You might be tired because you've played sixty games in a row, with just three or four days off. Maybe you've been on the road for a week and a half and it's wearing on you. Your mechanics might start to slide before you realize it. We didn't have hitting coaches early in my career, so I'd pick a guy on the bench who didn't play much and say, "Hey, could you do me a favor? Just watch me as often as you can to see if I'm falling into a bad habit." Or Joe Rudi or Sal Bando might check me out if they're hitting behind me and they might say, "Look, your hands are down."

There's no shortage of things that can throw off your mechanics. So you need to make them second nature. You need them to be there, solid, automatic—to be *part of you*, not only as a hedge against slumps and fatigue but so your mind isn't cluttered with all the technical stuff when you're trying to concentrate on what's coming next from that closer who throws ninety-seven miles an hour.

It takes repetition. Practice.

Bob Gibson

Early in a game, a pitcher might have an opportunity to tweak a thing or two, like the length of your stride, as long as it doesn't preoccupy you so much that it takes your attention away from the batter who's up there with runners on second and third. But if you shorten your stride for two or three pitches and you're not getting the results, there's no more time for that. You'll have to scratch your little experiment and take it up in the bullpen between starts.

That's exactly the kind of thing you'd work on in the bullpen. Your control depends a lot on where your front leg lands. If you're having a hard time getting the ball away from a right-handed hitter, chances are you're locking yourself out, not opening up your body enough. If you keep throwing it inside, inside, inside, and when you try to go away the ball comes back over the middle, it's probably because you're leaving your left foot a couple inches to the right of where it needs to be when you land. So when you're working in the bullpen, you can draw a mark where your foot comes down. If you land on that mark two or three times and you're still having a hard time getting the ball outside, draw a new mark a few inches to the left and see if you can make that work without flying too far open.

Reggie Jackson

A two- or three-inch difference at home plate can be a two- or three-hundred-foot difference when the ball comes down.

I once asked Catfish Hunter, "Catfish, why do you fix your hat every time? When you're on the mound, you adjust your hat on every pitch."

He said, "I do that because if my foot is not hitting in the same spot every time, then my hat gets a little cocked. So that's how I check myself." When a guy takes his stride and that foot and that spike mark start mating up over and over, he's right. He's going to hit that little three-by-five paperback book from sixty feet, six inches.

Bob Gibson

Catfish could monitor himself that way because he had worked it out in the bullpen and knew exactly where his stride had to be.

You can't be ready without enough practice. And at the same time, you can't get enough practice to make yourself ready for what you might face in a live game situation.

You might pitch and pitch and pitch in the bullpen and get to the point where your stride is dead-on and your control is impeccable *in the bullpen*. That's great, and it improves your skill level, but there's a little more effort involved when you're pitching against Willie Stargell or Lance Berkman. All of a sudden, what you were doing in the bullpen might not mean so much because now you've got to throw a little harder. Just that *ugh!*, that grunt, that extra little bit of *oomph*, will change your mechanics and change the direction of the ball. It will change your location.

You find that when you throw a little harder you tend to throw a little *higher*, and if you don't throw with that same intensity in the bullpen, you'll be out of sync in a game situation. And the fact is, you *don't* throw with the same intensity in the bullpen. You just don't. There are no consequences if you miss in the bullpen—just a gee whiz and a shake of the head. If you miss in a game, the party might be over. There's a tremendous difference, just like there's a tremendous difference between shooting a fifteen-foot jump shot alone in the gym and shooting that same shot with Dennis Rodman in your face in a close game with the clock running down and twenty thousand people screaming and waving things.

You need both. You need the practice to get the repetition, and to get your mechanics mastered to the point that they come naturally; and you need the game experience. There's no substitute for either.

Routine

Bob Gibson

I'm still waiting for a manager to put me in at third base. I took a lot of ground balls over there on the days after I pitched.

But the time wasn't wasted. Even in the major leagues, I believed that you had to throw a lot to keep your arm strong. The more you *run*, the *longer* you can run, and the same goes for throwing. That's how you develop your durability: throwing.

Most pitchers schedule a bullpen session midway between their starts, and that's fine, but my arm—my whole body—was always sore on the second day after a ballgame. For some reason, I was never sore the *next* day. So I'd go to third base and field at least fifty ground balls, probably more, and get them across to first with something on them. The following day, I'd hurt so bad that I couldn't do anything but sit around and agitate people. The day or two after that, I'd shag in the outfield and toss balls in from there, or take more grounders at third. When I was young I threw bullpens, but later on I was more concerned with saving my body—more so my knees than my arm—and stopped doing that.

At one point, fairly early in my career, there was a nun who took films of me when I was having trouble in the late innings. The films showed that my location was wavering because I was tired. So I started running stadium steps. But I didn't do that any longer than I had to. Later, it got to the point where I didn't like to run at all. We had artificial grass in St. Louis, with concrete a few inches beneath, and it was hard on the legs—and especially hard on *my* legs. My problem was a combination of age and injuries. I had three operations on my knee. Toward the end, I had no cartilage left in that knee, so things were just rubbing together in a way that compelled me to cross running off my to-do list.

That was why I liked third base. I could build up a sweat and get the kinks out of my arm and exercise my legs without putting miles on them. That was what worked for me. Nothing else I tried ever lasted.

Once, I polished my car in the morning and threw a one-hitter that night, so I thought I was onto something. I thought it loosened up my arm. But I did the same thing the next time and got lit up. So much for rituals.

Reggie Jackson

I was more a creature of habit—not just in my workout, but in the whole preparation before a ballgame. It's different for an everyday player. We're not on five-day timetables. It's the same agenda, game after game. There's a routine that you develop without even realizing it. Something works, or feels right, and you don't want deviation.

For example, I liked to wear two pairs of sanitary socks, and I wanted them new. I wanted two towels on my locker when I got in. I'd have a lucky T-shirt that I'd stay with for a long time if my luck held up. And that was about it.

My superstition, if you want to call it that—actually, I wouldn't, because I had a reason for it—was wearing a long-sleeved shirt under my uniform. In Oakland, especially, I had trouble with hamstring pulls and muscle tightness, so I learned to wear long underwear in cold weather to stay warm. But I also wore it in hot weather to stay cool. Got that from Dick Allen, who recommended it. Brother, when Dick Allen gave advice, I took it. We'd play back east in the humidity and a hundred degrees, and I'd be sticking to my long underwear.

Bob Gibson

I did the same thing. I always wore a long-sleeved wool shirt. Always. The breeze would blow a little bit on there and cool you off. Even now, when I go down to spring training with the Cardinals, I always have a jacket on underneath my uniform. I don't care how hot it is.

Reggie Jackson

There was something reassuring about getting ready a certain way every time. I liked putting my uni on. I liked getting taped up. I liked getting my hat and my glasses and my sweatbands on. I liked my number forty-four. I liked it all.

Bob Gibson

Hmm. I never thought much about it. I'd just put the stuff on and go get 'em, then take it off and go home.

Reggie Jackson

Pitchers have different considerations than everyday players, and different routines. For that matter, married players have different routines than single players, drinkers have different routines than nondrinkers, old players have different routines than young players.

Every day, I got up between nine and ten in the morning and made it a point to go to breakfast. I was single and didn't cook, so I always went out to a local diner. I'd get something else to eat around two o'clock—a lot of greens and rice—so I could head to the ballpark at three; games started at eight or eight-oh-five in my era.

When I got to the ballpark I'd read the paper, put my underwear on, walk around, put my shirt on, walk around, grab some cookies, have some milk, shoot the bull with the other guys, walk around, maybe talk to somebody from the media, put my pants on . . . I didn't get rubdowns or sit in the whirlpool until I was close to forty, but I just needed the time to be in the clubhouse. Some players—Bobby Grich was one—like to pull in at quarter to five if batting practice is at five. I couldn't do that. I needed to get into my routine and get ready.

Then, when it was over, I'd have a beer. If it was New York, I'd ride downtown, go to McMullen's for swordfish, relax, maybe drive through Central Park, listen to music. I didn't drink. I'd spend some time with a special lady and by twelve-thirty or one o'clock I was heading to the hay. I'd wind down by watching television, then be up again the next morning at nine or ten.

I only stayed out all night one time. That was in New York when I played for Oakland.

Bob Gibson

It's tough to stay out all night if you don't drink.

Reggie Jackson

It's tough to stay out all night unless you run around with somebody who stays out all night. I didn't do that.

Bob Gibson

I didn't raise much ruckus on the nights before I pitched. But I didn't try to get any extra sleep, either. I always got up early, and it wasn't because I kept myself on a strict schedule. I just didn't sleep long.

After I got up and had some breakfast, I might shop a little bit—mainly just look in windows. I'd have lunch about two o'clock, but didn't pay much attention to what I ate. I didn't know what a carbohydrate was; didn't know any of that stuff. I ate everything but fish. I didn't have fish at all until I was out of baseball. It was just my custom. As a black kid, I grew up eating a lot of pork and beef, a lot of beans and rice. We didn't have a regimen. I eat more greens now than I did then. But I always drank a lot of milk, and still do.

On the days I pitched, I didn't have to be at the ballpark at three—that was the way it was for everybody—so I'd get there about four-thirty or five. After batting practice, I'd wander into the training room, lie on the table, and get a rubdown. They'd massage my arm, try to loosen it up and stretch it, and I'd fall asleep. Sound asleep. The trainer used to put a towel over me because I snored so loud.

Reggie Jackson

For me, the off-season was a big part of the routine. I'd take it easy for about a month, a month and a half, then around December I'd get back at it, running and lifting weights. I was younger than the guys I hung out with in spring training—Billy Williams, Willie McCovey, Fergie Jenkins, and Ernie Banks— and they always told me that when you get to be thirty, things are going to be different; you need to pay attention to your conditioning. I trusted what those guys said, so I started working out more intensely when I turned thirty. There were winters when I did twelve hundred sit-ups every other day.

Bob Gibson

Exercise is a way of life for these guys now. They wouldn't know what to do if they weren't exercising.

Reggie Jackson

It was a way of life for *me*, and it still is. I can't run like I used to, but I lift weights six or seven times a week. Not heavy ones, though. I've got a bad back from being rear-ended in 2005 by a Ford Expedition doing a hundred. Flipped my car three times and destroyed it.

Bob Gibson

Rather than lift, I played basketball in the off-season until the Cardinals got wind of it and said they didn't want me to. If I were active today, I still wouldn't work out with weights—not in view of the fact that I accomplished what I accomplished.

Reggie Jackson

It's amazing to me that so many players are getting injured today in spite of all the conditioning they do.

Bob Gibson

I'm not sure that's a coincidence. I wish I knew whether all the weight training they do today was helpful or harmful. It seems to me that it's like stretching a rubber band. It'll hold at a certain point, but pretty soon it's going to get loose and lax. My instinct tells me that all the muscle building is contributing to players breaking down, because their bodies aren't getting the rest they need.

The body needs to recuperate. I don't think you need to work out year-round to be a good and well-prepared ballplayer. You play ball most of the year and when you're not playing you're exercising? I don't get that. If you listen to the exercise gurus, yeah, they'll tell you that you need to do this or that, and they'll keep you on an elaborate conditioning program. Naturally. They make their living by having people do that stuff. Meanwhile, the players today look good in their uniforms, but they're on the disabled list all the time.

I believe in downtime, and what I did worked really well for me. Of course, all I have is theories. Judging by the money they're making, I suppose that what these guys are doing now is working out all right for them.

Reggie Jackson

There's something to be said for taking a break. No doubt about that.

Over the winter I'd relax by working on my cars. I'd do Christmas shopping for my family. I'd read the Bible. Socialize. Have a nice time.

But I liked to be ready for spring training. I didn't go there to get in shape; I wanted to be in shape when I arrived.

Bob Gibson

I looked at that a little differently. To me, spring training itself was the time for getting ready. That's when you need to put your work in.

I did a lot of running in the spring to get my legs in shape, but mostly I was concerned about finding my rhythm and sharpening my hand-eye coordination. One year, after I was retired and helping out the Cardinals, they brought in this guy named Mack Newton to lead them in exercises. He's a martial arts expert and a conditioning authority who has done a lot for the Dallas Cowboys and Oakland A's and I don't know who-all, and he had the players performing these rigorous calisthenics. A lot of the guys were complaining that they were sore. So one day, when they were talking about this in a meeting, Tony La Russa asked me what I thought of those exercises. I'm sure it wasn't what he wanted to hear, but I told him that those things were pretty good, I guess, if you were a professional exerciser.

Obviously a ballplayer has to be in shape, but for my money, that's a matter of playing ball. It would drive me crazy when the regulars didn't want to be in the lineup for the exhibition games. I understand that everyday players are out there a lot more than pitchers, but they're probably only seeing ten or twelve pitches a ballgame. You need more than three or four days a week of that. I wanted them ready when the season started.

That said, there are things that spring training just can't prepare you for. A pitcher can go seven innings in the spring and feel no effects, and then after your first start in the regular season you hurt from your toes to your teeth. I might pitch a whole exhibition game without a breaking ball. I'm just trying to get control of my fastball, throw it over for a strike even if I have to let up a little bit. In spring training, you hold back. If the batter whacks one, you go, oh well, that's something to work on.

In the regular season I never, ever thought like that.

CHAPTER THREE

STUFF

Velocity

Reggie Jackson

They say velocity doesn't matter that much. That's bull.

They say that no amount of velocity is enough if you can't put the ball where you want it. Maybe so. But at the same time, there's no safe place to put a pitch that doesn't have anything on it.

Bob Gibson

There are very few guys who can consistently hit that ninety-five-mile-an-hour fastball that's up above the belt. Hank Aaron could. Aaron was a little different. A guy like McCovey swung with a big, long, sweeping arc, and maybe a little uppercut. Aaron swung down on the ball. He'd get backspin on it and hit line drives that would start off close to the ground and just keep going unless the fence got in the way.

But for the most part, when you throw that hard you're not afraid to throw it high. I actually preferred it.

Reggie Jackson

That's why velocity matters. A high fastball at ninety-five miles an hour is really more than you care to deal with. It takes everything you've got to hit it; and sometimes *that's* not enough. But if the ball's coming in at eighty-six miles an hour, even ninety, that's not a pitch that the hitter has to commit himself to in advance. At least I didn't.

Here's the thing. When a guy throws the ball ninety-five and above, you've got to be looking fastball and timing the fastball. If you don't look fastball, the ball is in on you right now. Or if it's up high in the zone, it's by you. Out of 120 pitches, eighty of them are going to be fastballs, so you'd better get on the fastball. At ninety-five miles an hour, sometimes the fastball is by you even if you *are* looking for it. You just can't get there. You're thinking, "Damn, how am I going to hit that?" And then Gibson or Randy Johnson goes to the other side of the plate and you've got a very long day.

Speed on the ball—if there's enough of it—can reduce your hitting options to one, basically. When a pitcher has a lot of velocity going for him, you can't try to time the slider. You've got to look for number one. You've got to set yourself for "dead-red," buddy, and hit it to the opposite field. With Gibson or Seaver, you just have to fight the slider.

Now, say a guy throws the ball ninety or ninety-one. If that's the case, I can look slider speed and I've got everything covered. I'm not saying that a guy like that can never get a fastball by you. That's not true. Even an ancient finesse pitcher like Jamie Moyer can sneak a fastball past you if he's got you off balance and thinking too much. But he won't throw it up in the strike zone unless he has you looking for a bunch of slop. He's going to be very judicious with his fastball.

The point is, if a pitcher doesn't have overpowering hard stuff you don't have to build your whole at-bat around that. Against that guy, if I'm geared for slider speed, to hit it to dead center field, I'm still good for the fastball and off-speed pitches. I want to be behind the fastball, but even at ninety-one I can keep it in left center (which to me, as a left-handed hitter, is the opposite field). I can keep the curveball and changeup fair even though I'm a little out in front of them. You can do that if you're looking slider speed.

Bob Gibson

And if we screw up on that slider, he can hit it out of the park to right field. But we're talking about the slider that accompanies a ninety- or ninety-one-mile-an-hour fastball. If the fastball's ninety-five, he's got to be looking for *that*.

A hitter can't set himself for two things at once if one of them comes in at ninety-five. Anything other than the fastball, he just has to react to it. A big-time power pitcher knows he has that advantage, and another one to boot: He knows he can get a good fastball past a good hitter who's looking for it. Just don't try to do it too often.

Reggie Jackson

If a guy's coming with the same thing all the time, no matter how hard he throws, I like those odds. If I'm looking for something and I get it, chances are I'm going to touch it.

Now, sure, you can look for it and foul it off or maybe swing and miss if a pitcher's throwing ninety-six and he hits a good spot. When a guy like Goose Gossage comes on in the ninth inning with a one-run lead and he's throwing to somebody like me or McCovey, somebody who can hurt him, we're going to get *all* of him, right *now*. He's going to empty the tank, and we know it. We're ready for it, and we might not square it anyway. We might just foul it off, and then foul another one off. Remember, he's got a hundred miles an hour in that gun of his. And then he breaks one on the outside corner. Forget it.

But it's probably good, for his sake, that he went with something different at that point.

Bob Gibson

One reason why they foul off that fastball is that the ball's usually moving some way or another. It's not just straight ninety-six. It's dipping in, dipping out, cutting, sailing, depending on whether it's a two-seam fastball or a four-seamer. That's why they don't quite hit it.

In the All-Star Game, 1965, I threw a high, four-seam fastball to Joe Pepitone and it sailed so much that Pepitone turned to Joe Torre, who was catching, and asked for another slider.

Reggie Jackson

The movement makes all the difference. I'd rather hit against ninety-seven straight than ninety-three with good sink.

Bob Gibson

I'd rather throw ninety-seven straight.

Reggie Jackson

That's a Gibsonism. I like that.

But I think I could hit that if it was away from me. Toward the end of my career the velocity would have been harder for me to handle, but when I was young I could have hit it if they'd shot it out of a .30–06. It's the same way with Allen, McCovey, Aaron, Mays, Frank Robinson, Manny Ramirez . . . When a hitter like that is in his prime, it doesn't matter how hard you throw.

Nolan Ryan threw ninety-eight, a hundred miles an hour, maybe one-oh-one. His fastball was the standard, and I got a charge out of facing it. On two separate occasions, Nolan told me that he was just going to throw me fastballs and let's see what happens. He'd walk right up between the mound and home plate, and in that Texas twang of his he'd say, "Reg, I want to see if you can hit my best fastball." I had a big reputation, he had a big reputation, and we were friends; we had the same agent. He just wanted to see. He did it once when I was with the A's and once when I was with the Yankees, both times when the game was in hand. I got a base hit the first time and lined out to left the second time. I hit the ball hard both times, but his version is different. In his, the first one was a bloop single. But that's what makes a great story.

In my day, they didn't have radar guns showing the speed of every pitch, but I could tell within a mile an hour or two. When a guy like Joba Chamberlain cuts the ball loose, you know it's over ninety-five. It's hard to differentiate ninety-nine from a hundred—it's just like, whoa, what was that?!—but I'm sure I saw Ryan and Gossage touch a hundred. Sudden Sam McDowell. Joe Sparma for Detroit.

A hitter like me, if a guy can throw a hundred, you're going to see it. And that is *fun*!

Bob Gibson

If I was about to pitch a game and somebody said to me, "You have your choice tonight: You can either give up five miles an hour of velocity or three inches of control," I think I'd hold on to my speed.

Don't get me wrong: I believe in spotting the ball. I wasn't a good pitcher until I learned to do that. My whole pitching philosophy was based on keeping the ball away from the hitter's strength. But throwing the ball ninety-five miles an hour is a gift. You can't teach somebody to do that, and there's no substitute for it.

Once you get up over about ninety-two or ninety-three, you're reaching the point where you can get away with some things that you can't get away with at eighty-nine . . .

Reggie Jackson

All right, we're back on the same page now . . .

Bob Gibson

But like everything else, that's not a hard-and-fast rule. If you've got a great seventy-five-mile-an-hour changeup, that could make an eighty-eight-mile-an-hour fastball play like a ninety-four-mile-an-hour fastball. It's the same thing if your curveball's so good that the hitters have to be watching for it. In cases like that, velocity is relative. But once you get up to ninety-five, there's nothing relative about it. I'll take my chances at ninety-five even if I miss the location. Missing your location at eighty-eight or ninety doesn't work very well. You just don't get away with it.

Reggie Jackson

As a hitter, I'd rather he had his best stuff than his best location.

To start with, if a guy throws eighty-seven, his best stuff isn't necessarily that big of a deal. If he doesn't have his location, he doesn't have much of anything. I don't mean to diminish a pitcher who has a lot of savvy and great changes of speed, or all kinds of breaking balls, or fabulous movement on his fastball; but it's not often that somebody who's missing his spots will beat you purely on the basis of stuff that tops out at eighty-seven miles an hour.

Now, with a pitcher like Ryan or Gibson or Koufax, or, these days, Jake Peavy, Brandon Webb, Johan Santana, Roy Halladay, or C. C. Sabathia, there are about three ways to consider this. If they have their best stuff *and* their best location, they're going to shut you out or maybe no-hit you. If they have their best location but not their best stuff, their stuff is still more than good enough to beat you. Your best chance is if they're off a bit with their location. That would mean they make mistakes. As hitters, that's what we ask for.

I have to admit, though, that I once faced Jack Morris—Anaheim, 1984, late in my career, which makes a big difference—when he was throwing ninety-seven in the ninth inning. It didn't matter where he threw *that.* You walk into Vida Blue when he's throwing ninety-nine, that's more than you want. That's like asking for a scoop of ice cream and the guy sets down a whole gallon in front of you . . . Whoa! I didn't want *that* much!

At least, not when I was approaching middle age.

Bob Gibson

Even to me, as a pitcher holding a bat, if you throw me eighty-seven over the plate, I'll hit it, and there's a pretty good chance I'll hit it hard. If you don't throw very hard, location *really* matters. But that extra five miles an hour means an awful lot.

It doesn't mean you can miss your spots all night long and get away with it; but it means you *might* get away with it, often as not, if you don't push your luck. It means you've got a little extra margin for error. Velocity can make up for a whole bunch of mistakes.

I'll take the speed any day.

Sliders

Bob Gibson

When I first started out, I thought my slider was my curveball. That was the only breaking pitch I had, so I just assumed it was a curveball. I didn't find out until I was in Triple-A that I didn't *have* a curveball. Johnny Keane, our manager, asked me to throw one, so I did, and he informed me, no, that's a slider.

The spin is different. You have to get on top of a curveball, and it usually has a bigger break than a slider, and isn't thrown as hard. A slider's a tighter pitch, and a lot easier to locate than a curve. When I developed the ability to spot the slider, I became a much better pitcher. I never developed the ability to do that with a curveball; and anyway, I didn't have much of a curveball to do it with.

Reggie Jackson

From the batter's box, it's hard to identify a good slider because it gets on you so fast and it's got a little short break on it. A bad slider has a hump in it.

Some guys say you can spot a slider by seeing a little red dot on the ball. That dot is the seams spinning together in a vortex. To me, it looks like a circle. When that vortex appears big in front of your eyes, you can pick up the slider early and send it on its way.

Bob Gibson

When you see the circle, or a *big* dot, it's not a good slider. It's just spinning, not biting. On a good, tight slider, you'll see a little bitty dot as the ball moves away from you.

I have to say, my slider was *nasty*. They could look for it and couldn't hit it.

Reggie Jackson

Amen. Big slider. Big, hard slider. Ouch!

Bob Gibson

Actually, I had two sliders. Other pitchers might grip them differently, but I held both of them between the seams, parallel to the seams at the closest point, with my fingers together and my thumb on the seam below.

My main slider was my hardest one, and it would just break abruptly and mostly downward.

Reggie Jackson

Electric slider.

Bob Gibson

And I had one where I'd twist my wrist a little more and give it a bigger break. That one didn't have the speed or suddenness of the first one, and I didn't throw it very often to left-handers; but if I got it where I was supposed to get it, a right-handed batter wasn't going to do anything with it.

The problem comes when your slider stays flat. You never want a horizontal slider. They can get the big part of the bat on that thing. It's the darting action that fools the hitter and makes him miss.

Reggie Jackson

I'll never forget that slider against Detroit in the World Series, the one that struck out seventeen.

Bob Gibson

I had a big slider that day.

Reggie Jackson

No sh— . . . shoot! Hard. Hard! With a slider that hard, even if you pick up the red circle, which I doubt you could, it gets in on the left-hander's hands so fast that he can't do anything with it, and it darts away from a right-hander's bat. That's the ultimate strikeout pitch.

Bob Gibson

I'm pretty sure batters didn't go up against me thinking slider speed. They missed the slider too far to be looking for it.

They'd be crazy to look for slider speed off me. You do that, you're not going to hit my fastball, which in my prime I'd estimate at ninety-five to ninety-seven. I'd say my slider was about ninety-two.

Reggie Jackson

J. R. Richard threw a slider at about that speed, maybe even harder, and he's another guy that you'd have to be looking fastball. That's a deadly combination. If a pitcher like that comes with anything other than the fastball, it's got to be a mistake for you to hit it square and fair.

Bob Gibson

I said that I'd show that inside slider to guys like Reggie who don't like hard stuff on their hands, but I'd make damn sure I didn't leave it over the plate. In fact, I'd come in tight to most left-handers. But not *down* and in, which is where sliders tend to be.

The bottom line was that I just didn't throw as many sliders to lefties, which is probably why I fared so much better against right-handers in general. But even against righties, I was reluctant to come inside with a slider. Once in a while, I'd do it with the thought that they'd quit on it before it came in to catch the corner. Never twice in a row, though.

After I learned how to pitch, it got to where I could backdoor a slider to a left-handed hitter. It was a matter of starting it so far outside that the hitter would give up on it, and then it would slip in and catch the outside corner. Whoops, that's a strike. Eventually, the backdoor slider was the one I was most likely to throw a lefty. Very seldom will a left-handed hitter swing at that pitch, as long as it's kept on the corner.

There was also a back*up* slider that I learned from Bob Purkey, but I rarely threw that sucker on purpose. Purkey was a veteran who had a little bit of everything, including a knuckleball and a slider that would look normal but hold its line or even back up a little like a screwball. I'd done it accidentally a few times, and Purkey explained to me that it would happen if I overthrew my slider. He showed me how to do it purposely by raising your arm a little too high and then throwing it like mad, as hard as you can. Sometimes you'll send up a hanging slider so bad, so far up in the strike zone, that the hitter can't get to it. This is sort of like that. Hitters will pick up the spin—especially in day games—and that's what sells it to them as a traditional slider. If you start it out over the plate, a left-handed hitter thinks it's going to break in for a ball, and it just floats away from him while he stands there wondering what happened. Purkey had it perfected, but it takes a lot of guts to throw something that stays over the plate and doesn't really do much. The vast majority of the time, I wasn't that courageous. It's not a pitch that children should try at home.

Reggie Jackson

Hank Bauer, who was our manager in Oakland in 1969, gave me a talk after a game in which the Royals had struck me out two or three times with breaking and off-speed pitches out of the strike zone. He mentioned to me the need to understand the strike zone and lay off of balls that aren't in it. That's not so hard to do with fastballs, but it's a little different when the pitch is darting, dipping, and off-speed.

Before a pitch is halfway to home plate, you need to recognize whether it's going to be a strike or not and what it's going to do. You've already started moving toward the ball *as if* it's going to be a strike, and there's a critical instant when you have to commit yourself one way or the other. If the ball's got a hump coming out of the pitcher's hand, it's going to be a breaking ball. But there are some guys—Koufax, Ryan, Bert Blyleven—with stuff so good that the breaking ball is coming on the same plane as the fastball, without a hump. Then it fools you. You can't move. You break your bat. You look funny. All because you couldn't recognize the pitch soon enough.

Bob Gibson

When I changed speeds on my slider, I was able to get away with something you're really not supposed to do. I actually slowed my arm motion down a little. That's against the book, and understandably so. Everything—fastball, breaking ball, changeup—is supposed to be thrown with the same motion. If you alter your delivery, the hitter doesn't have to wait until the ball is halfway there to figure out what's coming. But I got away with the changeup slider, because the difference in speed was so different from my other stuff, and it was so unexpected coming from me.

Normally, you throw a slider with a stiffer wrist than a curveball. It's still wrist action, but you just kind of cut through the ball to effect a quick, tight break. You give a little twist like you're turning a doorknob, about a ninety-degree turn. If you use a bigger twist, more like a one-to-seven move—pulling the ball down more—the slider's going to be bigger and slower, between a slider and a curve. That was my changeup slider. A slurve, I guess you'd call it, with both horizontal and vertical break.

Reggie Jackson

I'd have handled that pitch better after I was about thirty.

Bob Gibson

I'd keep it high, especially to a left-handed hitter. I prefer the slider high.

These days, you see right-handed pitchers throwing a lot of low inside sliders to left-handed hitters. I watched when the Reds brought up Jay Bruce, a good-looking left-handed hitter, and for a couple weeks he was clobbering everything in sight. Then they started throwing him that inside slider that would break down toward his shoes and he'd be practically falling over whaling at it.

Time after time. That's great for the pitcher, but it's not going to work for very long. A hitter like Bruce will adjust to that, and a few of those pitches will end up in the right-field stands; and then he won't see much of that pitch anymore. Down and in is not a good pitch. You can get guys to chase those if the pitch is off the plate, but if you make a mistake they'll murder it. They just drop the bat on it.

The only time I'd throw down and in to a right-hander was when I wanted a double-play ball. The *only* time. I'd throw a two-seamer and hope they hit it on the ground.

Reggie Jackson

And no doubt they did, more often than not, because they were so excited to see a strike on the inside part of the plate.

Bob Gibson

When Mike Shannon was moved in from the outfield and started playing third base for us, he said to me, "I want you to move me around depending on who's hitting."

I said, "Mike, you're never going to get the ball unless it's a double-play situation."

Sure enough, a situation came up with a man on first and a right-handed hitter at the plate. I went down and in, and the guy hit it right to Shannon for a nice double play. After the inning, he came over and sat down next to me in the dugout, all perplexed, and asked, "How do you know when they're going to hit the ball to me?"

I said, "I'm smart, Mike."

Assorted Fastballs

Reggie Jackson

About the time I figured out when to look for slider speed and when to sit on the fastball, pitchers started throwing the split-finger. That was something *more* to think about.

Bob Gibson

The split-fingered fastball is really difficult to recognize, because it looks like a fastball and all of a sudden the bottom drops out. You'll see guys swing at it when it's in the dirt because they think it's just a low fastball, probably a two-seamer.

Reggie Jackson

I think there are more checked swings in the game today than there were when we played, because of the split-finger.

Bob Gibson

You throw the split-finger with the index finger and middle finger in a V-shape grip, holding the ball along the seams at the widest point. You need big hands, or long fingers, to do it right.

The two-seamer is a totally different pitch. It's just a sinking fastball—not that nasty thing that Bruce Sutter made so popular. You hold a two-seam fastball along the seams where they come together at the narrowest point.

Reggie Jackson

One of the things that makes hitting so hard is that pitchers have the advantage of being able to come up with new stuff. They can create, innovate, invent. All we can do is react.

Now hitters have to deal with the cutter, too—Mariano Rivera's bread and butter.

Bob Gibson

A four-seam fastball will often take off and sail like a cut fastball. Joe Pepitone might mistake it for a slider, but it's harder than a slider and doesn't have the vertical break. I didn't throw a cutter, per se, because I got the same kind of movement from my fastball. You hold the cutter a little off center, and it has a sideways rotation that makes it travel horizontally one way or the other.

My four-seamer was more old-school than that. I held it across the seams where they're wide, and that way you get the resistance of all four seams as the ball rotates. That puts a little hop or lateral movement on the ball. And you could alter that movement by just sliding your grip a smidgen or two.

Reggie Jackson

The four-seamer is the fastball that you have to set yourself for when you're up against somebody like Gibson, Ryan, Palmer, Roger Clemens, Josh Beckett, or C. C. Sabathia.

The velocity of the two-seamer isn't that much different than the four-seamer. Some pitchers—Chien-Ming Wang is a good example—can throw it just as hard.

Bob Gibson

Generally, though, the fastball down low, which the two-seamer had better be, isn't going to hit ninety-five miles an hour. You can put just as much effort into it and the ball simply won't be arriving at top speed. It's the four-seamer, up high, that comes in the hardest.

People often said that I had a little extra when I needed it in a tight spot or in the ninth inning. They said that if I'd been throwing ninety-three, I could reach back in that situation and blow one in at ninety-seven if I had to. That might be true, but it wasn't a matter of having a little extra. That implies that I'd been holding back. I never held back on a fastball.

What would happen would be that I'd been throwing two-seamers, or maybe sliders, and then, in the do-or-die situation, I'd turn to the four-seamer and bring it up there high in the zone. But it's not a matter of reaching back a little further and grunting a little louder and letting it all out. Every once in a great while, there might be a special occasion for that. As a rule, though, trying to throw the ball harder leads to *over*throwing it, which might cause you to lose command and actually might cause you to lose velocity, as well. You might tense up too much—tighten up—and the pitch doesn't come out of the hand as fast as the one before when you were nice and loose. It's all a matter of self-awareness.

Most of the time, there's no extra. It just *looked* like that.

Reggie Jackson

The four-seam fastball is more of a strikeout pitch than the two-seamer. A two-seamer is good for getting the batter to hit the ball on the ground, but it usually doesn't make him swing and miss like a four-seam or a split-fingered fastball.

Bob Gibson

A forkball is another good two-strike pitch, because it drops so much. Sandy Koufax got a lot of strikeouts on forkballs. Elroy Face, a great little relief pitcher, lived by it. So did Lindy McDaniel, who was our top reliever when I came up with the Cardinals.

The splitter is thrown a little harder—it's not jammed between the fingers so much—and after Sutter came along, you didn't see the forkball as often. Jack Morris was one who got a lot of mileage out of it. Dave Stewart.

Reggie Jackson

The way a forkball tumbles down, it's sometimes not much different than a spitball, except drier. A spitball has more of an unnatural, unpredictable fall because the ball is weighted on one side.

Bob Gibson

The spitball is different because it's cheating. I'd throw it, though, if I thought it would be to my advantage.

The reason I didn't was that the ball would do all kinds of unpredictable things and I didn't feel like I could command it. On a spitball, you don't hold any seams. If you grab the ball between the seams, most of the time you can't throw it straight anyway; it's going to do something. The thing was, I didn't really know *what* when it came to the spitball.

But I did actually throw it for one game. It was against the Mets, and I just wanted to see if it would work. It was nasty, all right.

Dave Ricketts was catching me. I used to work on it on the

sideline, and one day I said, "Dave, I'm gonna throw a spitball today, and I'll tell you what I'll do. Whenever a guy gets two strikes on him and he fouls one back, I'm gonna throw a spitball the next pitch. Because when he fouls the ball back, everybody cranes their neck to see where it's going. Nobody's watching me, so that's when I'll spit into my glove and I'll load it up when the umpire tosses me a new ball." So that's what I did. Jesse Gonder was the catcher for the Mets, and he was bitching and moaning to the umpire about it. I forget who the umpire was, but finally he said to Gonder, "Come on, Gibson doesn't throw a spitball."

I did that day. And I won.

Reggie Jackson

If it's a good spitball, it's pretty impossible to hit because it has abnormal flight and you can't tell where it's going. But a guy can throw a bad one. You can hit one on the dry side now and then. A spitball has that tumbling spin to it, and you can at least identify it.

Bob Gibson

A spitball is thrown harder than a forkball, and even harder than a split-finger. Most spitters go whissht, straight down, from the speed and weight.

I don't know how he did it, but Lew Burdette could somehow throw a spitter and make it go *up*. He had a couple different spitballs. He could make it go both ways.

Reggie Jackson

Some of the best spitballs probably come from pitchers you didn't know threw one. I'm sure there are guys who get away with it who aren't even suspected. There are a lot of guys who sweat enough naturally that they don't need anything else. That's the one who's got the best spitball. Watch out for guys who wear long sleeves in ninety degrees.

Everybody knew that Gaylord Perry threw a spitter—he *wanted* you to know—but there was no telling how he did it.

Against Gaylord one time, I asked the umpire to check the ball on eleven straight pitches and he still didn't find anything.

A lot of times, what we call a spitball is actually a scuff ball. There are all sorts of methods for scuffing or nicking it. Rick Honeycutt had a razor or a nail or a tack or something on his glove. There are guys who have sandpaper in their gloves. There are guys who'll cut out a little circle of sandpaper and attach it to their glove hand so they can scratch the ball when they rub it up. When Mike Scott pitched, players on the other team would sometimes gather up a few of the balls he threw and sit in the dugout examining the scuff marks on them. There was a president of one team who kept a collection of balls scuffed by Don Sutton in his desk drawer.

Bob Gibson

Some guys throw over to first like they're trying to pick off the runner, and the first baseman will scratch the ball for them before he tosses it back. Johnny Roseboro, the old Dodgers catcher, used to cut the ball on his knee pads for certain pitchers. Drysdale, Sutton.

One time Sutton was pitching a game against us in St. Louis, and the first inning we just knocked the tar out of him. We must have gotten three or four runs and were still rallying. And he called time-out and walked into the dugout and disappeared. Went into the clubhouse. He was gone five minutes. Everybody was waiting for him. He'd started out naked and didn't have his good stuff, so he went back in there and got outfitted.

Reggie Jackson

He may have had a tip before the game that somebody was going to check him.

Bob Gibson

We hardly touched him the rest of the way.

Reggie Jackson

When Gaylord Perry went out to the mound, he would pick up the resin bag, cover his hand with resin, and leave it on. The first pitch he'd throw, there would be this little cloud of powder when he released the ball. That was his puff ball.

I saw a lot of spitballs, and I saw a lot of them from Gaylord alone. When he didn't throw it, he'd fake it. He'd touch his cap, touch his glove, touch his belt, everything, and then throw you a curveball. He threw a Vaseline ball. Had it all over him. Around his neck, in his sideburns, wherever. There are all kinds of places where pitchers can hide their goop. They can put it in the stripe of their pants. They can put it inside their belts so that when they hitch up their pants they can get some. Sometimes, Perry loaded the ball so much that it was too slippery for the catcher to throw it back; he'd have to walk it out there. Gaylord also had a good forkball, which confused the matter a little further.

He was throwing me spitters one night in Seattle, my first year with the Angels. This is in one of the baseball bloopers highlight films, and one of my great moments, if I may say so. It was the usual routine. He kept loading it up, and when he didn't he'd go through all his gyrations. I kept swinging and missing. The umpire was David Phillips, nice guy, and finally I called time and said, "Dave, check him out, would you? Look at the ball. Look at the *flight* of the ball. It's not normal. It's a spitter. Everybody in the ballpark knows it. Why don't you call it?"

He said, "I can't. I can't prove it."

I said, "Well, I'm *telling* you."

He said, "Well, Reggie, he's gonna tell me he's *not.*"

Of course, Gaylord was just looking in there and laughing all this time. Eventually, I struck out after about an eight- or nine-pitch at-bat. Instead of heading back to the dugout, though, I started shrugging my shoulders, throwing my hands up, arguing with the umpire, jawing with the catcher, and pointing at Perry, who's just having a great ol' time. Somehow I didn't get thrown out of the game for all that. But I wasn't finished. I walked over to the bench, grabbed the water bucket, and carried it out toward the mound. When I got to the foul line, I took the top off and started shoveling ice and water at Gaylord. That's when I finally got thrown out of the game.

Bob Gibson

Taking more water out there for Gaylord to throw his spitter with. That's a good move.

Reggie Jackson

On my way back to the clubhouse I walked past one of my teammates, Mick Kelleher, looked at Mickey, and said, "How was that?" He about doubled over.

You know, only one time in his career did Gaylord get tossed out of a game for throwing a spitball. That was later that year in Boston. The umpire was Dave Phillips.

Bob Gibson

Joe Niekro had sandpaper in his back pocket once, and when the umpire came out to ask him what he had back there he reached into his pocket and said, "Nothing." And the sandpaper fell out on the mound while the umpire was standing there watching. Kicked him out of the game.

To me, though, throwing a spitball falls under the category of gamesmanship. It's like an outfielder who traps a ball and knows he trapped it but holds it up to convince the umpire that he caught it. That's part of the game. It's not *exactly* the same, because there's no rule against trapping a ball and saying you caught it; but the point is that everybody tries to get away with whatever they can. I don't have a big problem with that. It's competition.

Curveballs

Bob Gibson

My curveball didn't bite. It would just sort of peter out. It was terrible. That's why I only threw it to left-handers, and only rarely.

It was almost always a hanger. Always, *always* up. A right-handed hitter would feast on that curveball, because he was probably bailing out to begin with and then the stupid thing would just stay right there where he could get lucky and lay into it. But more often than you'd think, I'd get away with hanging a curve to left-handed hitters. Left-handers would see it rolling in, slow and fat and tumbling right to them, and they'd get excited and take a mighty rip, but it wouldn't break as much as they thought, or they couldn't quite reach it, or they'd jump out there and jam themselves because they were so eager, and they'd hit it about twenty feet and go, "Damn!"

Joe Morgan was one. I couldn't throw a fastball by Joe Morgan. He'd pull it foul. Then I started throwing him that slop curveball and he'd hit nice little grounders to second base and shortstop.

So I saved my curve for lefties, except for the couple I threw to Dick Allen.

Reggie Jackson

I grew up in Philadelphia, and I'd go watch Dick Allen—he was called Richie back then—at Shibe Park—well, it was Connie Mack Stadium by then—at Twenty-first and Lehigh. He'd be hitting home runs over that 447-foot sign in center field.

Bob Gibson

He hit one out there on me. Curveball.

But it's a two-part story. The first time, I'd gotten two strikes on him, and he didn't know I had a curveball since I never threw it to right-handed hitters. But I just got the idea to throw one to Dick Allen and he kind of did a double take and cursed. "Strike three!" He just *looked* at me. That was back in St. Louis. The next time I faced him was in Philadelphia—this was in June 1964—and he was just looking for that curveball. First two times up I struck him out, nothing but fastballs, and he hadn't swung yet. Third time, I threw him the curveball and he hit it over the flagpole in center field. He gave me a look when he got to second base, and I thought, "Yeah, you'll never see another one." He set me up.

That was the last curveball he ever got from *me*. It was also the last and only home run he ever hit off me.

Reggie Jackson

The curveball became hittable for me when I learned to look for slider speed and adjust. That meant I was waiting longer and was willing and able to take a ball to the opposite field. It was the same approach that helped me against all kinds of off-speed stuff.

When I came into the league, the Orioles had a little relief pitcher named Stu Miller who was famous for his changeups, and his changeups off his changeups. The first time I faced Stu Miller was my rookie year, 1967. I didn't have a prayer. He had me crawling on my knees.

Baltimore always seemed to have crafty little guys—usually lefties—who gave me fits. Tippy Martinez had a good fastball but got me out consistently with a tough breaking pitch that I just couldn't stay with. Scott McGregor wasn't small, but he was a left-hander with a great knowledge of pitching, and he tied me up in knots. For years, I couldn't even touch the ball off McGregor. Then, in 1982, I hit three home runs against him. I guess I finally figured him out.

I can say that now, but I wouldn't say it at the time. It may sound strange coming from me, but you can get too cocky if you make an assumption like that while you're still playing. If you think you've got something figured out in baseball, you're asking for trouble. I found it wise to remember the age-old saying: Take it one day at a time. There are no guarantees about tomorrow.

Eventually, when I refined my approach and become more patient, I did better against the finesse guys. I can't brag about how I handled the off-speed stuff, but if you look at a list of pitchers I did the most damage against, it includes the likes of Wilbur Wood, Doyle Alexander, Bill Lee, Geoff Zahn, Bob McClure, Mike Cuellar, Jerry Augustine, Luis Tiant, and Dave McNally.

You had to be on your game against those characters, because they knew how to pitch . . . and win.

I managed to hit a home run off McNally—another Oriole— early in my career, in Oakland, and I distinctly remember touching first base and thinking, "I just got me a real twenty-game winner!" It was a real lefty, besides. In fact—to my surprise, actually—a lot of the guys on that list were left-handed.

When you're a left-handed hitter up against a left-hander, that means you can't bail out on the curveball. You cannot give *anything*.

Bob Gibson

And that's not easy. All through youth ball and college I was a switch-hitter, so I never had to face a curveball breaking away from me. I was still switch-hitting in Triple-A ball, and in fact the first home run I hit was from the left side. But the Cardinals said they didn't want me batting left-handed because it would expose my pitching arm. I thought that was dumb, because if a ball came in on me I would have turned away and probably been hit in the *left* arm; but that's what they said, so I stopped.

After that, I started seeing those breaking balls that would start out right at me. That was horrible. Sam Jones struck me out with a pitch that I thought was going to hit me in the middle of the back. I fell down and the umpire said, "Strike three!" The ump was Frank Dascoli, and he was looking straight down at me while I was lying on my back. I was embarrassed to death. I said, "That ball hit me!" Dascoli just laughed and said, "No, it didn't."

Sam Jones had a curveball you could actually *hear*.

So did Koufax.

Reggie Jackson

Hearing a pitch—now, that's a cut above.

What I heard was Nolan Ryan's fastball hitting the catcher's mitt. You could hear that if you were eating peanuts in the second deck.

Knucklers

Reggie Jackson

Sal Bando taught me how to hit the knuckleball. I was struggling with it early in my career. Sal was our captain, and he was a good knuckleball hitter, so I just asked him, "How do you *do* that?" He told me to just stand at home plate and follow the speed of the ball to get it timed.

The next knuckleballer I saw was old Hoyt Wilhelm. It was in Milwaukee, because it was 1968 and the White Sox were playing part of their home schedule there. I was just a kid, and when Wilhelm came in they announced, "Hoyt Wilhelm is now making his nine hundred and seventh appearance, which breaks the all-time record held by Cy Young . . ." The first pitch he threw, I hit the ball over the right-field stands at County Stadium.

Sal's advice was just right because, as far as I knew, there was only one guy who *changed speeds* with his knuckleball. That was Phil Niekro, and he was in the National League. Niekro had a little blooper knuckleball and a soft one and a hard one. That's probably why he won more than three hundred games. The only knuckleballer within a hundred of him was his brother, Joe.

A few years ago, I started paying attention to Tim Wakefield of the Red Sox. Every pitch he throws is sixty-six, sixty-eight miles an hour. Against a speed like that, you have time to adjust. So when I faced a knuckleballer, I'd just stand there with the bat on my shoulder and not get into a hitting position until the guy released the ball. I always got a good home-run cut against knuckleballers. In fact, Wilbur Wood, a knuckleballer, is the pitcher I hit the most home runs off of.

Bob Gibson

Knuckleballs, incidentally, aren't thrown with your knuckles. They're thrown with your fingernails. The reason they call it a knuckleball is because that's what the hitter sees when you dig your fingernails into the seam.

If I threw one—and I hardly ever did—I'd use it like a changeup. Our pitching coach my first year in St. Louis was Howard Pollet, and his best pitch had been a changeup. He wanted me to learn it and worked and worked with me. Told me I couldn't pitch in the big leagues without a changeup. But I just didn't have a good one. Every time I threw a changeup, somebody would whack it over some fence or in between the outfielders. Unfortunately, my knuckleball wasn't much better.

I was afraid to use it in ballgames, but one day when Hank Aaron was batting I floated that baby up there—anything to avoid throwing Aaron a fastball—and he hit a ground ball to the second baseman. As he ran back to the dugout, he yelled to me, "What the hell was that?" I laughed and told him, all proud, that that was my knuckleball.

CHAPTER FOUR

CORNERS

Location

Bob Gibson

Home plate is seventeen inches wide, and most of that is of no interest to the pitcher. When I concerned myself with the middle ten or twelve inches, it was only because I had a serious problem with the count and circumstance. In that case, the response would probably involve my best fastball and the upper portion of the strike zone.

Reggie Jackson

And see, that foot or so in the middle is what I had my eye on, although my hitting zone wouldn't be exactly centered. Shift that region an inch or two toward the outside corner and now we're in business.

Bob Gibson

The diameter of the baseball is a fraction less than three inches, so you could squeeze about six of them across the plate. But the strike zone is actually wider than that—or *should* be—because all a pitch has to do, to be a strike, is catch any portion of the plate with any portion of the ball. So, technically, if you divide the zone into slots the size of baseballs, you've got eight of them to work with, counting the two just touching the edges.

I'm satisfied to split those eight slots with the hitter. I'll take the one farthest inside—make it one and a half—and about two and a half on the extreme outside. As long as I restrict myself to those areas, I figure we're fighting the battle on my turf. If I venture into the fat territory toward the center, the home-plate advantage swings to the batter.

Reggie Jackson

That's fair.

Bob Gibson

The average pitcher is going to put the ball where he wants it maybe fifty percent of the time. When I say where he wants it, I'm talking about *close*. Three inches. The width of the ball. That's pretty close.

Unless you've pitched yourself into a bind and left no room for error, you're always aiming for the corner or just off the corner. If you miss a couple inches either way, that's okay. It's still okay to miss by more than that *off* the plate, but it's not okay to miss *over* the plate by more than that.

Reggie Jackson

I'd go to the plate expecting the pitcher to throw the ball within four to six inches of where he wants to. Six inches is a pretty good miss. A good control pitcher should be able to put it within a four-inch space most of the time—or even closer than that if you throw like Jamie Moyer does, with his fastball in the low eighties and his changeup in the mid-seventies.

A guy like Gibson could afford to miss his spot more than most pitchers, because he had enough speed to get away with it. On top of that, his control was good enough that you couldn't *count* on him missing. It wasn't the norm for him to miss, so it wasn't that big a part of your approach as a hitter. But generally speaking, if a pitcher misses by more than four inches—and especially if he makes a *habit* out of missing by more than four inches—he can be hit out of the ballpark. Gibson could get away with being a little wild in the strike zone at times. Most pitchers can't.

If I know a pitcher is wild in the strike zone, I'm going to be on him quick. I'm going to step on him right away, going to put a number on him immediately, going to be *on* him. That's why some guys get hit even though they're throwing the ball close to a hundred miles an hour. Hitters can expect them to miss in the strike zone, so they go up looking for that and ripping at it.

Bob Gibson

If you're going to be wild, be wild outside the strike zone.

Reggie Jackson

I'd much rather that a pitcher be wild *in* the strike zone. If a guy's all over the place, especially at ninety-five miles an hour, it puts a lot more uncertainty into a hitter's head—emphasis on the *head*. Ouch! It makes me less likely to step into a pitch on the outside part of the plate.

Bob Gibson

The only trouble with being wild out of the strike zone is that it puts you behind in the count. There's a domino effect. If you're behind in the count, you can't afford to work the corners quite as adamantly. And if you're bringing the ball in over the plate, you *really* can't afford to miss and bring it in too far.

That's a bad position to be in if you don't have good command. You're *going* to miss. You just have to hope you don't miss in the wrong spot. If you're wild, you have to be lucky.

Reggie Jackson

I was watching one of our young Yankee pitchers, and he was missing the target sometimes by two and three *feet*. Jorge Posada was setting up outside, and he was missing *inside* in the dirt. Now, that is not good. He was knocked out of the game the next inning.

Bob Gibson

I've done that. I've missed by three feet. You have some days, man, when you do that. You just can't have too many of them.

On those days you think, damn, how can I miss by that far? There are reasons for it. You may be opening up a little bit too soon. Your arm might be dragging. You might not be releasing the ball at the right point. You know what you're doing wrong—*after*wards.

Reggie Jackson

If you catch a Gibson or Seaver or today's Halladay on a day like that, you'd better jump on it. If you catch them in an *inning* like that, you'd better jump on it.

Bob Gibson

Most starting pitchers—good pitchers or not-so-good pitchers—are the most vulnerable early, because they don't quite have their control yet. They haven't found that spot where they want their foot to hit or haven't gotten comfortable on the rubber or just haven't figured out how their body's functioning that day. They don't have full command of the mound yet, and consequently they don't have full command of the ball yet. In the first inning, I'm a lot more apt to throw a fastball out over the plate than I will be later.

Sometimes I was locked in by the first inning, but not too often. There were times when I'd come in from the bullpen and tell my teammates, "Guys, you're going to have to get a whole bunch of runs today, because I wasn't throwing squat down there." Then I'd walk out to the mound and the ball would go right where I wanted it to go and I'd pitch a one-hitter for seven innings. I don't know if it's adrenaline or what. It's just that foot coming down in the same spot every time.

Most of the time, though, I tried to survive the first couple innings by just throwing hard, overpowering the batter, because I wasn't sharp yet. Then, around the third inning, you don't have to overpower him because you're boom, boom, boom—right on the spot.

Reggie Jackson

A pitcher can get along fine with a hard, moving fastball in a good location. When he can add to that—with either stuff or control—he's something special.

Some guys could dot an *i* with a slider. Ferguson Jenkins could do that. Mickey Lolich had a slider like that. Steve Carlton. Ron Guidry. Sparky Lyle would come into a game and throw twenty-five pitches and twenty-four of them would be sliders. And they were right where he wanted them.

You don't expect a curveball to be as precise, but I've seen pitchers who could locate their curves as well as other pitchers could spot their fastballs. Those are folks like Koufax—after he settled down—or Blyleven or Camilo Pascual. David Wells could locate a breaking ball. A guy like Seaver didn't have to. He had enough mustard that he could make you sit on that, then come with a curveball and say, "Here, hit this."

Gibson didn't even fool with it.

Bob Gibson

For most pitchers, control isn't quite as precise as you might think. I didn't even try to throw to the catcher's mitt. I picked out a square between the catcher's knees and shoulders and focused on that. That's why, for me, the toughest pitch to locate was the backdoor slider to left-handers—because there was nothing to aim at. If you can pull it off, that's an outstanding pitch.

The location that really matters is the corner, and the control that really matters is the ability to put the ball there. To me, the corner *starts* at the corner and extends about the width of the baseball beyond that. Of course, a lot of it depends on the umpire; and the rest depends on what the hitter is willing to swing at. The two of those go hand in hand. Umpires don't seem to call those strikes on the corner as much as they used to, and consequently the hitters are less compelled to swing at them. When the pitcher is forced to move the ball over the plate, that results in home runs and other bad stuff.

Control pitchers like Greg Maddux and Tom Glavine are more likely to get the corners called than most other pitchers. They've earned the benefit of the doubt because they're always there, always in the same spot. I'd estimate that Maddux and Glavine are within two inches of their target ninety percent of the time. With that consistency, they've carved out strike zones that might extend an inch or two beyond the plate. And when the ball is an inch or two off the plate, in a good spot, the hitters can't center it on the bat. No way. They'll moan and complain about the calls, but they know what's in store. It's always there, and it's usually going to be a strike.

And if it's not a strike, it's still a damn good pitch.

Outside

Bob Gibson

In all the years I pitched, nobody ever made an issue when I threw the ball a few inches off the *outside* corner. So why all the fuss when I missed that much *inside*?

I promise you, I spent a lot more time outside than inside. It's where I made my living. The importance of pitching outside was the main reason I ever pitched inside. You can't do one without establishing the other.

Reggie Jackson

As much as I preferred the ball away, I'd have to prove to a Gibson that I could hit *him* away before he'd change his approach. Hoot, Seaver, Maddux, Roger Clemens—the great ones are on their own programs until you give them a reason not to be. I'd have to hurt him a couple times before one of those guys would say, well, hell, let's try something else.

Bob Gibson

I start with the fact that a hitter can't square a pitch on the outside corner. Period.

Unless he cheats. What I mean is, unless he leans in and dives at that outside corner. Obviously, I can't let him do that, because that's where I'm trying to pitch. So if he tries it, I have to stand him up a little bit. Think of the hitter as a dog with an electronic collar—you just administer a slight correction, as they call it, if he tries to get out of his yard. Throw the ball inside so he can't wander into the wrong area. Don't let him lean where he shouldn't be leaning. If you throw it inside and he's still leaning, it usually hits him. Or, the way I look at it, the batter hits *himself.* Ouch! Jump back!

Roberto Clemente was a diver. For a great ballplayer, though, I found Clemente to be comparatively easy to pitch to. First off, he was a right-hander, and right-handers generally didn't give me a lot of trouble as long as I kept the ball where I wanted it. With Clemente, I would just throw it down and away, down and away, and he couldn't do anything with it. So he'd get frustrated and start jumping out at the ball. Then I'd knock him down, tick him off. Not trying to hit him or anything. All I was trying to do was make him mad. When he was mad, he'd swing at *everything.* I'd put him on the ground, and he'd pop up determined to kill me.

Some guys—Frank Robinson—were dangerous doing that, but Clemente was only dangerous in that situation if you screwed up unnecessarily. He'd just hack at the ball. Down and away, down and away, down and away. Not *up* and away. That was the mistake I didn't want to make against Clemente. And no strikes inside if I could help it.

It worked pretty well until he broke my leg with a line drive in 1967.

Reggie Jackson

I'm sure he'd say he wasn't trying to hit you.

Bob Gibson

They pitch a little differently today than we did. You hear all the time that today's pitchers are afraid to come inside, but that's not what I see. They throw inside. But not the way I did. Not the way Don Drysdale did. They pitch inside because they're unable to take away the outside.

These days, pitching inside means working the inside part of the plate. In our day, pitching inside meant pitching *inside*. Off the plate. At least, that's what *I* meant by it. I wasn't throwing for inside strikes so much as I was throwing to set up my *outside* strikes.

The pitchers today seem to think that hitters can hit the ball on the outside corner as well as they can hit the ball on the inside corner. I don't believe that. When you see guys belting walk-off home runs in the ninth inning, not many of them are to the opposite field. The great majority are pulled, because the pitchers are coming right into the hitters' power. I guarantee that most of the home runs today are coming on pitches over the inside part of the plate. You see little-bitty second basemen hitting forty home runs because the pitchers pitch inside but don't have the will or the control—either one—to get the ball as far inside as it needs to be. That wasn't going to happen to me.

My general plan was to stay on the outside corner and break up the pattern now and then by coming inside to drive the batter away from the plate. That's the way the old-timers did it. That's part of the reason why Nolan Ryan became so popular when he was in his forties—because he pitched the hard-nosed, old-fashioned way. You don't see that style anymore. The game itself has discouraged it. Nowadays, hitters can get away with leaning over the plate because the umpires protect them. So a lot of pitchers stay in, in, in—by today's standards, not mine—then go away, then back in.

That's the opposite of what I did. The outside corner was my bread and butter.

Reggie Jackson

For those reasons, I suspect that, if I played today, I'd have less trouble with pitches in on me. They wouldn't be as *far* in. Today's pitchers would be more likely to leave the ball out over the plate.

Bob Gibson

You should pitch with the conviction that you're going to do your business in a certain region of the plate, and then ensure that the hitter doesn't encroach upon that area. You'll make mistakes and he's going to get there once in a while, but you can't allow him to constantly, or comfortably, look for the ball in a certain spot—much less in the spot that *you've* staked out. Make an honest man of him.

But be realistic about it. I hear a lot about pitchers owning the inside corner. No pitcher owns the inside corner. If you're going to own anything on the plate, it's going to be the outside corner. The reason's obvious: Most hitters like the ball from the middle in, so they can turn their hips and yank it into the seats and get on *SportsCenter* and make a lot of money. So you pitch them away. It's pretty simple stuff, and hard to beat if you back it up with the force of your convictions. If the guy starts looking for the ball away in a manner that's disrespectful of what you're trying to do—if he chooses to venture out there aggressively, without any apparent concern for the consequences—there should be a pretty good chance he'll get hit.

When I was pitching, the hitters knew that. It's just the way it was. Not because I was throwing at them, but because I was trying to keep them off the outside corner.

Of course, when you do that, they call you a headhunter.

Reggie Jackson

I met Bob in Los Angeles at the Martin Luther King game, and went over to introduce myself. I'm Reggie, you're Bob, yada yada. And then I said, "I understand you like to come inside on guys."

He said, "Yep."

I said, "If you came inside on me, I'd be out there."

He said, "Well, then I guess we'd roll in the dirt, wouldn't we?"

--- **Inside** ---

Bob Gibson

There are several ways in which a hitter lays claims to his territory at the plate. To some extent, his stance will let you know where he wants the ball. His history tells you a lot. And of course his stride.

Every hitter has an area where he wants to operate, just like every pitcher has one. If I want to throw the ball outside and Ryan Howard wants it on the inside corner to pull, I do my thing and he does his and everything's lollipops and rainbows. At least for me. The conflict arises if both parties are interested in the same turf.

Some pitchers are quick to defer. If they see that a batter is setting himself up to hit the ball away, they'll keep it on the inside corner. That's the modern style. It's also the passive style.

What made me an aggressive pitcher was not simply that I would bring the ball farther inside, as a general practice, but that I was insistent on having that outside corner. I expected the batter to defer to *me,* not vice versa. And to arrange that, I might have to miss the inside corner to an extent that could sting a little.

Another way to put it is that the inside fastball was the hand grenade I used for blowing the enemy out of his foxhole.

Reggie Jackson

Gibson felt about pitching the way I felt about hitting. You have to take what's rightfully yours. He was the most feared pitcher out there because he'd do whatever he had to do to win.

Bob Gibson

It didn't matter who was up there. Bill White was one of my best friends in baseball, but he was also an uncompromising pull hitter. He'd wade into anything, and I told him, when we were teammates in St. Louis, that if he ever did that to me he'd be hearing from my representative.

He got traded to the Phillies in 1966, and the very first pitch I threw him was on the outside corner. And sure enough, he reached out there and *pulled it foul* down the first-base line. The next pitch hit him in the elbow.

He told me I was crazy, but what's crazy about doing what you said you'd do? Doing what you *have* to do? He got over it. It didn't hurt our friendship a bit.

Reggie Jackson

In those days, you got drilled for a reason. We expected it and respected it.

The game has changed in that regard, but at least some of the unwritten rules have stood the test of time. If you hit a home run and strut around the bases when you're up 8–0, or when you're down 8–0, you're asking for it. If you steal a base with a big lead and you're not in Fenway Park, where no lead is big enough, there will be consequences. If a guy slides too hard, or calls too much attention to himself, or if he's guilty of certain antics that aren't "kosher"—aren't part of the game or don't fit in with how a player should act socially on a ballfield—he pays the price. Even his teammates will tell him, "Hey man, you should have seen that coming. Look what you did. You showed this guy up. You showed their team up. You're going to hear a little chin music." You pay for your "shows."

I was a player who liked to savor some of my home runs. At the same time, I realized that pitchers didn't always appreciate that. I'm pretty sure John Denny didn't when he was pitching for Cleveland. I once hit a long one against him in Yankee Stadium and checked it out for a couple seconds. By the time I started running around the bases, there was Denny walking after me, screaming at me. He caught up at home plate and they had to pull us apart.

Ordinarily, though, a pitcher would share his feelings by sending me a message the next time I came up. So be it.

Bob Gibson

And so it would be.

Reggie Jackson

A lot of times when you get hit, it's protocol. Or, with somebody like Bob, it might just be the pitcher trying to get into your head, trying to make sure you understand that he's the one with the baseball. He's going to make you stand back, move your feet, stay where you belong.

All the great pitchers—even the ones today—will do that. They have to. They'll knock you down to make you respect them.

Bob Gibson

I wasn't in the business of hurting people, and when it happened I felt badly. But it happened, and I couldn't allow myself to feel badly enough that I'd give in to a hitter. I'd feel *worse* about that.

For a few years after the Dodgers moved to Los Angeles, they played in the Coliseum, where the left-field fence was only 251 feet away. They put up a high screen, but that fence was still a target. Duke Snider was a left-handed hitter and he didn't go to left field very often, but one day I threw him a ball away and he just stepped in and stroked it over that screen. At least he didn't try to pull it. I wasn't all that upset until the next time he came up, when I threw him a ball farther away and he hit it over that screen again, only this time foul.

When he leaned into the next pitch, it broke his elbow. I wasn't trying to hit him. I was trying to get him off the plate. Anyway, I went over and apologized after the game. He said, "Yeah, I know."

That's how baseball was played. There was a mutual understanding. It was understood, also, that you weren't trying to hurt anybody too much.

Most pitchers try not to hit a guy in the head. That's just something you don't do.

Reggie Jackson

It's generally agreed that if a pitcher is going to hit someone, he hits him in a big-muscle part of the body—the back or the butt or the side. Hitting somebody in the ribs and hitting somebody in the head are two entirely different discussions.

I was never afraid that a pitcher might hurt me, and never felt that anybody was trying to. That doesn't mean you're unaware of what could happen. You just can't let fear take you over in the batter's box. That can be a challenge when you're up against a guy who throws about ninety-five and has a reputation for being wild; or toward the end of the season, after call-ups, when you're standing in against a young pitcher just up from the minor leagues who's a hard thrower and doesn't have any idea where the ball's going. Then, yes, fear will try to creep in. But if you let it govern you, you're not going to be a good hitter. You have to go to the plate fearless.

The time you have to really focus on suppressing that fear is *after* you've been hit. I was thrown at fairly frequently in my career, but the most frightening was in 1976, my year in Baltimore, when Dock Ellis tried to hit me in the head and succeeded.

Bob Gibson

When I said most pitchers won't throw at your head, I wasn't talking about Dock Ellis.

Reggie Jackson

I'd been yelling at him from the dugout, so I knew I had *something* coming. But I had no idea he was going to hit me in the head. The three or four other times I was hit in the head during my career, I was protected by my helmet. That time, I took it in the face.

I missed a couple of games afterwards. On the day I was going to play again, against Detroit, I made a point of getting to the ballpark at one o'clock so that I could have the batting-practice pitcher throw balls at me. If you do get hit in the head, you're very conscious of it the next time you're in the batter's box. Don't let anybody tell you differently. I was uncomfortable.

Luckily, the first time I came up that night the pitcher, Dave Lemanczyk, threw me a fastball down the middle of the plate and I hit a home run. I was fine from then on.

Bob Gibson

If I wanted to plunk a batter, I would throw at his ribs, just slightly behind him. Batters usually have a tendency to step back a little bit when they see the ball coming their way, and if you throw just behind them it'll hit them in the side or maybe in the back.

In my view, when batters get hit in the head it's basically their fault. First of all, they're not expecting a pitch in there—which is especially the case these days—and aren't protecting themselves like they should. A lot of guys get lost in the confrontation and don't prepare themselves, mentally, for the ball coming inside. The head should be the easiest thing to move.

Reggie Jackson

There's a way to get out of the way, to avoid getting hit in the head. Most players, the first thing they do is duck down rather than turn away. Don't do that. Turn your face away from the ball and let the helmet protect you. Turn your back toward the pitcher. Don't try to duck and run. That's when you get hit.

Willie Mays was one of the hardest guys to hit because he did it right. He turned away. You couldn't hit Willie.

Bob Gibson

I certainly couldn't. I don't think I ever hit him. But I don't think I ever threw at Willie, either. There was no need.

It probably traced back to a little episode we had my rookie season. Bill White had been with the Giants before he got traded to the Cardinals, so he was friends with Willie and took me to

Willie's house in San Francisco when we played there. I was standing behind Bill when Willie opened the door, and I was wearing my glasses, like I always did off the field. I'm sure Willie had never seen me with them on. Anyway, he's got this loud, high-pitched voice, and when he opened the door he looked around and asked Bill, "Who's that?"

Bill said, "That's Gibson."

And Willie said, "Gibson! You wear glasses? Man, you're gonna *kill* somebody out there!"

After that, I never had to bother too much with Willie.

Reggie Jackson

If you *are* thrown at, it's not like you don't have any recourse. I went to the mound six or seven times.

There was a game against the Twins, in 1969, when I hit two home runs against Dave Boswell, then came up against a rookie named Dick Woodson. The rookie made me duck twice. After the second one, I headed out and tackled him.

Bob Gibson

And then the Oakland pitcher would've had to knock down one of the Twins. It goes back and forth like that. Retaliation.

That was about the only reason I ever used for actually throwing at somebody. Bear in mind, I make a distinction between throwing at a batter and what I did to Duke Snider, for instance. I didn't knock a guy down just because he hit a home run off of me. I may have *looked* at him in an angry way, like, "Damn, I can't believe I screwed up and laid one in for you like that." But I was mad at myself, not him. Those were usually my mistakes. The guy hit a home run because I made a bad pitch.

You shouldn't knock a guy down because you made a bad pitch. That's on you. Make a better pitch.

Reggie Jackson

I truly wish it had been left like it was in the old days, when retaliation was accepted as part of the sport. I wish the game could manage itself. But it all went over the top, and baseball has seen the need to step in.

Bob Gibson

Lou Brock and Curt Flood got hit all the time, so I'd have no choice but to retaliate. The fact is, I hated it.

Brock, especially, made it tough on me, because he was a nuisance to pitchers with his bunting and his stealing, and he got them riled up. We'd be up ten runs with two outs, and he'd steal third base because the third baseman was playing back. Then they'd hit him. I'd say, "Damn it, Lou, now I've got to knock somebody down." He got me in a lot of trouble because I was obligated to protect him. He'd say, "I didn't ask you to do that," but it didn't matter. I *had* to. It was my job.

There was the day in 1967, for example, when we scored seven runs in the bottom of the first inning against Milt Pappas and then Don Nottebart came on in relief for Cincinnati. The next time Brock stepped up to bat, Nottebart hit him. And then he threw at Lou on first base. Threw the ball right at his head while he was over there taking his lead. Nottebart didn't like Brock very well, for whatever reason. Well, I guess we all knew the reason. Anyway, Tony Perez was the first man up for the Reds the next inning, so I buzzed one back against the screen, about three feet over his helmet. Just wanted to let them know. Right away, Perez started woofing at me. Woof, woof, woof. He made such a fuss that I thought, well, hell, I can get closer than that. So on the next pitch he went down, and his hat went up, and the ball went between. I yelled in to him, "*That* was a knockdown."

Perez eventually flied out, and on his way back to the dugout he jogged past the mound and said something in English. I could understand his Spanish better than his English. He kept walking and talking, and I told him, "If you've got something to say, don't run away!" Then I went over to meet him. The guys from both benches trotted out onto the field at that point, but we were getting along okay until a big relief pitcher named Bob Lee came charging out of the Reds' bullpen. We fought for twelve minutes, but it seemed like fifteen rounds. I hit Perez over by the Reds' dugout, and Tommy Helms came up behind me and I happened to catch him out of the corner of my eye and took a swing, and he went head over heels. Then I jumped on Pete Rose and was pounding on him when a couple guys—it might have been Perez and Helms—piled on top of me. It's not real smart to fight in the other team's dugout, but I didn't mind; I grew up in the projects. It was quite a melee, though. There were policemen out there with billy clubs. An old cop tried to break us up in the dugout and Dave Bristol, the Reds' manager, fractured the poor guy's jaw. Half the players on the Cincinnati team had to be treated for cuts and bruises. I came out of it all right and ended up pitching into the eighth inning.

For the most part, though—and this was why I had to respond to Perez's yapping—hitters in those days didn't dispute our right to come inside. In all my seventeen years, nobody ever charged the mound against me.

If they had, I'd told my guys not to come running in to help right away but to stand back and watch, and if it looked like he was kicking my butt, *then* run over and help.

Reggie Jackson

I recognized that the pitcher had to protect his turf, but I also reserved the right to fight for mine. I particularly objected when a pitcher threw at me for merely doing my job, which was hitting the ball out of the park.

In August of 1971, I hit a couple home runs against the Red Sox on a Saturday and we had a doubleheader Sunday. In the first game, Roger Moret hit me in the arm. In the second game, Sonny Siebert knocked me down. I charged the mound. In retrospect, that might have been a little hair trigger, since Siebert kept the ball well below my head. But I was young and full of piss and vinegar, so I went out there and got corralled by the Red Sox. I said, okay, it's cool. So they let me go and I started up again. I don't know who I punched, and I don't know who punched me, but I remember that big George Scott—one of my favorite people in the world—had me wrapped up in a bearhug. Somehow, I managed to stay in the game. In fact, I ended up winning it in the bottom of the ninth inning with an inside-the-park home run off of Siebert. I got fined, played the next day, and that was that.

Bob Gibson

Fights don't carry over. It's just the heat of the moment. What carries over is when you *don't* fight and it just simmers.

Here's an example. John Milner was a pretty good left-handed hitter for the Mets and Pirates, and a guy who would dive over the plate to reach the outside corner. To let him know what I thought about that, I went inside and hit him in the body during spring training. A few months later, around midseason, we were playing the Mets and Seaver threw at me three straight times. I yelled out something about him having better control than that, and he yelled back something about *me* having better control than that, too. He was remembering what I did to Milner back in March.

Reggie Jackson

I could never wait that long for my revenge. In 1981, I had a good series in Minnesota, and one of the Twins' pitchers, John Verhoeven, knocked me down. Then I hit a home run and made a point of walking halfway to first base on my way around. In the newspaper the following morning, Verhoeven said something like, "The next time Reggie Jackson does that, I'm going to hit him in the head." So I went to the ballpark at two o'clock that afternoon, walked into the Twins' clubhouse, and sat in his chair. I mean, I was absolutely nuts when I did that. Finally our manager, Gene Michael, came over and got me, and he and a few others ushered me out of there before Verhoeven showed up. They said, "Reggie, you're out of your mind." Looking back, I can't believe I did that. But I'm kind of glad I did—for the sake of the story, if nothing else.

Bob Gibson

I don't believe I ever announced ahead of time that I was going to hit a batter.

Reggie Jackson

There's no need if you already have a reputation. That changes everything.

Everybody knew Gibson's reputation. He started the All-Star Game in 1972 and I batted third for the American League, so I faced him in the first inning. It was common knowledge that Hoot didn't like to be bothered with All-Star Games because they got in the way of the job he was trying to do for the Cardinals. So he always wanted to get out of there as quickly as he could, and wasn't in the best temperament. Well, he hung me a slider and I hit it off the fence in right center. As I pulled in at second base, he was *staring* at me.

I wouldn't look back at him. Would *not* look back. I just kept my helmet down over my eyes and minded my own business. I was scared to death.

Bob Gibson

I don't remember staring. I *do* remember that double.

Reggie Jackson

I wouldn't think of doing to Gibson what I did—or started to do—with John Verhoeven.

And then there are guys you try to intimidate and just can't. For me, that was Mike Caldwell of the Brewers. Caldwell had my number, and frankly, it made me mad. Once, after I popped out, I tried to get to him by cutting across the pitcher's mound on the way back to the dugout, which you're not supposed to do. The next time I came up, he knocked me down. The pitch after that was a fastball and I popped it up again, only this time I tossed my bat about halfway to the mound. After the ball was caught, Caldwell walked over, picked up my bat, and snapped the handle off. That started the brawl.

On that occasion, I'd say there was a personal element to it. Caldwell and I fought for a long time. I damaged something in his rib cage, and he was out for six weeks. But he still wasn't intimidated.

Bob Gibson

To me, it was almost never personal. People thought I had some kind of grudge against Jim Ray Hart of the Giants, but that was just the press carrying on.

I happened to hit Jim Ray in the shoulder once. The book was to pitch him inside. He was a guy, like Reggie, who'd kill you if you got the ball away from him, which was another reason to pitch him *way* inside—to keep him from diving. So I was making sure that he wasn't going to kill *me*. I went up and in, and he was leaning and it broke his shoulder. After that, word got out that I was throwing at him, which I wasn't.

Years later, I was playing in an old-timers game in Montreal and Jim Ray was on the same team. Those games sometimes end sooner than you expect, and when it looked like we were going to cut it off before I got into the game the manager sent me in to pitch for the other team, just so I could make my appearance. Well, of course Jim Ray was the first guy up, and he was going, "Whoa! Hold up here! I'm not gonna hit against *him*!"

I said, "Oh, get in there. I'm not gonna hurt you." He actually thought I wanted to get into the game just to throw at him one more time.

Reggie Jackson

See, that goes even beyond reputation. It's that air of mystery. Once you establish it, it keeps working for you.

There were times when I lost my cool and was out of bounds with my behavior. I acknowledge that. But the fact is, I didn't mind if pitchers thought I was a little crazy. It could only help me, just like it helped Gibson.

Bob Gibson

Guys like Reggie couldn't be intimidated. But there were hitters who could. If not intimidated, at least thrown off their game, like Clemente.

The Cubs had a skinny outfielder, Adolfo Phillips, whom I could get to. I'd knock him down in the first inning and he'd be done for the day. As good as Ron Santo was—and he hit three home runs against me—he was a guy who didn't like to be brushed back.

More than being afraid, guys like that get angry and they're going to *show* you. They get overanxious and swing at things they shouldn't swing at. There it is—go right ahead. Once they start that, you've got them.

Reggie Jackson

It can work the other way, too. Hitters can intimidate pitchers, or at least get in their heads.

Darrell Jackson was a 150-pound left-hander who also pitched for the Twins. He'd knocked me down during a game in Minnesota, and when the writers asked him about it afterwards, he'd made a statement that if Reggie Jackson does so-and-so, I'm gonna do such-and-such. So the next time they came to Yankee Stadium, we were taking batting practice—I always went last, which meant the other team would be taking the field as I hit—and Minnesota's pitchers were running in the outfield. When I was finished hitting, I strolled out to left field and walked right up to Darrell Jackson to see if there was something he cared to discuss. He Mister-Jacksoned me for the next five minutes.

I like telling that story.

Bob Gibson

I've even had a *manager* try to intimidate me. Gene Mauch.

Mauch was always doing something or other to get under my skin. In May of 1964, we were beating up on the Phillies early in the game and Mauch had their starter, Dennis Bennett, throwing at our guys, trying to get me to retaliate. By the fourth inning, Jack Baldschun was pitching in relief for the Phillies, and before I came to bat Mauch called down to the bullpen to have somebody ready in case Baldschun got thrown out. The first three pitches almost hit me and the fourth one got me in the thigh. That was excessive. I flung my bat toward the mound and then headed to the Phillies' dugout, looking for Mauch. Baldschun didn't get ejected, but I did. It cost me a victory, and as it turned out, that would have given me twenty for the first time.

Reggie Jackson

We all understand when a knockdown pitch is part of the game—at least we *did*—and we all get angry when it crosses the line. At my best, I turned that anger into focus. It was an I'm-gonna-get-this-guy mentality. Get him paid back.

My model was Frank Robinson. He fed on getting thrown at. You hit Frank Robinson and all he's thinking about is murdering that next pitch.

Bob Gibson

Frank Robinson was a pain in the butt. The records show that I hit him one time, but that can't be right. I hit him a *lot*. I must have hit him twenty times, about sixteen of them on that left arm of his that hung out into the strike zone. It made me mad, because the pitches that hit him weren't that bad. I remember yelling at the umpire, "He's standing on the plate! That's a strike!" Of course, it wasn't a strike. It would be four or five inches inside, but that shouldn't hit anybody. And Frank would be jogging down to first base.

A few years ago, I asked him about it. I said, "As much as I hit you, how come you never got mad?"

He said, "Because you weren't throwing at me."

He was right. I wasn't throwing at him. But I hit him all the time anyway, and there wasn't much else I could do. I pitched him away once at Crosley Field and he took it out of the park, so after that I just threw him fastballs to the elbow. If he couldn't hit it with his bat, he'd hit it with his elbow. Drove me crazy.

Reggie Jackson

Frank Robinson could intimidate equally well at home plate or on the bases. He was a hero of mine. He taught me a lot about how to play the game to *win*.

Bob Gibson

The way baseball is played today, there aren't many Frank Robinsons anymore. There aren't many Don Drysdales, either.

The changes in the game have not all been for the better, in my estimation. These days, if you throw the ball in and off the plate—not trying to hit anybody—the umpire'll yell at you and the batter'll come out and beat you up. If the ump thinks you're intentionally throwing at a guy, he can kick you out; he can kick the manager out; they can fine you, suspend you, take away your Blockbuster card, whatever.

The reality is, the ball's going to hit somebody now and then. You throw 125 pitches a game and there's a pretty good chance you're going to hit somebody even if you're not throwing at him. And when the batters are not expecting it—when they think they're protected and get too comfortable in there—they can be hurt really badly. You've got to watch for that ball in on your body, and the hitters today don't. They're constantly looking for something they can hit with their arms extended. I'm afraid that somebody's going to get killed because they don't look for the ball in on them anymore.

Reggie Jackson

Maybe Frank should be in charge of discipline in the commissioner's office. Sometimes they forget that this is good old hardball.

CHAPTER FIVE

SCENARIOS

Bob Gibson

Most of the time, I was happy to see a little guy up at the plate. I wasn't going to walk him, because there was no reason to. Throw him strikes. The worst he could do was hit a single.

But now and then you find yourself in a spot—with the bases loaded, or with a runner in scoring position late in a tie game—when the little Punch-and-Judy hitter is just the guy you don't want to deal with. In that situation, I might actually rather pitch to Willie McCovey than Pete Rose, or to A-Rod than Ichiro.

Reggie Jackson

In a spot like that, a home-run hitter might have to make himself a singles hitter.

Bob Gibson

As much as I respected a big guy like McCovey, and went to great lengths to prevent him from hurting me, that situation calls for a strikeout, and I had a better chance of striking him out than Rose. Maybe, with McCovey or Reggie, I don't have to be quite as accommodating in the strike zone. Maybe I don't *have* to throw a strike. They're not looking for a strike; they're looking for a ball they can hit. They're not quite as particular. A power hitter might swing at a pitch that he really shouldn't swing at, because there's always the chance that he'll hit it, and if he hits it there's always the chance it'll leave the park. In some circumstances, those guys can be easier to handle than the irritating hitters who are going to hold out for a nice little pitch right where they want it.

When I've got really good stuff, I'd rather take my chances in that situation with a guy who swings at a lot of pitches. I need that strikeout.

Reggie Jackson

I loved to hit with the bases loaded, but there's some merit to Bob's argument. I always felt that I was the guy who should drive in the runs. For that reason, if there were men in scoring position I'd sometimes expand the strike zone. That's what Bob's hoping for.

At the same time, I didn't want to do it selfishly. I wasn't interested in handicapping my team with a dumb, self-defeating at-bat. So I'd try not to go out of the strike zone *too* far. I didn't want to look foolish and play into the pitcher's hands by taking a bad swing. I'd also know who was on the mound, who was on the mound for *us*, what the game situation was, how important the run was, and who was hitting behind me.

It's all about circumstances. You might have the prettiest swing on the planet—you might have the quickest hands, the sharpest eye—but you can't be a great hitter unless you understand circumstances. As strange as it sounds, hitting is a team sport.

It's not enough just to recognize *your* circumstances. You also have to understand the pitcher's. This isn't the backyard, and we're not playing for a beer. We're professionals. If he has a cozy lead and time is running short, he may give up a run in exchange for an out. His priority then is to make sure I don't keep the inning going: Don't worry about the guy on third; let's just get Reggie to hit the ball on the ground. That tells me I might see a breaking pitch in the dirt, or a two-seamer at the knees.

The situation is fluid. It might change in the time it takes me to get from the on-deck circle to home plate. There's a lot going on for me, and a lot going on for the pitcher, too—what he's got working that day, what he doesn't have working that day. Maybe the first two times up I've gone boom, boom, two seeds, on a slider *and* a fastball; so he may have a different plan in mind this time. Every little nuance has the potential to change both his approach and mine.

Bob Gibson

That right there tells you why Reggie was a great hitter.

Reggie Jackson

When you get into the situation where he needs a strikeout and I need to strike a blow, that's when it really gets fun. Now he's going to give you *all* of it. He's going to step off the mound, grab the resin bag, and pull his hat down. The guys in the dugout are saying, "Uh-oh, don't let the man pull his hat down now."

Bob Gibson

If my back's to the wall and I can't walk him, he's going to get the fastball, and it's got to be over the plate. You just try to make sure it's not over the plate and at the belt at the same time.

With a guy like Reggie . . .

Reggie Jackson

I'm a tough situation, aren't I? I can end the game. You can think strikeout against me, but at the same time you don't want to make a mistake and give up *two* runs. Or four.

Bob Gibson

With a guy like Reggie, that might be the only time all night I try to strike him out. But it's just so hard to generalize. It depends so much on your wiggle room. It depends so much on the score.

There's some satisfaction in striking out Willie Stargell with

115

the bases loaded, but for the most part you really don't go out there to strike people out. At least I didn't, unless there was an important run at third that could score on a fly ball or groundout. Or unless I got two strikes. With two strikes, yes, you do think strikeout. But there were times when I had the bases loaded with nobody out and struck out the side, and it wasn't because I was *trying* to but because the situation called for my best fastball and it happened to be good enough to strike people out.

I was considered a strikeout pitcher, and I struck out more than two hundred batters nine times, but you know *who* I'd strike out? I'd average about eight a game. I'd get the seven, eight and nine hitters twice each. That's six right there. I *lived* to get the pitcher and those two guys in front of him. I'd swallow them whole. *That's* who you strike out. The bottom of the lineup and whoever comes up with a man on third and less than two outs.

Reggie Jackson

I certainly contributed my fair share to the strikeout totals of a whole lot of pitchers. Most home-run hitters do.

That was hard for me to accept at first. Early in my career, striking out would infuriate me. Then Dick Allen told me not to worry about it, because it was going to happen. Frank Robinson told me the same thing, and Carl Yastrzemski told me the same thing, as well. I wished I had struck out less, but eventually I learned not to obsess over it. It came with the territory.

When all was said and done, I had struck out nearly 2,600 times. I'd covered a *lot* of territory. Too much, really. I definitely struck out more than I should have.

Bob Gibson

Everybody loves to watch the big matchups when the strike-out pitcher is throwing as hard as he can and the home-run hitter is swinging as hard as he can. It's great stuff—power against power, Hall of Famer against Hall of Famer and all of that—but I never had the kind of ego that made me want to get Hank Aaron out when the game was on the line. I was a little more practical than that. I gave those guys a wide berth in those situations. I'd rather end the game against somebody I *knew* I could get out. Hey, let's try Joe Adcock.

Reggie Jackson

It's too bad, but you just don't have many high-profile, Hall of Fame showdowns anymore. Not with *starting* pitchers. Back in the day, you could face Gibson in the ninth inning with everything on the line. You could take on Jenkins, Palmer, Seaver, Carlton—any of the great ones—in that scenario. But how many times will Johan Santana still be around at the end of the game? How many times will Josh Beckett, C. C. Sabathia, Brandon Webb, or Jake Peavy come out for the ninth inning?

Even when I was playing, the big confrontation late in the game would usually come against a reliever—for me, usually a *lefty* reliever. The percentages were with that move, but I liked my odds anyway. The tighter the spot, the better for me.

Think about it. The manager just brought the dude in to face a left-handed hitter, handed him the ball, and slapped him on the butt with a big "go-get-him." That's why the guy's on the team. Okay, kid, there's Reggie, do your thing. More than likely, he's going to grit his teeth, throw a fastball, and throw it for a strike, if he can. I'll get one whack at it, maybe two.

I'd look for a ball to hit early in the count, and I would put that baby in play. I would *not* foul it off.

Bob Gibson

A left-hander would come in and throw you a fastball? Damn. I would have thought you'd see a breaking ball ninety percent of the time.

Reggie Jackson

Nope. I looked for a fastball. I didn't want to take too big of a swing and foul the sucker off, because I was going to get a cookie in the first two pitches. The reliever comes into the game to *pitch* to you. I tried to take advantage of that. That would be my best shot.

I was going to run right into it. All my timing, everything, was set up for a fastball to hit to left center. If I could get it in the air and square it, I had an opportunity for four "steaks" (rib eyes). I didn't want to get complicated or fancy. Don't overswing. Don't try to hit it over the fence. Don't pull it over the dugout. Don't foul it back and have it rolling up the net behind you. Don't wind up making frustrated gestures that everybody in the ballpark can read. Don't end up thinking, "Oh man, that was the *one*! How could I miss that? I shouldn't even *be* here!"

None of that. Put it in play. Square the ball.

Bob Gibson

If Reggie Jackson is going to beat you with a bases-loaded, ninth-inning single, more power to him. It'll happen, because he's a good hitter and you have to throw him a strike.

But if he hits a home run to beat you *leading off* the ninth, or with two outs and nobody on, there's no excuse for that.

Reggie Jackson

There would be games when not much was going on for either team, we'd get to the late innings, and the great pitchers I played behind—Catfish, Guidry, Palmer, Kenny Holtzman—would tell me, "I don't want you going for no single now. Give me a whack at it. You got one in you?"

I always believed I did. People say you shouldn't ever go to the plate trying to hit the ball over the fence, but that's bull. I've done it. Sometimes the situation calls for it.

Bear in mind, I don't recommend it for a kid, because it could lead to bad habits. It could make you open up your shoulder trying to pull the ball, jerk your head out of the strike zone, get your hips moving too soon—all the things that constitute bad mechanics. But at the major-league level, in a home-run situation, an accomplished power hitter not only *can* try to hit one, but he *should*.

I won't say for sure that I hit home runs at a higher percentage when I went up there gunning for one, but there were times when I owed it to my pitcher and to my team to try. There were times when I ended ballgames that way.

For me, that's the ultimate. With one swing, you get the results that you play for and the gratification that you live for. Hit a home run to win a ballgame and you own the world. At least until tomorrow.

There are games, also, when you can just feel, from the beginning, that a home run will do the trick. When Mike Norris made his first start in the big leagues I told him to take it easy, just pitch like he did in spring training, and I'd get him a tater. I hit a three-run shot in the third inning and he shut out the White Sox.

If you caught one early with Guidry on the mound, you could practically take the rest of the day off. Sometimes he'd walk over in the first or second inning and tell me, "I've got it today. Just give me one."

Catfish would say, "If you can just get me one, we're going to be all right today. Gimme a shot, Buck." (That was my nickname when I was with the A's.)

Bob Gibson

That's what I always wanted. We had some great teams with the Cardinals, and we were loaded with winning ballplayers, but it seemed like we never hit a home run. In 1967 we got Roger Maris, who had set the record with sixty-one for the Yankees, and he hit nine for us. The next year, he hit five. Orlando Cepeda led us with sixteen. The next year, Joe Torre led us with eighteen.

Guys on the Cardinals told me I was grumpy all the time. Grumpy? The score's 1–0, for crying out loud. With our team, it seemed like you had to grunt your way to the ninth inning every single time. That's as hard on you mentally as it is physically, knowing that if you give up a run, you lose. I'd leave the ballpark and have to go lie down. I always wondered what it would be like to get seven or eight runs now and then.

In 1970, we traded for Dick Allen and he hit thirty-four home runs and we thought we had Babe Ruth. He always seemed to come up with them at just the right time, too. It's no coincidence that I won twenty-three games that season, my highest total ever.

So yeah, hit me one, big fella. Win me a ballgame.

Reggie Jackson

In 1977, my first year with the Yankees, we were playing the Red Sox in mid-September and trying to hold on to first place. It was a 0–0 game going into the bottom of the ninth inning, Ed Figueroa for us and Reggie Cleveland for Boston.

Thurman Munson led off, and before he went up to hit he told me he was going to single between third and short and it would be up to me to get him home. I told him I would. He did his part, just like he said. But when I got to the plate, Dick Howser, our third-base coach, called me down and told me I might get the bunt sign. I got it on one-and-one, but the pitch was ball two and they took the sign off. Then Cleveland left a slider over the plate a little bit. That was his out pitch, but not in that spot.

It went out, all right.

Bob Gibson

That should not have happened. If Willie Randolph beats you with a ninth-inning home run, hats off to him. But in that situation, Reggie Cleveland had no business leaving a slider over the plate for Reggie Jackson.

Game Not in the Balance

Reggie Jackson

For a hitter, there's a big difference between a tight spot and a tough spot. In fact, I'm not sure there's such a thing as a tough spot for a hitter, other than facing a guy with a hot hand and too much stuff. In terms of circumstances, the hairier it gets, the easier it ought to be. Bases loaded—the pressure's on the pitcher. He's the one who has to throw a strike.

When I was fortunate enough to find myself in that situation, the game would heighten. It would come to me.

A hitter should be in his element when the game is close. That includes the first inning. In the early going, I was always sharp and bright-eyed, bearing down to see what the pitcher had and trying to set a tone—maybe take advantage of him right off the bat, before he could find his rhythm. And late in the game, when the action had built to a crescendo and the crowd was screaming, I'd be in a zone. In those moments, all the distractions would fade away and the task would become more distinct. It would come into focus.

What's hard is concentrating in the fourth inning when the score is 7–1.

Bob Gibson

A six-run lead should be a weapon for a pitcher. The other team is just trying to get baserunners on, trying to work walks, not trying to hit the ball seven hundred feet. The pitcher can, and should, take full advantage of the situation. He does that by challenging every hitter. He does it, basically, by throwing strikes.

But it's not as simple as it sounds. He can get in trouble if he takes too *much* advantage. A lot of pitchers confuse throwing strikes with just throwing the ball over the plate. They think it means throwing safe pitches. Well, there's no such thing. That's a bad way to go about your business.

I'd pitch just as hard with a six-run lead as I would in an even ballgame. I'd be less likely to pitch around the Aarons and the Reggies, because you don't want to extend innings and pile up baserunners in that circumstance; but that would be about the only difference in my approach. I'm going to challenge them by throwing strikes, but not with anything less than my best stuff. I know what'll happen if I let up. One of the surest ways to lose a lead is to change your way of pitching.

I had this discussion with Tony La Russa. Of course, Tony was never a pitcher, but he has a lot of ideas about how to win ballgames, and he's won a lot of them in ways that I wouldn't. He was talking about those get-me-over pitches when you have a nice lead and fall behind in the count.

To me, get-me-over implies two things I don't like. It suggests that you're unconcerned with your location within the strike zone. And it suggests that you're holding back on your stuff in the interest of getting the ball over the plate.

Anyway, Tony asked me if I ever threw a get-me-over pitch, and I said no.

He said, "Never?"

I said, "Never."

He said, "You don't believe in that?"

"Absolutely not."

"Why? Why risk walking a batter in that situation?"

"For one thing, I don't consider it a risk because I'm pretty sure I can get my best fastball over the plate. And for another thing, I know that if I throw Barry Bonds a get-me-over fastball on two-and-oh, he's going to hit it into McCovey Cove."

Then I don't have a six-run lead anymore.

Man On

Reggie Jackson

In 1987, my last year with Oakland, we were in a hitters meeting and Tony La Russa was talking about the proper approach with a runner on second or third. Mark McGwire and Jose Canseco were in the room, among others, and Tony wanted them to hear my perspective on the subject. So he asked me, in Tony's serious style, "Reggie, what are your thoughts when you're at home plate and there's a man in scoring position?"

I didn't miss a beat. "Skip," I said, "I feel that when I'm hitting and there's *no one* on base, there's still a man in scoring position." Everyone roared laughing—even Tony. But that was pretty much the way I saw it.

Since I believed so fervently that I could bring home any runner from anywhere, including myself, my preference was not to have a base stealer on first when I was doing my thing. I mean, I appreciated Bert Campaneris and Billy North and all the speedy guys I played with. They won games for us. All the same, I didn't want them running when I was hitting.

In fact, when they were dancing around off first base, stretching their leads and scheming to steal second, there were times when I stepped out of the batter's box and gestured to them not to do that. I don't need you on second to drive you in. And it certainly wasn't that I wanted that hole to hit through—the hole created by the first baseman holding on the baserunner. I wasn't thinking about hitting the ball in the hole. I was thinking about squaring the ball on the barrel, and I didn't want anything to divert my attention from that. I was going to *make* a hole. So I don't want you jitterbugging around out there. And when you're on second base, I don't want you stealing third, either.

Just stay where you are. If you don't distract me, I can drive you home.

Bob Gibson

But a fast runner works to the hitter's advantage. I've seen Lou Brock distract a lot of pitchers, and I've had to pitch to Tommy Davis and Frank Howard and Ron Fairly with Maury Wills in the starting block over at first. It can disrupt a guy's rhythm and throw him off his game. You might forget where you were with the hitter; you might quicken your motion to the plate; you might lose something on the ball.

So keep those guys off the bases. If you're pitching to Maury Wills, for heaven's sake don't walk him. I learned to not be too fancy with the little guys who couldn't hit home runs. Make them take their cuts. Here's a high fastball—have at it. If they can hit their way to first base, congratulations. But don't *give* it to them.

Honestly, though, when Wills was on base it didn't bother me as much as you might think, because I was resigned to the fact that Tim McCarver, my good buddy and catcher, wasn't going to throw him out. I loved pitching to McCarver, but we both know that he wasn't *about* to throw out Maury Wills. What I did was hold the ball when Wills was on. I'd bring it to my stretch position and just wait there. He'd be inching away trying to get a good jump, and a lot of times he'd get impatient and start running while I was still standing there holding the ball. I'd just turn around and throw him out at second. I had him all screwed up. I never picked anybody off, but I successfully messed with a few guys.

Looking back on it, though, maybe my attention to Wills explains why a guy like Fairly could knock me around the way he did. Fairly was a professional at the plate, but even so, I could never understand why he should have more base hits off me than anybody else. Maybe I was preoccupied. Maybe I was just pitching from the stretch a lot when he came up. He usually batted behind both Wills and Willie Davis, who was faster than Wills and hit me a lot better. Every time I looked over, Willie Davis was on base.

I don't advise pitching that way. When you're throwing out of the stretch, you don't have all those arms and legs working for you; but that's not necessarily the biggest problem. Your concentration might be compromised, but that's not necessarily the biggest problem either. If there's a fast man on first, the biggest problem is that the hitter is probably going to see more fastballs, and they're not going to be your best ones.

I'm sure Reggie is in favor of that.

Reggie Jackson

I *would* rather hit with a man on base, as long as he stays where he is. Let's take the pitcher out of the windup and split his focus. Maybe he'll neglect the fact that I can hit the ball out of the ballpark.

Bring that fastball in here.

Bob Gibson

There *is* a flip side that works to the pitcher's advantage. If Brock or Wills or Rickey Henderson is on first, I can pour strike one right down the middle because the hitter is more than likely going to take it and see if the runner can steal.

Most hitters, anyway.

Reggie Jackson

If I've got Rickey Henderson on first, or Vince Coleman—guys who stole huge numbers of bases—my thinking's not going to be any different. I was trying to drive him in from there. I was trying to square the ball and hit it on a line. I wanted the ball in the air for three and a half seconds. Then it's a souvenir.

Bob Gibson

Unless it's an awfully high pop-up.

Reggie Jackson

Of course, with two strikes it all changes. Then I'm playing defense. My order of business is to become a baserunner myself.

Bob Gibson

There are some hitters who *go to the plate* playing defense, and I hated it. I'm talking about the guys who take you deep in the count and foul pitches off and hang in there and hang in there and make a general nuisance of themselves. I'd much rather a batter hit the first or second pitch. I don't want to use up fifteen pitches on one little guy who can't hit the ball to the warning track.

The worst was Richie Ashburn. What a pain. He's a Hall of Famer and I salute him for that, but I couldn't stand to pitch to that guy. He couldn't put the ball in play off of me—he only had two hits against me his whole career—but he'd stand in there and foul off ten pitches and I'd end up walking him. I walked him ten times. These days the announcers would drool all over themselves telling everybody what a great at-bat that was, and maybe they're right. But I never thought of it as a great *battle*. I thought of it as a pain in the butt.

Whether I give him credit for that, I don't know. I probably should, but I'd rather not. The way the game is played today, that sort of thing has a lot more value because it runs up the pitch count and gets the starting pitcher out of the game quicker. But back then, we weren't taken out based on a pitch count. Richie

Ashburn wasn't going to get me out of the game. He was just going to tick me off.

Reggie Jackson

It takes some skill to stay alive like that in the batter's box. I wish I'd been better at it. But when a guy hangs in there with two strikes and fouls off pitch after pitch, he's not doing it on purpose. I don't know of anybody who can do that on command—stand at the plate and make up his mind to foul the ball off. Maybe a contact hitter like Luke Appling or Rod Carew or Nellie Fox could handle the bat well enough to do it if he tried, but that's not the plan. The plan is to put the ball in play. A foul ball means he couldn't do it.

It's possible that a great all-around hitter like Aaron could foul the ball deliberately, but it's not likely that he'd try. He was about hitting the ball hard somewhere. You think Willie McCovey went to the plate to foul the ball off?

Bob Gibson

The only guy I've seen do it deliberately was Jose Cardenal. He did it just to mess with Brock. Brock would be halfway to second base and Jose would just slap the ball in the direction of the dugout. You need talent to do that, and Jose had the talent.

One night I told him that I knew he was doing it on purpose. He just smiled and said, "Did you see that?"

"Yeah, I saw that. Why'd you do it?"

"I don't know."

Who knows why people do certain things? Maybe he wanted to steal more bases than Lou. We all dance to different tunes.

October

Reggie Jackson

The World Series was everything I wanted it to be. Come October, it was all you heard or read about. That put it front and center in my world. It was innate for me to be a hundred percent zoned in and primed for the World Series. I wish I could have done it during the regular season.

The postseason became practically a part of my life cycle. I played in eleven playoffs and six World Series. That is, our *team* played in six World Series. I played in five.

Oakland went to its first Series in 1972, but to get there we had to make it through a tough playoff against the Tigers. It went to the fifth game, with Blue Moon Odom pitching for us against Woodie Fryman. We were down a run when I came up in the second inning. I walked, stole second, went to third on a fly ball, and then stole home to tie it on the back end of a double steal with Mike Epstein. But in the process I tore my left hamstring, kept running, and ruptured it.

I was so distraught over having to miss the World Series that I cried, and my friends Dave Duncan and Joe Rudi cried with me. When we beat the Reds, it should have been the happiest moment of my career to that point. But I couldn't even run out onto the field and dive on the pile and jump around with my teammates. It was a sick, horrible feeling, and that feeling stuck with me. I wanted to be out there!

The next spring, I kept telling everybody on the team that we were going back to the World Series. I felt like I *had* to play in it. I honestly believe that sitting out the '72 Series was the thing that pushed me to win the MVP Award in 1973. I also believe that it had at least something to do with us repeating as champions of the American League.

The '73 World Series went seven games. We were forced to win the last two to pull it out. In game six, the Mets had Tom Seaver going, and he'd fanned me three times in game three with the best combination of stuff and location I'd ever faced. This time, though, I caught up with Seaver for three base hits, two of them RBI doubles into the gaps. That's a badge I wear on my heart to this day. That was Tom Seaver, dude—an all-timer! But Catfish Hunter beat him 3–1. Then, in Game Seven, Bert Campaneris, of all people, gave us the lead with a two-run homer. I hit another one a few batters later, and that was enough for another great pitcher on our team, Ken Holtzman.

I was named the MVP of the Series. Nobody had yet called me Mr. October, but that was the start of it. Let it be known, though, that Campaneris could just as easily have been the MVP.

The next year we beat the Dodgers, which grew into a habit when I went to the Yankees in 1977.

Bob Gibson

As much success as I had in the World Series, I have to say that it comes down to the hitter more than to the pitcher. I'm going to make my share of mistakes in the World Series, just like I do in the regular season. It's a matter of whether the hitters are on their game enough to take advantage of those mistakes.

Obviously, Reggie was a guy who could focus all his abilities in that situation and actually feed on it. Lou Brock was the same way. Brock was something else in the postseason.

Reggie Jackson

I watched Bob Gibson beat the Red Sox three times in the 1967 World Series and strike out seventeen Detroit Tigers in the opening game of the 1968 World Series. *Yes!* It made such an impression on me that he was in my Hall of Fame speech. Gibson was an inspiration. After watching him put everything on the line in two straight Octobers, I was driven to play with the will to win that he exemplified when he pitched.

I'd have loved to face Hoot in the World Series, because that's when I'd *know* I was going to be on my game.

Bob Gibson

That would make two of us.

Reggie Jackson

I might not *do* anything, but if ever I was going to be able to make my mark against one of the all-time greats, that would be the time. I was going to be on it. And if I did something under those circumstances, nobody could ever say, well, you caught him on a bad day. Uh-uh.

Bob Gibson

I don't know that I ever pitched a bad game in the postseason. I got beat; but pitching a bad game—I don't think that happened.

The atmosphere, no doubt, had something to do with it. I didn't care for all the distractions that came with the territory, but the excitement surrounding the whole thing served to help me forget how tired and worn out and beat-up I might be.

Reggie Jackson

I didn't consider them distractions. I saw all that stuff as the stage being set. Set for *me*.

Bob Gibson

My first World Series victory came in Yankee Stadium. It was the fifth game of the 1964 Series, and I'd lost in Game Two in St. Louis. That was a wild pennant race that year, and toward the end of it the Cardinals had pushed me up to three days of rest instead of the four we usually got. My last start was on the final Friday, and Al Jackson of the Mets shut us out 1–0. We still needed to win Sunday to take the pennant, and I had to go four innings of relief. That was twenty-nine innings in a stretch of eleven days, and four days later the Yankees beat me in our park.

But nothing energizes a ballplayer like Yankee Stadium in October. I had a cold and sore throat and wasn't throwing worth a damn in the bullpen, but none of that mattered. In the ninth inning, Joe Pepitone lined a ball off my backside and I sprinted toward the third-base line, grabbed it, and whirled around as I threw him out. He couldn't believe the call or the play I made, either one; but he was out, and we went to the tenth inning and Tim McCarver hit a three-run homer to win it.

For Game Seven, I only got two days' rest and went nine innings, which left me closing out the season with fifty-six innings in twenty-two days. There's no way I could have done that without the adrenaline I got from the pennant race and World Series. Competition brings out the best in a competitor, and also the *most*. Fortunately, our offense produced seven runs in the seventh game. I gave up a three-run homer to Mickey Mantle in the sixth inning and solo homers in the ninth to Clete Boyer and Phil Linz, which tells you how much stuff I had left. Johnny Keane had every reason to take me out but he didn't, and he explained it to the press with the comment that he was committed to my heart.

Reggie was saying how his reputation, and really his career, was built on the first World Series he played in. It was the same with me. Before that Series, I'd never won twenty games and I'd only pitched in one All-Star Game. But to win it all under those circumstances, against the New York Yankees, and to hear my manager talk about me in those terms . . . well, I walked a little taller after that. In 1965, I won twenty for the first time. No coincidence there.

I set a World Series record for strikeouts in that '64 Series, and they gave me the MVP Award. My prize was a Corvette from *Sport* magazine. I ended up selling it, because I needed the money and because I was a little ticked off after a policeman pulled me over when I was driving it through a small town in Missouri.

Reggie Jackson

The 1977 Series is the one that I'm most often associated with. Just like my 1977 *season*, it started out with a little tension. Billy Martin had benched me for the final playoff game against Kansas City, and I would have liked to make a statement about that right away. I singled my first time up in the opening game of the Series against the Dodgers, but in the ninth inning, when we were ahead 3–2, Billy replaced me with Paul Blair for defensive purposes. I didn't like it, but I can't blame him for that one. Blair was a great outfielder, and eventually he singled in the winning run in the bottom of the twelfth.

A lot of people have speculated that my spat with Billy was what motivated me in that Series. But to get amped for a World

Series, I didn't need coffee, bennies, amphetamines, or disrespect from Billy Martin. My times in the World Series were in the moment. When I was standing in the batter's box, there was nothing going on except getting the barrel of the bat in time with the baseball. There was no clutter in my head. I was going to get the barrel in the pay zone, as I call it.

Bob Gibson

It's a little different for regulars than it is for a pitcher. A starting pitcher is only out there every fourth or fifth day, so you don't get into the same kind of grind during the season that everyday players might. I imagine that a guy who plays a hundred and fifty games every year could get a little bored after a few months of going at it seven days a week. But for a pitcher . . . eighty percent of the time, I'm sitting in the dugout calling people names and having a ball. I didn't have much problem getting up for a start in the regular season, so the World Series wasn't much different for me.

But it was different enough.

Reggie Jackson

If a hitter doesn't do much in a World Series game, he has as many as six more to make up for it.

In 1977, the Series only went six games, but I waited until the latter part to crank it up. In Game Four, which we won 4–2, I homered to left center off Rick Rhoden. My second home run came off Don Sutton my last time at bat in Game Five, but we lost that one. Burt Hooton started Game Six for the Dodgers and walked me my first time up, which was disappointing because I'd been swinging extremely well in batting practice and really felt like I could light up Yankee Stadium. Then I hooked one off Hooton for a home run in the fourth inning to score Munson and give us a 4–3 lead. In the fifth, I homered against Elias Sosa with Willie Randolph on base. I didn't know anything about Sosa, so I called up to the press box to Gene Michael and he told me what to look for. It was an inside fastball, and I was ready.

In the eighth, when we were looking good, I got hold of one of Charlie Hough's knuckleballs and hit it way out to center field. By that point, I was just living out my fantasy. When it was over, I had three dingers on three swings. Including the one the game before in Los Angeles, it was four home runs on four swings—five first-swing homers in all, counting the one in Game Four. I also picked up a bunch of Series records and another MVP Award. Munson and Howard Cosell were calling me Mr. October.

What felt best, though, was doing it in New York. Especially after all that we'd been through that season; all *I'd* been through. It was like I'd unloaded the burdens of the summer on three fat pitches. To top it off, my dad and sister were there, and George Steinbrenner, the man who brought me to New York—The Boss—was saying, "I told you so . . ."

Now, nobody could talk about all the heroics of all the great Yankees—Ruth, Gehrig, DiMaggio, Yogi, Mickey, Maris, Whitey Ford—without including me in that roll call. I believed that what I'd done couldn't or shouldn't have been done anywhere but Yankee Stadium. I had become part of the tradition.

That felt *good.* God's sunshine surely hit me that night.

Bob Gibson

We weren't much like the Yankees. There was plenty of World Series tradition in the Cardinal organization—Dizzy Dean, Enos Slaughter, Stan Musial, Grover Cleveland Alexander—but that wasn't what we played for. We played for *us.*

The Cardinals were an uncommonly close and interesting group of guys. There wasn't the drama that Reggie dealt with in the Yankee clubhouse. People like McCarver and Curt Flood and Bill White were great friends of mine, and I thought the world of them. Brock, Ken Boyer, Mike Shannon, Joe Torre, Orlando Cepeda, Roger Maris—all those guys. You played for your teammates.

Did I get a kick out of being the best pitcher in the Series?

Yeah. Being the MVP? Yeah. But it wasn't really about me. It was about all of us.

Then, in 1967, we played the Red Sox. As much as we liked the guys in *our* clubhouse, we didn't like the ones in theirs.

Reggie Jackson

As a Yankee, that's music to my ears.

Bob Gibson

They seemed to think the Series was all about them. Carl Yastrzemski had won the Triple Crown and Jim Lonborg had won the Cy Young, and frankly, they were cocky about it. The whole city of Boston was cocky about it.

But you know, it was an ideal situation for me and the Cardinals. There's nothing better than being the underdog in the World Series.

Reggie Jackson

I was usually on the other end of that. But I could say there's nothing better than being a *Yankee* in the World Series.

Bob Gibson

I came in pretty motivated anyway, because that was the year Clemente clipped me with the line drive and I missed a couple months. I felt like I hadn't done my part, and I was determined to make up for that.

And then, with two outs in the bottom of the third inning in Game One, the Red Sox pitcher, Jose Santiago, lifted a little fly to left field and I started to walk toward the dugout and heard all this racket and turned around to see something dropping into the screen that caught balls that cleared the Green Monster. Fortunately, that was the only run they got.

I shut them out in Game Four and was good to go in Game Seven. George Scott, their big first baseman, predicted that "Gibson won't survive five." Meanwhile, they had Lonborg ready. He lasted six, and it was too bad he stayed around that long, because we scored three off him that inning to make it 7–1. I ended up with another MVP Corvette (and sold it again). In three games against me, the Red Sox never had more than one hit in an inning.

Afterwards, they weren't talking nearly as much as they had beforehand.

Reggie Jackson

Does my heart good.

Our rivalry with the Red Sox was never more intense and crazy than it was in 1978, when we came from fourteen games behind to pass them in September, then fell back into a tie on the last day of the regular season. We won the one-game playoff, 5–4, when Bucky Dent hit his famous three-run homer to give us the lead in the seventh inning and Goose Gossage got Yastrzemski to end the game on a pop-up with two men on. I had a home run in the eighth and two more in the playoffs, when we got past Kansas City, and three hits in the first Series game against the Dodgers. Then, in Game Two, at Yankee Stadium, I had driven in all three of our runs when I came up in the ninth inning against a rookie right-hander named Bob Welch.

Welch was only twenty-one years old, and Tommy Lasorda had brought him into a tough spot. The Dodgers led by a run, but we had two on with one out and Munson at the plate, followed by me. Thurman flew out, but I still liked our chances, because I was swinging the bat well. It was the kind of scenario I played for. Even now, I still think of it as one of my great moments in baseball. I *loved* it—even though I struck out.

Rather, Welch *struck* me out. The count was two-and-two for a long time, and the kid was just making pitch after pitch, ninety-five-mile-an-hour fastball after ninety-five-mile-an-hour fastball. I kept fouling them off, and he finally threw ball three. I was so focused on Welch that I lost track of the count and was surprised when the runners broke off the bases on the three-two pitch. I blinked and the ball got by me for strike three. It wasn't until I watched the tape that I realized the crowd had been on its feet the entire at-bat. I was so locked in that I didn't hear a thing. I guess

I was *too* locked in, because it was very unusual for me to lose track of the count. But I don't want to discredit the job Welch did. He was throwing high fastballs into a space that I'd been taking care of extremely well, and I just couldn't get there against him. I didn't lose that at-bat. He just beat me.

As much as I loved hitting home runs, there was also satisfaction in playing the game at a high level, and playing it right. I reveled in the pure baseball aspect of that matchup with Welch, and I was pleased with a little play in Game Four that helped turn the series in our favor. The Dodgers were up two-one in games (they won the first two) and ahead 3–0 in the sixth inning of Game Four when I singled to drive in Roy White and move Munson to second with one out. Then Lou Piniella hit a little liner to Bill Russell, the shortstop, but Russell dropped it and forced me at second. I was stranded halfway between first and second and decided to just stand there in the way of Davey Lopes's relay to first. I might have ever so slightly let my hip drift out in the direction of the ball. The throw hit me and bounced away, and Munson scored to make it 3–2. They called it the Sacrifice Thigh. I never really got credit for a smart baserunning play on that one, so I'll go ahead and take the credit right here, right now. Anyway, we tied the game in the eighth and Piniella won it with a single in the ninth.

In the sixth game, we were ahead 5–2 in the seventh inning when I came up against Welch again with a runner on first. As I left the dugout for the on-deck circle, Catfish said, "Get even with him, Buck." I got my revenge. This time, I dropped a big fly on him into the back of the bullpen at Dodger Stadium. We won, 7–2, and that was that.

Bob Gibson

My Bob Welch was Mickey Lolich. That might sound a little strange, because it wasn't like we went after each other, one-on-one, tooth and nail, from sixty feet, six inches. But we had a fantastic battle, and he beat me.

In 1968, after two World Series MVPs and seven straight

World Series victories and a single-game World Series strikeout record (in the opener against the Tigers) and two World Series *series* strikeout records (I broke my own record from 1964 in the seventh game), and after we blew a three-to-one lead in games—in part, possibly, because my teammates felt deep down that we'd win Game Seven anyway since I'd be pitching it—I was beaten by a left-hander with a big gut and lots of guts.

I'm glad, at least, that it wasn't Denny McLain. He won thirty-one games that year, while I was only winning twenty-two with my 1.12 ERA, and he was on all the TV shows and magazine covers—which was all fine with me until he said before the World Series that he didn't want to just beat the Cardinals, he wanted to humiliate us. That helps explain my seventeen strikeouts against him while throwing a shutout in Game One.

The other thing that explains those strikeouts is that, even though it was my third World Series, the Tigers' scouting report still said—apparently—that my game was my fastball. So I kept striking them out with sliders, as I usually did. I guess they thought they were fastballs. In the ninth, I got Al Kaline, Norm Cash, and Willie Horton, and the third strike to Horton was an inside slider that he claimed he never saw.

McLain was also my opponent in Game Four, which we won easily. But we all remembered that, during the season, when McLain was ripping off one victory after another, Roger Maris had told us that the guy we had to worry about in the World Series was not McLain but Lolich. Sure enough, Lolich had beaten us in Games Two and Five, and although it should have been McLain's turn in Game Seven, the Detroit manager, Mayo Smith, went with the right guy.

I retired twenty of the first twenty-one batters in the seventh game, but we couldn't break through against Lolich, even though he must have been physically exhausted. It was 0–0 until the seventh, when, with two outs, Cash and Horton singled and Jim Northrup hit a two-run triple to deep center field. That was enough for Lolich, who proved that pitching under pressure is as much about brains and attitude as anything else. Of course, he had pretty good hard stuff, too. The winner of that game would surely be the Series MVP, and he was the best man.

And don't think that's easy for me to say, even forty years later.

Reggie Jackson

Here we are, Mr. October and the greatest World Series pitcher of all time, and we both lost our last Series. Mine was 1981, against the Dodgers again. Backing up a bit . . . In the first round of the playoffs, against Milwaukee, we'd dropped two straight and blown a two-game lead. George Steinbrenner roared into the clubhouse and gave us holy hell. We were very close to falling apart, and I remember telling a writer that we'd find out in the fifth game about this Mr. October business. I ended up with three hits in game five, including a home run off Moose Haas that tied the score in the fourth inning. We survived to play the A's for the American League championship.

Oakland was Billy Martin's team now, and a lot was made of our personal relationship. But that didn't have anything to do with us beating the A's in three straight. The series, in fact, wasn't especially sweet for me: I pulled something in my leg early in the second game and couldn't play the last one. Then, in the victory celebration at an Oakland restaurant, I took out my frustrations with Graig Nettles. There was a misunderstanding and a tussle—no big deal. But I can't say that we were in the best frame of mind for the World Series. Maybe the drama was finally wearing us down.

My leg kept me out of the first two games of the Series, and we won them both. I could have played in the third, against Fernando Valenzuela, but Bob Lemon didn't put me in the lineup. It occurred to me that George had probably made that call. It would be my last season in New York, and my guess was that the front office wanted the Yankees to win a World Series without me, just to prove they could.

Maybe it would have been different if I'd played in that game. There were chances to win it, and I had no doubt that I could have gotten the job done. I always had before! As it was, the Dodgers beat us 5–4. Then they took two more one-run games with me back in the lineup. In Game Six, they gave us a pretty good drubbing. It was the first time I'd been on the losing end of a World Series.

I wouldn't get another shot. And there's no way to measure what I would have given for one.

CHAPTER SIX

THE OTHER GUYS

Scouting Reports

Reggie Jackson

Today, teams have advance scouts, video, charts, computer printouts, and all kinds of data designed to tell you how you're supposed to pitch a certain batter. I have to say, all that information does help. But the great pitchers don't really need all those reports, unless you're talking about a hitter who just came up from the minor leagues. They'll file them in their memory banks for information, but generally the good pitcher already has a plan of his own.

Seaver, Gibson, Maddux—they're on their own programs. They understand their success and what they're going to war with. And they understand the hitters they've been pitching to and have been getting out for years. Regardless of the scouting report, a guy like that *knows* how he'll pitch me. I'd have to make an adjustment and hurt him a couple times before he'd change his approach and move on to something else.

Bob Gibson

I think my best friend in the World Series was the scouting report. Nobody really looked for my slider when we played in the

World Series. They all looked for that ninety-five-, ninety-six-mile-an-hour fastball that I probably threw about eighty to eighty-five percent of the time during the regular season. The scouts just saw the fastball, and they heard about it by word of mouth or whatever, and that's what went down on their reports. Fine.

I had a lot of regular-season games that were better-*pitched* than some of my best games in the World Series. The difference was that, in the World Series, the batters didn't know me nearly as well as they thought they did by reading my friend, the scouting report.

Reggie Jackson

I had the same experience. That scouting report was the best thing I had going for me in the postseason.

They had a book on how to pitch Reggie, and the book said to go inside. That was all well and good, but teams like the Dodgers were so hung up on that scouting report that they couldn't see what was happening in front of their eyes. They couldn't tell that I was cheating back in the box. They couldn't see that, for a while there, I was hitting a home run every time I swung the bat.

Bob Gibson

About the worst thing a pitcher can do is swear an oath to the scouting report. There are just too many things to consider.

Albert Pujols is kind of like Reggie, for example. You can get him out by pitching him in, too. But they'll trot out some guy throwing the ball eighty-seven or ninety miles an hour, and he's trying to pitch Albert Pujols on the inside part of the plate. That ain't gonna work. It's just not going to work. You've got to realize, pal, that some pitchers can pitch him in, but not *you*!

It's just a fact that all pitchers are different and very few of them can succeed exactly the same way. A scouting report can be helpful to a pitcher if he understands its limitations, but as a blueprint to getting somebody out it's not worth much, as far as I'm concerned. Sam Jones might be able to get a batter out with that great curveball of his, but that doesn't mean I should throw curveballs to that same batter, because my ragtag curveball was nothing like Sam Jones's. By the same token, I would be able to pitch Reggie, for instance, in ways that other pitchers couldn't because I had command of two good fastballs and a hard slider and confidence in them all.

How could some other pitcher be expected to approach a batter the same way I do when, if I got in trouble, chances are that I wouldn't even stick with that plan *myself*? If, say, you're a sinkerball pitcher and the batter is a good low-ball hitter, when your back's against the wall you've got to go with the sinker regardless.

Reggie Jackson

All that aside, if I'd never faced Bob Gibson before and somebody handed me a scouting report on him, I'd definitely look at it. I don't have to pledge allegiance to it, but I'd take a look. I can use all the information I can get.

Bob Gibson

Sure, you want to get an idea. But that doesn't mean it's going to happen the way they say it's going to happen.

In 1965, the Cubs had a little rookie infielder, a Dominican named Roberto Peña who was about five-foot-eight at the most. The scouting report said that this guy could pick the ball up and hit it four times and couldn't get it out of the ballpark. It said to throw the ball right down the middle and let him hit it as hard as he can. And the very first pitch, I threw it right down the middle and wham, he hit an opposite-field home run to right. His first career home run. The next night, he hit his second career home run, against Curt Simmons. In 1968, he hit his third career home run, against Steve Carlton. In 1969, he hit his fourth career home run, against Carlton. I don't think our scouting report on Roberto Peña was very good.

Reggie Jackson

The best scouting report is your own history with the other guy, if you have one. When you first get into the league you might keep your own little black book on how pitchers throw to you, but after you've been around for a while the book is in your head—at least, when you're facing the guys you've seen over and over. In my last year or so, I'd go to the ballpark in, say, Baltimore, and up on the scoreboard they'd have my lifetime statistics against the Orioles. It looked like a season. I'd have like 580 at-bats, 120 runs scored, 40 home runs . . . After all that, the Baltimore pitchers and I had a pretty good idea of what to expect from each other.

I saw Jim Palmer from 1969 to 1982. I knew how he was going to pitch me. I faced Nolan Ryan for almost twenty years. When you've battled somebody for that long, your rivalry is at a different level. Your plan is already complete. There aren't many nuances left to think about. There's not much cat and mouse going on anymore. It's almost easier, really, because you've swallowed so much of the guy's bread and butter. You've come to anticipate the taste of his cooking.

Being a smart hitter is knowing how you're going to be pitched. You can do that more intelligently against a familiar foe you've batted against for a dozen years. Being a smart hitter is knowing what the pitcher's going to do in certain counts with certain scores. Certainly he's going to pitch you differently when it's 6–1 than when it's 1–0. And he's going to pitch you differently depending on what pitcher he's pitching *against*. If Palmer's up two runs and we have our number-four starter going and there's a runner at third base, he's not going to be worried about that run. He knows he's in good shape. But if he's matched against Bob Gibson, Ferguson Jenkins, Roy Halladay, or Johan Santana, then you're going to be pitched differently because he can't count on any more run support. He's going to protect what he has and be a lot more careful.

None of that stuff is in a scouting report. It's in your head and your history.

Of course, it's a different story if you're talking about a rookie pitcher or somebody you're unfamiliar with. In that case, I'd listen to the scouting report but I'd also do my *own* scouting by watching the guy throw in his warm-ups. I'd check him out in the on-deck circle. You don't stand there moving and timing him, but I tried to get a feel and a rhythm for what's going on. I did that by paying attention.

Bob Gibson

You hear all the time that young hitters have an advantage their first time around the league because there aren't good scouting reports out on them yet. And it's true, it seems to happen that way a lot. But it really shouldn't. As a pitcher, I feel like it's easier to pitch to a hitter I haven't faced before—and who hasn't faced me, which is more to the point—because I can assume that he's going by the scouting report. He just knows what I *usually* do, not what I'm *likely* to do. I consider that a big advantage.

As a rule, though, I think scouting reports are more useful for hitters than they are for pitchers. At least they tell you how hard a pitcher throws and what his other pitches are like and how good his control is on most nights. That's information you can use. But whatever they tell you about a *hitter,* they tell you in the context of a pitcher who isn't you. As far as I'm concerned, about the only scouting report worth anything to a pitcher is the one that comes from the last time you faced that batter—or better yet, the last fifty times.

When we played Boston in the 1967 World Series, they said you couldn't throw Carl Yastrzemski high fastballs because he was a high fastball hitter. I thought, *really?* Well, I was a high fastball pitcher. The first game, I just kept throwing the ball up there and he kept hitting it straight up in the air. I never struck him out. He'd get a good swing at it. But he couldn't quite catch up with it. If somebody had been writing up a scouting report from that game, it would have said to get Yastrzemski out with high fastballs. But that wasn't going to work the next day for Dick Hughes. Yastrzemski had two home runs the next day.

In the 1965 All-Star Game, I faced Harmon Killebrew in the bottom of the ninth with the tying run on second base, in his home ballpark. They told me you couldn't throw Killebrew a high fastball. Is that right? Struck him out with a high fastball, as I recall.

They told me the same thing about Sadaharu Oh when we toured Japan after the 1968 season. They said you couldn't throw him a high fastball. Well then, what am I gonna do? I threw him three high fastballs. Whoosh, whoosh, whoosh. Never touched the ball. We got back to the dugout and Cepeda said, "Was that the guy you weren't supposed to throw high fastballs to?"

I said, "Yeah, I think it was."

Matchups

Reggie Jackson

There was a pitcher from Kansas City named Steve Busby who actually figured out and had the guts to pitch me inside. He threw mid-nineties and had an electric slider that crawled up the label. I hated facing him. Also Dave Stieb for Toronto. Stieb had a mid-nineties fastball that I could hit, but he had a slider that looked like it was right down the middle and when I swung it either cracked my bat or I'd foul it off the handle. Sometimes I'd look around and think, man, I hope nobody saw that. Both of those guys caught on. For all I know, it might have been a mistake the first time they figured out about working me inside— sort of like the way Bob figured out how to pitch Eddie Mathews. But I'm sure I looked funny swinging, and I'm sure they thought, *ohhhh . . . yes!*

On the other hand, Bert Blyleven was a pitcher who hardly ever tried to come in on me. Blyleven had great stuff. Nasty curveball. Hitting Blyleven's curveball was like trying to drink coffee with a fork. It was like Nolan Ryan's. The two best curveballs in the game belonged to Bert Blyleven and Nolan Ryan. Just like Willie McCovey was the standard for raw power, you measured the curveball off Bert Blyleven, because he would use his a lot more than Ryan used *his*. But I liked facing Blyleven. He gave up as many as forty or fifty home runs in a season, and I usually felt like I was going to click one. I only got six off him, though, in 140 plate appearances. I had more at-bats against Blyleven than any other hitter did, and at the same time he was the pitcher I faced more than any other. As well as I knew him, and as good as I felt standing in there when he was on the mound, I actually only hit a little over .200 against Blyleven for my career. I must have seen two hundred great curveballs in those 140 plate appearances. But I always thought I was going to get something to cut at. Looking back on it, maybe that's what he *wanted* me to think.

You know, I just now figured that out. It took me about thirty years. Kinda slow, eh?

Bob Gibson

Koufax had a curveball like that. It would start in the same spot as his fastball and then just disappear.

Reggie Jackson

As much as Blyleven threw his curveball, he didn't hang many. The home runs I hit off him were fastballs that missed his spot. Usually when you get a guy, it's because he missed his spot.

Bob Gibson

Here's the fine line you have to walk as a pitcher. Roberto Clemente just couldn't hit the ball down and away. But get it *up* and away, and he'd knock the pee out of it. Just a few inches made all the difference.

There were little subtle things with so many batters, things that you wouldn't know unless you watched them and sparred with them for a while. Rusty Staub was interesting. He was a left-handed hitter you could pitch away, but only until he got two strikes. Then you'd have to come in on him, because with two strikes he'd try to hit the ball to left field. I knew that. So I'd go boom, boom, hard outside, then beep, he'd shorten up a little and here it comes on his hands. Break his bat.

You just have to study these guys, and you have to remember. And you have to respect them.

Reggie Jackson

Tommy John was interesting to me. Before his elbow surgery he threw about ninety-two miles an hour, and post-surgery he became a sinkerball pitcher. He always had excellent location. I could never hurt Tommy. Even when I hit a home run against him in the 1978 World Series, he was already way ahead in the game. We became teammates on both the Yankees and Angels, and I watched and admired how well he was able to manage a game from the mound. You might feel comfortable against Tommy, and even enjoy batting against him, but that didn't mean you could beat him or hit him.

On the other hand, Luis Tiant was a guy I looked forward to, and with better reason—eventually. In his heyday, he threw ninety-five and pretty much had his way with me. But after being in the league eight or ten years, he showed me balls to hit and didn't throw hard enough to get them by me. Tiant had a curveball I could time. He liked to throw his curveball to surprise you, like two-and-oh, three-and-one, something like that.

His style was kind of like Marichal's. The dance was similar on the mound; but the effect wasn't quite the same. Tiant was good. Marichal was great.

Bob Gibson

I thought Marichal was the best *pitcher* in our era. He didn't have the best stuff, but he was the best pitcher. He could throw strikes from anywhere. And he could throw a different pitch from anywhere. He was tough.

Reggie Jackson

There are plenty of guys who throw hard, but you've got to be able to put the ball in certain places. Sam McDowell was an example of one who had great stuff but wasn't a good *pitcher*. He just tried to strike everybody out and threw the ball right over the plate. He was "wild in the strike zone." You can throw a hundred miles an hour and you're not going to win if you keep serving up balls right over the plate. Sudden Sam also had a great curveball on top of all that speed. But if you could keep the game close, he'd beat himself.

For a lot of pitchers with great stuff, the book said that if you could stay close they'd give you a ball to beat them with. There will be a loud bang in the seventh or eighth inning.

Bob Gibson

To me, Frank Howard was the hitter's version of McDowell. He was a big, strong guy who swung hard, and every once in a while he was going to hit one eighteen miles. But he wasn't a good hitter in the way that the really good hitters were. He had those massive long arms and he liked the ball out over the plate. I would just stay from the middle in, good hard stuff. Then sliders away.

I got him out pretty well, except one time he hit a ball over my shoulder and I went to catch it and missed, and when I turned around it was heading into the bushes up in center field. Into the *bushes.* I just got it in the wrong place. You can't do that.

Reggie Jackson

Denny McLain always gave you a ball to hit. I think he liked home runs almost as much as hitters did. He didn't mind giving them up as long as he won the game. Late in 1968, the year the Tigers won the World Series, I hit two homers off him one game. Both of them put us in the lead, but true to form he ended up winning, 5–4, and it was his thirtieth victory of the season. Denny McLain was out there to win games.

Nolan Ryan was another one who didn't seem to care if he gave you something out over the plate. To this day, I don't know that Nolan threw for spots. I felt like *he* felt he could throw so hard it didn't matter where he put it; all he had to do was throw strikes. And to a great extent, he was right. He could get away with pitches that virtually nobody else could. But because of that, he wasn't so careful with his control.

Of course, he threw a curveball that matched his fastball. You couldn't hit his curveball. The only reason he ever got hit was because of his control.

Bob Gibson

When I was coaching in Atlanta, we used to have pretty good luck against Nolan Ryan. We hardly ever scored on him early, but then he'd start getting smart with the curveball and trying to trick you with it. He had, whomp, this great big old curveball, and he'd try to change speeds on it and do various things. The guys wouldn't even pay any attention to him for the first three or four innings, when he was throwing heat. They'd just be in there talkin' and spittin' and waiting for the fifth to roll around. Then in the fifth inning they'd grab their bats and be ready to go, and here comes Nolan with that trick curveball and they'd just rip at it. They knew what was in store.

Reggie Jackson

On the other hand, Jim Palmer didn't have much of a breaking ball, but he had a little tight slider, a big high fastball that he threw about ninety-five, a big high leg kick, and a lot of smarts. Palmer threw what I call a slop curveball. It was a spinner that he'd just try to get over for a strike. But he was definitely a great pitcher.

Bob Gibson

That was the same curveball I had. I hardly ever threw it, except occasionally to left-handers. Just like Palmer, it sounds.

Reggie Jackson

I never swung at that curveball, because when a guy throws ninety-five you can't look for a rolling breaking ball that's seventy miles an hour. Mostly, Jimmy pitched me away, where I liked it, but a little up where I couldn't quite get to it. I did hit two home runs off him one game, and we lost the game 3–2. He'd pitch around me a lot of times, and be satisfied to get out the right-handed batters who hit behind me.

Palmer once told me, "I didn't care to pitch to you." He threw a no-hitter against the A's in 1969 and walked me three times. Whenever I faced him with the game on the line, he either walked me or I went after a ball that was up in the zone and hard as he could throw it. I'd swing and miss that high fastball, foul it off, hit a hard ground ball at the shortstop.

Bob Gibson

That was roughly how I pitched Willie McCovey. McCovey was a guy who had all the power you'd ever want, and he was a low-ball hitter. I don't think it's a great idea to throw guys down and in, period, but if you threw one there to McCovey he'd drop the barrel of that big bat and hit it about seven hundred yards.

With Willie, though, I made one exception: I'd throw him a slider down and in—*way* down and in—if it was the first pitch. He wasn't about to take it. I could count on him swinging. But then I'd work him up the ladder. The next pitch would be about belt-high, and the next one was letter high or higher. I used to laugh because when I'd get two strikes on McCovey he was so determined to hit that ball at his neck that he'd go up on his toes to get it. He couldn't—no way—but he was damn sure going to try.

Reggie Jackson

Hoot may say he didn't like to pitch inside too much, but you can bet he would have buried the ball in on me. He'd have shown me the ball away to make me *think* something might be there, then he'd have thrown it as hard as he could inside. With two strikes, that slider that starts at the middle of the plate and breaks down and in—lefties swing over it. If we hit it hard, we hit it into the home-team dugout.

I never had the privilege of facing Gibson, other than that one at-bat in the '72 All-Star Game. I wish I could have, just for fun.

I'm a baseball fan, and that would have been a pretty awesome thing to do.

Bob Gibson

I threw my slider a couple different ways, and I don't know that I'd give Reggie the big one that broke more. I had a quicker one that got right in on your belt buckle. That's what I would have shown him. That's what I did with McCovey when I threw him a slider.

I pitched Willie Stargell a lot like I did McCovey—hard stuff, sliders way in tight, maybe go up the ladder. Most of the good hitters like that—those big, strong lefties—I'd work pretty much the same. Try not to give them anything down and in on the plate.

On Opening Day, 1969, Stargell had three hits off of me. I threw him inside and wham! Just knocked the devil out of it, out of the park to right field. It was a pretty good pitch, I thought. The next time I pitched him away and whoom! He smoked one right up the middle. Next time up, I thought, I'm tired of this, and bam! Hit him right in the back. Next time up, he scorched one to left field. I thought, well, hell. I had to give it to him. He was just hot that day and I wasn't going to get him out.

Big Sticks

Bob Gibson

More times than not, I reserved most of my worrying for the cleanup hitter. The number-four batter is supposed to be the one who can hit the ball out of the park, and for that reason the number-three batter, generally speaking, is going to get some pitches to hit.

There are exceptions to that. The three-hole hitter typically has the best all-around bat on the team, and he might be so much better than the cleanup hitter that *he's* the guy you don't let beat you. Babe Ruth hit third. Hank Aaron hit third a lot. So did Barry

Bonds. The Cardinals bat Albert Pujols third, and that's part of the reason why Ryan Ludwick had such a big year in his first season as a cleanup hitter. Pujols was on base almost three hundred times, so they had to pitch to Ludwick. To his credit, he responded.

Reggie Jackson

I batted in both spots at various times, but I preferred cleanup. Either way, I always had the advantage of solid RBI people following me in the lineup. In Oakland, it was Sal Bando and Joe Rudi. In Baltimore, I hit third in front of Lee May, who led the league in RBIs the year I was there. Lee May might have been the most effective guy who ever batted behind me. He wasn't a high-average hitter, but he had dynamite in the barrel. In New York we had Graig Nettles, Chris Chambliss, and Oscar Gamble, and if Lou Piniella hit fifth he could handle the bat and drive in a run. Don Baylor followed me one year in Anaheim. All good hitters.

Had I not had those guys behind me, smart pitchers might have made easy work of me in RBI situations. They'd have taken advantage of my natural aggressiveness. They'd have exploited my instinct to feel personally responsible for driving in the run, which compelled me to expand my strike zone. If I hadn't been able to trust in Sal and the rest, I suspect I'd have gone too far in that respect, to the point of getting myself out on a regular basis. As it was, I could be selective enough to take the walk if they gave it to me. It was hard, but prudent. At the same time, though, I was more likely to get something to hit than I would if the batter behind me was a soft touch.

A pitcher like Gibby is not going to give me much to swing at if it's late in the ballgame and he's got lesser hitters following me, especially right-handed hitters who don't handle him very well. That said, there might be other games when he's having his way with me but not the batter behind me, in which case I might get a crack at one. The scenarios change dramatically from game to game, inning to inning, and batter to batter.

Bob Gibson

I played most of my career before expansion, when the talent was more concentrated, and at that time the great hitters—I'm talking about the guys in the middle of the order—seemed to come in pairs or triplets, which was no coincidence.

The Giants had Mays, McCovey, and Cepeda. The Cubs had Williams, Banks, and Santo. The Braves had Aaron and Mathews. The Pirates had Clemente and Stargell. The Reds had Frank Robinson and Vada Pinson, and then the Orioles had Frank and Boog Powell. The Yankees had Mantle and Maris. The Tigers had Kaline and Cash. Yastrzemski always had some other slugger with him, whether it was Dick Stuart or Tony Conigliaro or George Scott or Ken Harrelson or Reggie Smith or Rico Petrocelli. When two great hitters come up back-to-back, you have to deal with at least one of them.

These days, it's rare that you find a lineup with two of those guys. When there's only one big hitter, and say he comes up with a man on second base, I have no problem throwing him some bastard pitches and walking the guy if he won't chase them. For that matter, I'd almost always pitch to the right-hander instead of the left-hander, unless the right-hander was Aaron.

If it was Hank, I might just go ahead and pitch to Reggie. Well, no *might* about it. I *would*. Anybody but Aaron.

Reggie Jackson

Not a bad guy to be second fiddle to.

There was a tough situation in Boston with Ramirez and David Ortiz. If they put runners on base in front of those guys, you had a problem on your hands. Pick your poison.

It's impossible to calculate the difference that the guy behind you makes, but it's enormous. If I had a bad year, I couldn't blame it on the hitter behind me; but you could chart the changes in your success. The strikeouts and walks would go up and down.

In that light, it makes what Bonds did all the more amazing. He had a year when he walked 232 times, and he still hit forty-five home runs. That's almost unimaginable.

Bob Gibson

I'd have probably walked him 232 times myself. He would have been my Aaron, the guy who wasn't going to beat me under any circumstances that I could control.

There's a hitter like that in every lineup, but there's no particular formula to tell you how to pick him out. Most of the time it's pretty obvious—who can hurt me with a home run?—but your gut feeling trumps the numbers. You go with a combination of personal experience and common sense. Billy Williams probably hit me better than anybody, but even so, and despite the fact that he was left-handed, I went ahead and pitched to him because he had Ron Santo and Ernie Banks behind him and I didn't want either of them hitting two-run homers. If Williams had batted cleanup, I'd have probably pitched around him more.

As it turned out, Billy Williams drove in more runs against me than Banks and Santo combined. He hit ten home runs off of me, and *that* was more than Banks and Santo combined; and if you throw in Jim Hickman, George Altman, Randy Hundley, Don Kessinger, Glenn Beckert, and Adolfo Phillips—all the best hitters the Cubs had—you're still two homers short. Strange as it sounds, though, I don't know that Williams ever really *hurt* me. I was more concerned with Banks.

Reggie Jackson

It's respect for the home run. That's what that is.

As you might expect, I have the same kind of respect. In my day, probably more than today, home runs were a big deal. Your batting average can dry up overnight, but those taters stick to your bones. They don't evaporate.

Even so, I wish I'd have hit for a higher average—and not for the sake of singles. Hitting for a higher average would have meant more home runs.

I realize now that I should have been a consistent .300 hitter. The only time I made it was with the Yankees in 1980, and that was also the only season in my last eighteen that I hit forty homers. I don't think it's a coincidence. There doesn't have to be a trade-off between home runs and base hits. Contact is a good thing. Eventually, I learned not to lose my cool over strikeouts—which was handy, considering that I struck out more than anyone else in history, by a wide margin—but if I had it to do over again, I'd try harder to keep them to a minimum. If you don't strike out, you put the ball in play more often. If you put the ball in play more often, and you're a natural home-run hitter, you hit more home runs.

I don't see how Dave Kingman could hit thirty-seven home runs and bat .204, and hit thirty-five home runs and bat .210. The kind of season I admire—the kind of season that makes sense to me—is the kind that Alex Rodriguez put together when he hit fifty-four home runs and batted .314, or when he hit forty-eight home runs and batted .321. Hank Aaron batted .305 for his *career*. Willie Mays was a career .302 hitter. I should have done that. I should have hit for a higher average.

I just didn't give it the care that I should have. I didn't realize that base hits and home runs can go hand-in-hand, if you're good enough.

Bob Gibson

If I've got a bunch of guys on my team who can hit home runs, I'm not worried about singles or walks or stolen bases or anything else. I don't care about any kind of speed-and-power combination in the lineup.

If I don't have power, sure, I'll take speed. I'll take Brock. I'll take Rose's singles and Don Mattingly's doubles. But if I've got a choice, give me Aaron and Mays and Mantle. Give me McCovey and Mathews. Give me Bench and Banks. On that team, I'll put Reggie at second base and pitch the left-handers outside.

But you know, it's a little odd that I'd feel that way about it, because the guys who wore me out were the left-handed banjo hitters. Ron Fairly, Willie Davis, Al Oliver. I used to break Al Oliver's bat and he'd still drop the ball right over the in-field. Made me nuts.

Of course, I wouldn't put Billy Williams in that crowd, except that he swung the bat from the same side. That was the common denominator. Nearly all the guys who hit me were lefties. Part of it was because I had a hard time keeping the ball elevated on the outside corner against left-handers. It would tend to come down when I threw to my hand side. I didn't want the ball down against lefties, so I'd end up pitching them inside more than I would have liked.

Other than Aaron, who had eight home runs against me, right-handers just didn't bother me much. Even Aaron batted only .215 against me. I didn't give up more than four home runs to any other righty, except for Deron Johnson, who had five; and he batted .154. Frank Robinson had four, and his average against me was .229. Clemente had four, and his was .208.

Reggie Jackson

I hit better against right-handers, but the difference wasn't as significant as some of my managers seemed to think. Billy Martin used to sit me down against lefties now and then. Billy also batted me seventh a few times, so I'd come to expect almost anything from him.

But I didn't expect to be on the bench for the final game of the 1977 playoffs, when the Royals went with a left-hander named Paul Splittorff, whom I actually hit fairly well. In fact, earlier that year, my first home run as a Yankee had come against Splittorff.

Oh well.

Bob Gibson

If I'd have been Paul Splittorff, I'd have applauded that move. Get *all* those home-run hitters out of there.

Reggie Jackson

It must have been motivational genius on Billy's part, because after that game we went straight to the World Series and I was MVP. That was the Series when I hit five home runs, four of them without swinging at another pitch in between. Of course, none of them was against a lefty.

In reality, I didn't find it easy to handle a tough left-hander. I considered it something special when I homered against one. I got one against Mickey Lolich in 1968, my first full year in the league, and I felt like I'd taken God out of the park.

But here's something Billy couldn't have known. I hit eleven grand slams in my career, and eight of them came against left-handers. Figure that one out.

CHAPTER SEVEN

THINGS THAT A FELLOW JUST HAS TO DEAL WITH

Umpires

Bob Gibson

Umpires tend to have their own strike zones. That's sad, but it's true. I always had a problem with that.

There's supposed to be *a* strike zone, not an *umpire's* strike zone. But you have to live with it. The worst was 1969, when they lowered the mound and tightened the strike zone at both the top and bottom. That was hard enough, but some umpires made the adjustment and others didn't, or they'd make them in different ways. It was disorienting. After a while, it seemed like there was almost no such thing as a high strike anymore.

I always made sure to find out, in the first few batters, what the umpire considered a strike that night. But it's not right that you should have to do that. A strike should be a strike.

Reggie Jackson

Baseball at least tried to address the issue with the QuesTec system, which was designed to compare each umpire's strike zone with the actual strike zone. But it was only installed in about a third of the major-league stadiums. In the ones that had it, cameras were stationed at various points to track the path of the ball and put each pitch within the framework of the batter's stance. The purpose was to make the strike zone uniform. It was a noble cause, and it accomplished its objective to some extent. The studies showed that a lot of umpires were calling a strike zone that was wider than the plate and smaller vertically than it's supposed to be.

For the 2009 season, QuesTec was replaced by a new system called Zone Evaluation, which was put in all the parks. That's an improvement. But whatever the system, I'm not a big advocate. I'm too much of a traditionalist for that.

Bob Gibson

Put the umpire back there and let him screw it up in the way he wants to. That's how it's been played all these years, and I don't know why they should have some kind of machine telling you what a strike is.

Reggie Jackson

I suppose the quality of umpiring is as good as it *can* be.

Bob Gibson

It could be better if the umpires would stop thinking that they were such a big part of the game and that they need to be seen and recognized. Just call the balls and strikes. We don't care about all this other stuff. A good umpire should be like background music, just kind of there. Now you get "Steeeriiiiiike!"

Come on. "Strike one." That's all you want.

Reggie Jackson

I'd prefer "Ball one."

I'm not as concerned with an umpire's style as I am with his strike zone. It's a tough deal for a hitter when you've got a guy back there like Ed Runge, who didn't issue many walks. He wanted to get the game over with. You'd walk up to the plate and he'd say, "You'd better be swinging."

Bob Gibson

Ed Runge. Oh yeah. Heh-heh.

Ed Sudol was another one who had a big strike zone, a pitcher's strike zone. If you saw Sudol you'd remember him because he had his own way of showing if a ball was outside, like he was shooing it away with both hands. But if he called it outside, it was *outside*. You could throw the ball four inches off the plate and Ed Sudol would shoot that hand up and go, "Strike one!" I thought, man, I love this guy. Love him! You didn't have to come *close* to the plate. "Strike two!" Guys are swinging and bitching and woofing at him, and I'm just out there smiling.

Reggie Jackson

You're not going to hit the ball if a guy's throwing it ninety-five miles an hour and getting calls off the plate.

Bob Gibson

No, you're sure not. But for every Ed Sudol, there's an Al Barlick.

Al Barlick was very consistent, but he had a small plate. He *never* gave me a pitch.

And then there was Doug Harvey. He called himself God.

Doug Harvey used to drive me crazy. He was considered one of the greatest umpires of all time, but he had a very difficult strike zone. You'd throw a ball on the corner and he'd call it a ball, and you'd complain that it was on the black and he'd say, kind of smart-alecky, "The black is not a part of the plate."

If the ball's that close, they should be swinging at it.

Reggie Jackson

You have to be aware of everything to be a good hitter. You have to know if the umpire has a high strike zone, a low strike zone, or a wide strike zone, or if he calls one side of the plate better than the other.

Frankly, I like the fact that a hitter has to learn the umpires, just as he has to learn the pitchers. Every ump has a strike zone, and that's part of the game. I think it's a *good* part of the game.

Bob Gibson

It's hard to judge or measure how much of a difference a guy like Harvey ultimately makes in the final outcome, but I was definitely more exhausted, mentally, after a game that he called. If I've got a Harvey back there, or a Barlick, I know I'm going to have to bring the ball over the plate to get a strike. That takes a toll, because I don't *want* to bring the ball over the plate. I make my living by not doing that. If you throw the ball over the plate, hitters are going to hit it. If you *have* to do it, that puts you in a bind. It eats at your confidence. But if you *don't* do it, you're behind in the count. That's not a very good arrangement for a pitcher.

Reggie Jackson

There are all kinds of umpires. Some are just bad umpires. Others want to put on a show, so you have to be mindful of that with two strikes because you know the guy's looking to run out there and make a big call. There are umpires you can't question, because if you do you'll be paying for it the rest of the game. Joe Brinkman would get mad in a heartbeat if you said something that he thought was out of line.

I didn't argue much, mostly because Dick Allen told me not to. There was one particular umpire who apparently appreciated my manners at the plate, because he gave me the benefit of the doubt on every close call. He once told me, "You'll get your pitch when I'm behind the plate."

I had umpires say to me toward the end of my career, "If you don't swing today, it ain't a strike."

Bob Gibson

I knew there was something wrong with those guys.

Reggie Jackson

When I was trying to hit home run number five hundred in California, Durwood Merrill was the umpire, and he knew exactly what was going on. Most of them did. I got breaks toward the end of my career, for sure.

There were times when I'd be hitting late in a ballgame, a close game, and the umpire would call a *ball* that I actually questioned. I'd say, "Not now. Don't do that now. I need everything fair and clean."

Bob Gibson

Sounds like Bob Uecker, except Uecker wasn't quite that serious. He was catching against us for the Braves once and the umpire was Billy Williams, and Williams called an outside strike on Mike Shannon. Uecker ripped off his mask and argued with him.

Reggie Jackson

I didn't want the *pitcher* to have an advantage, and *I* didn't want an advantage. I wanted it to be straight, because in that situation—late innings, game on the line—I think I can get him. Just leave everything fair. Don't give *him* anything, don't give *me* anything.

Bob Gibson

I'd take whatever I got. But other than Ed Sudol, I never thought I got much. Maybe it was because my etiquette wasn't quite as refined as Reggie's.

When I struggled with the strike zone, I usually thought it was the umpire's fault—especially when I was young and wild. In college, the strike zone was different than it was in professional ball. Once I got to the minor leagues, I couldn't figure out what the strike zone was. I was thinking, what's up with this? I'd throw a pitch between the belt and letters and they'd call it a ball and I'd think, what in the hell is going on? I'm sitting there reading the rule book and it tells me the strike zone is from the knees to the letters. It was *never* the letters in pro ball. I'd throw that thing up there and they'd call it a ball and I'd go crazy.

Eventually, I got used to it. The fact is, if you're bad that day, it's not the umpire's doing. But it does make the umpire a little less likely to pull you out of trouble. If your pitches are all over the place, you're probably not going to luck into the strikes that you might on a better day. The umpire is sitting right over your catcher's shoulder and he knows the ball's not going where it's supposed to go. If the catcher sets up on the inside corner and you happen to hit the outside corner, there's a pretty good chance he won't give it to you.

Reggie Jackson

It's possible to work the umpire. You have to learn how to talk to him. It's an art. A hitter can reach down to get some dirt, with his back to the umpire, and say, "That ball was a little outside, wasn't it? That ball a little outside?" I might be turned the other way, adjusting my helmet, and say, "Damn it now, don't tell me that ball was a strike. That ball's *not* a strike. Don't tell me it's a strike. That ball's *not* a strike!" You can do all that, but you can't turn to him and say anything. You can't look at an umpire. You can look forward, you can call time and look the other way, but don't look *at* him. He'll respect you for that.

Bob Gibson

As a pitcher, you can't say much, and you can't say *anything* from the mound. That would show up the umpire, and they'll nail your butt for it because they don't like to be shown up. That's the kind of thing they hold grudges over. When the umpire would make a call I didn't appreciate, I'd kind of cock my head and look in like I must have seen it wrong or something. Then, when I came in to hit, I might say something like, "You know, those balls are strikes." But that's about all you can do. Hopefully, your catcher's getting in his two cents' worth.

I remember Tom Gorman, a big ol' umpire. One day I was

throwing high strikes, just above the belt, and he kept calling them balls. I came in to hit and the other pitcher was throwing the ball in the same spot and ol' Tom Gorman says, "Strike one."

I said, "Damn it, Tom, that's the same pitch you keep calling a ball on me." And he wouldn't say a word. He just kept tapping his indicator. And here it comes again.

"Strike two."

And I said, "Damn it, Tom, if that's a ball from me, it's a ball from him."

And he said, "Bobby, you take it *again*."

After that, I was swinging at everything.

Reggie Jackson

An umpire can make you do that. What's worse is when there's a combination of an umpire who calls a lot of strikes and a pitcher who works the ball just off the plate, like Greg Maddux or Tom Glavine. A smart pitcher with great control, plus a wide strike zone . . . whew. You're in for a long, tough night.

Bob Gibson

Maddux can throw a pitch three or four inches outside, and the umpire will say, "Striiike!" Because he's always there. If the umpire calls *that* one, Maddux will come right back to that spot, or maybe stretch it out another half-inch. His control is just that good. The umpires know who's out there, and they have a tendency to give you a break if you have good control and you're always right there where you want to be.

The hitters always complain about it, but that's the way it is. It's that way because guys like Maddux and Glavine—and there aren't many of them—are so consistent. Those two are probably within about two inches of their target ninety percent of the time. It's not always a strike, but it's always *there.* They know they're going to get the call, in all likelihood, and the hitters *ought* to know it.

It's the same with hitters. I'm not sure about Ted Williams, though. He might have had the best eye in the history of baseball, but the umpires didn't like him. He didn't have the manners. But guys like Tony Gwynn, Pete Rose, Joe Morgan, Albert Pujols, even Barry Bonds . . . you get a great hitter up there, a guy with a good eye who doesn't swing at the ball off the plate, and they're apt to get the call just like the great pitcher does.

Reggie Jackson

No matter who you are, though, or who the umpire is, you can't take anything for granted with two strikes. You can't expect the umpire to bail you out, and you can't let him beat you, either. A hitter has to make sure it's just between him and the pitcher.

All you can ask of an umpire is that he leaves it that way.

Bob Gibson

You just don't want him to upset the natural flow of the game. For the most part, I don't think anything is thrown out of kilter by an umpire acknowledging the skill of the best pitchers and hitters.

A really tough game is one where the umpire calls a pitch a ball and then calls the same pitch a strike. Inconsistency is hard on everybody concerned. The pitcher doesn't know where he has to throw the ball, and the hitter doesn't know what he has to swing at. Everybody gets out of rhythm and you've just got a bad ballgame.

An umpire can also impact a game when he *is* consistent, if he's consistent one particular way or the other—tight or loose with the zone, for instance, or high or low with it. Harvey and Barlick were examples of that. They would set a tone by the way they defined the strike zone. That can be the difference between a low-scoring game and a high-scoring game.

It sounds as though that wouldn't give one team an advantage over the other, but it might. If the umpire has a small strike zone, it could favor the better-hitting team, because that's the team more likely to take advantage of pitches over the plate. Those are the days when a pitcher might wish he were in another line of work. On the other hand, if I knew an umpire was going to give me a strike three inches off the black, I sure as hell wouldn't throw the ball any closer than that. So I'd consider that an advantage for me, more than the other pitcher.

Reggie Jackson

A *major* advantage, with that fastball and slider. An unfair advantage, I'd say.

Bob Gibson

And every now and then—not very often—you'll get an umpire who calls the entire nine innings just like they're supposed to be called, from the first pitch to the last one. There was one night in particular when I thought Harry Wendelstedt didn't miss a pitch all night, and I told him so. I lost that game, by the way.

Of course, Wendelstedt was the home-plate umpire for five no-hitters, which tied a National League record. He was considered a pitcher's umpire.

Like I said, he was a *good* one.

Catchers

Bob Gibson

The most critical thing a catcher does is call the game. That's much more important than blocking pitches and framing pitches and throwing out runners and all that other stuff.

That's why Tim McCarver was such a good catcher. He had a terrible arm, but my goodness, could he call a game. All he had to do was catch you for an inning or so and he was on the same page. He'd know what you wanted to do in just about every situation. When a pitcher can place that kind of trust in his catcher, it puts his mind at ease. You don't have to wear your brain out deciding what to do on every pitch and shaking off the catcher and battling him all the way.

Reggie Jackson

You don't want stuff rolling around in your head when you're trying to play ball. You know what you want to do, and you want to just *do* it.

Bob Gibson

I was so sure what Tim would call that I once balked in a run when he surprised me and asked for something different. A lot of times I'd start winding up before he was even finished giving his signs. What he would do is put down one . . . two . . . three . . . And when I started winding up, that was the pitch. That was sort of my signal to *him*. Well, this particular time I started winding up and he wasn't finished giving his signs yet. I thought, uh-oh, and stopped for a second, then tried to start up again. Everybody in the whole ballpark yelled, "Balk!"

I'd occasionally shake Tim off, but more often I'd just stand there and wait for him to put down something else. The thing you can't do is shake a catcher off *twice*. If you do that, the hitter knows it's a fastball. The second shake is probably for location, and that's the tip-off that it's a fastball. A catcher usually won't signal for location on a breaking ball, unless maybe it's a slider. Partly for that reason, I generally didn't shake off location.

With McCarver, sometimes we didn't even *need* a sign for location. He knew, for instance, that if it was a left-handed batter I'd probably want to jam him with the fastball.

Reggie Jackson

As far as the second shake-off meaning it was a fastball . . . That was especially true for a pitcher like Hoot, who was mostly all hard stuff. If it was Luis Tiant or Juan Marichal, two shakes wouldn't mean as much. Those guys had so many pitches, it might take more signs for them to settle on one.

Of course, with Gibson, I'd be focused on the fastball anyway, hoping to hit it to left center—or pull the slider if he came with that instead. I wouldn't be paying much attention to anything else.

Bob Gibson

I was fortunate in that I always threw to good catchers. But sometimes it took a while to get in sync.

My first two or three years, I let the catcher call the game for me. The first one was Hal Smith, and he did a nice job of it. Gene Oliver caught every now and then, but he wasn't quite as sharp back there. I once hit him right in the chest. Don't know what happened. More often, though, Carl Sawatski would catch when there was a nasty right-hander pitching for the other team.

One night, around my third year, Sawatski, who'd been around for a long time, kept calling fastball, fastball, fastball. I shook him off. Fastball. Shook him off. Finally, he called time and trotted out and told me I was going to throw a fastball. I said I just threw the guy five in a row; I want to change it up. He said, nope, you're going to throw a fastball. So I threw the guy a half-assed fastball and he hit a home run. Now I'm blaming Sawatski. That's when I told myself I'd never, ever do that again: When I want to throw a pitch, that's what I'm going to throw. If the catcher wants to fight about it, we'll fight about it. But I'm not going to throw something I don't want to throw.

Once a pitcher reaches a point where he knows what he's doing, the catcher's not really *calling* the pitches anyway. He's suggesting. He's just making a recommendation. Now, with a young pitcher who just came up and an experienced catcher, yeah, the catcher does and should call the game. The pitcher, at that point, doesn't know the hitters and doesn't fully understand the situations and circumstances. But once you learn how to pitch—if you know how to pitch *at all*—you don't let the catcher call the game.

The worst thing is to give up a hit or a home run and lose a ballgame and second-guess yourself on something a catcher called. That's what I learned from Carl Sawatski. You don't want to blame anybody but yourself when you lose a ballgame.

Reggie Jackson

A while back, somebody with the Yankees was telling me that our young pitchers were nervous about being in the big leagues and were trying to be too fine with their stuff and location. I asked the guy what he meant, and he said, "They're throwing a lot of changeups. The other day, Ian Kennedy threw a three-two breaking pitch."

I said, "Who was catching?"

He said Posada.

I said, "Why didn't Posada put down a fastball?"

He said he did, and Kennedy shook him off.

I said, "Well, why didn't Posada put it down again? This kid's twenty-three years old. Posada should walk out there and say, 'If you're dead set on that and think you have to throw it, then you should throw it. But here's what *I* think you should do in this situation.' "

You explain it to the guy, let him swallow it, digest it.

Bob Gibson

The one with experience should take the lead. Both the pitcher and catcher need to recognize which of them that is.

Ted Simmons used to drive me crazy when he was a young catcher. One day he called time and came out to ask if I was giving him a hard time. I said, "Giving you a hard time?"

"Yeah, you keep shaking me off."

I said, "You know what I'm really trying to do?"

He said, "What's that?"

I said, "I'm trying to win the friggin' ballgame. I don't have the luxury of giving you a hard time."

Simmons was a bright guy, and he learned. It took him a while, but he caught on. As a rookie, all he thought about was hitting line drives, which he did very well. You can forgive a catcher for a lot of sins when he clears the bases with a double.

Reggie Jackson

Bob views the catcher from the specific vantage point of working with him, but I see the role as a little broader than that. I've always thought that a catcher should be a team leader, as well—a lot like a quarterback.

We certainly had that with the Yankees in Thurman Munson. I had my troubles with Munson when I first got to New York, and they were magnified because of the admiration and support he had from his teammates. They stood by him when they perceived me as a challenge to his stature on the club. Later, he and I worked things out and developed a mutual respect. Munson was a proud man, and a good leader.

I like Posada's leadership skills, as well. That's an important quality when you're handling a pitching staff.

Bob Gibson

You know, they made so much out of the business of me not wanting the catcher to come out and talk to me. The truth is, I didn't mind that much. It broke my rhythm, and I didn't appreciate that, but a pitcher needs somebody back there who will keep him from drifting, to read his body language and get him back on track if he's straying from the plan. I used to give McCarver a hard time just to give him a hard time.

He'd come out and I'd say, "What the hell are you doing out here? *What?*"

"Well, you got a man on first . . ."

"I know that. I *put* him there."

"Give me a shot at him."

"Give you a shot at him? Who're you kidding? You're not going to throw him out."

"Aw, the hell with you."

And then he'd trudge back and on we'd go.

When Johnny Keane was the manager, he'd give a signal from the dugout that meant Tim had to come out and calm me down. Tim knew that I saw the signal, too, and he'd look at me and I'd be glaring at him and he'd just as soon walk on glass as come on out to that mound. He'd go about halfway and pretend he was telling me something.

If there was strategy involved, that was a different thing. McCarver would lumber out to make sure everybody was straight on the way we were playing it. All the infielders—including Dal Maxvill, our shortstop—would gather around, breaking my rhythm a little more. There'd be runners on first and third, and Tim would tell me, "Maxie's covering second, go for two."

I'd say, "No, I'm going home."

"Why?"

"Because you guys can't score and I'm not giving up another run."

He'd say, "Well, that's not the way you play the game."

"Well, that's the way *I'm* playing it. Now, get on back there."

Thankfully, McCarver understood me. Hell, he even understood Steve Carlton.

Signs

Bob Gibson

Batters cheat. They watch the catcher and try to pick up the signs.

Sometimes they peek. Other times a catcher will set up his target too quickly and the hitter, with his peripheral vision, can see him moving over to the outside part of the plate or wherever.

Reggie Jackson

It's not always cheating. If a catcher's shuffling around too much or making a lot of noise back there, you can sense what he's up to even if you're not looking. Good catchers will move to their target late.

But yeah, some hitters will try to see what they can see. Steve Garvey was always checking his bat when he was up there, like he was making sure the label was in the right place. A lot of people thought he was really checking out the catcher.

Bob Gibson

I'm convinced that Hank Aaron did it. He was always looking around, looking back, looking down, looking, looking. He bothered me doing that. I'm watching him and I'm thinking, "Is that sucker looking at the catcher? What's he *looking* at back there?"

Sometimes I'd have the catcher set up away and I'd bring the ball inside, just to see. McCarver would put his target on the outside corner and I'd buzz one under Aaron's chin. It would go back to the backstop, because Tim wasn't going to catch it if I crossed him up. That was just my way of telling Aaron to be careful now, you might be looking at the wrong thing.

I'd have to say, though, that Aaron was more subtle about it than Mays. Back in the fifties they'd just use fingers for everything, and then catchers began to touch their shinguards for location and sometimes for the pitch. One time McCarver was going through all this rigmarole back there, and Willie calls time out and turns to him and says, "What the hell was *that?*" He couldn't figure it out.

Oh yeah, they peek.

Reggie Jackson

I didn't *want* to know what the sign was. I honestly didn't pay attention to that, because I needed the whole count, the whole context, to figure out how I was going to hit. I couldn't gear myself for a certain pitch. If a guy threw it and it was a ball and I couldn't hit it, I'd think, okay, *now* where am I? I'd gotten off my pattern.

Teammates would say that so-and-so is tipping his pitches. I didn't want any part of *that*, either. Some of them were good at reading the catcher and then signaling the hitter somehow. Graig Nettles, for one. He'd give you the location more than the pitch. But there are guys who sit in the dugout and whistle to tell the batter if it's a fastball or breaking ball.

They do that until the pitcher hears it a time or two, and then the next pitch somehow hits the guy in the ribs.

Bob Gibson

Gene Mauch used to whistle all the time when I was pitching. Every time I'd wind up, he'd start whistling. He had me doing all kinds of stuff to try to throw him off.

Mauch used to coach third base when he managed, and one day I walked by him and said, "Gene, if you keep whistling, you're going to get somebody killed in there." It got kind of quiet after that.

Reggie Jackson

I don't think it's cheating if a runner on second base picks up the catcher's signs. It's up to the catcher to make sure he doesn't. As a hitter, if you're smart enough to get 'em, then get 'em, any way you can. Some guys like to have that advantage, some don't. Personally, I didn't. Jeter doesn't, either.

Mostly, a runner on second will watch where the catcher goes and give the batter the location, in or out. The batter watches where the runner puts his hand, or some other signal. But some catchers will deek you. They'll set up in one spot and then slide somewhere else if they see the runner flash a sign to the hitter.

Catchers love to take advantage of a hitter they think is trying to pick up the pitches. There are some who will pound their glove right under the batter's ear so it sounds like the ball's coming inside, then scoot over real fast to the outside corner. Even if there's a runner on second who's watching it all, it's too late by then to get a signal to the hitter.

A guy can get messed up if he plays that game. Make sure you *know* what you *think* you know, or don't do it.

Bob Gibson

If the runner at second picks up on the location, he might take his lead with one arm or the other sticking out, and that arm tells the batter where the ball is coming. The runner probably doesn't know the signs, but he can certainly see where the catcher sits. That's why the catcher should start in the middle and not move until the pitcher begins his motion.

But you still have to be careful how you give your signs with a man on second. Maybe we'll add one to whatever the sign is, or add two. Then, say, the second place the catcher touches will be the location.

We wouldn't have to be so tricky if these guys didn't cheat.

Reggie Jackson

There are players who can read the pitcher's grip on the ball and determine from that what they're throwing, but I couldn't do it. At least, I *didn't* do it.

If it's a curveball, the pitcher will sometimes raise the ball differently while it's still in his glove. Maybe you can see his wrist turning a little bit. Sometimes, you might be able to tell from the angle of his forearm whether it's a fastball or a breaking ball. Or it could be that, because of the way a pitcher wraps the ball for a curveball, he won't come down as low when he starts his motion.

I might have been able to pick up on all that if I'd tried, but I wasn't interested. I didn't want to be looking in several different places when I was up there. I didn't want to get in the way of myself, which I could do pretty easily if I thought about too many things at once.

I felt I had a lot of gifts, and I didn't want to clutter them. That said, there's always a guy who is so bad about tipping his pitches that you just can't help but know what's coming.

Fielders

Bob Gibson

I complained a lot about the Cardinals' hitting, but I never complained about our fielding. For me, it started with Curt Flood in center, because I was a fly-ball pitcher.

Not long after the 1968 World Series, some woman actually came up to me and asked if I still spoke to Flood. She was referring to the long triple that Jim Northrup hit in Game Seven, and the fact that Flood took a step *in* before he went back on the ball. I said, "Lady, how could you ask me something like that?"

My goodness. If Flood couldn't catch that ball, nobody could. And even if he *had* misplayed it, there's no way on earth that I would ever complain about anything Curt Flood did in center field. It's not just that he was a great friend and outfielder. I'd never complain about *any* teammate who busted his butt out there like Flood did.

Reggie Jackson

A pitcher can really tick a guy off by turning around and staring at him for making an error. The first thing the fielder's going to think is, "Well, if you're so great, buddy, don't let him hit it to me."

Actually, that'd be the second thing. The first wouldn't be as pleasant.

Bob Gibson

What aggravates a pitcher is a fielder making a mental mistake. That tells you his heart and head are not in the game while you're out there pitching your arm off. But errors are going to happen, just like hanging sliders are going to happen. If your fielders turned on you every time you made a mistake, you'd have a mess on your hands. So you can't throw any tantrums out there when *they* make one—as long as it's physical. And you can't complain about them when the game's over. That's no way to rally the troops. You need those guys.

I trusted my fielders. They knew what they were doing. I didn't tell them what to do or where to play.

Reggie Jackson

Only Jim Palmer did that, and most of the time he was right. But it looked kind of weird. Some players didn't like it.

Bob Gibson

The coaching staff moves them around from the dugout, anyway. They have spray charts showing where guys are likely to hit the ball.

I didn't think a lot of those, though. They're like scouting reports: They assume that a hitter is going to do the same thing against every pitcher. They also assume that you're going to throw

174

the ball where they expect you to throw it. Sorry, that doesn't always happen.

Reggie Jackson

If I were playing right field behind Bob, I'd position myself well off the line against certain left-handers, because I'd know they weren't likely to pull him into the corner. That's just common sense. I'd know I might see some balls off the bats of right-handed hitters, because a lot of them would swing late. Plus, he'd be pitching away from them. I'd also move around, depending on the count. If he's behind two-and-oh or three-and-one on Frank Robinson, I might shade toward center because Frank probably wants to turn on a fastball in that situation.

Then, late in the game, I might take into consideration that he isn't throwing as hard.

Bob Gibson

Don't assume *that*.

Reggie Jackson

I'd watch. I'd pay attention.

Bob Gibson

That's what *I* assumed. I just left the fielding up to the fielders.

I looked at it like my old teammate, Curt Simmons. He'd just tell everybody, "When you see those great big ol' guys up there, play deep. With the little bitty guys, come in a step or two."

Parks

Bob Gibson

There was really only one thing about a ballpark that mattered to me: the size of it.

In small parks, I tended to pitch guys away more often so they couldn't pull the ball for cheap home runs. I'm talking about left-handers, for the most part. Normally, I tried to come in on left-handed hitters, but if they could just poke the ball over a short right-field fence, never mind. In old Busch Stadium, for instance, where we had that damn roof in right field, they could step back on an inside pitch and dump it up there real easy.

Reggie Jackson

I didn't want the ballpark to change my approach. At pretty much all times, I preferred to keep the ball toward left center. For example, when we played in Detroit, where they had a short porch in right field, I tried not to think right field because it would hurt my swing. Fortunately, Tiger Stadium also had a short porch in *left* field.

My best hitting park, all around, was probably Fenway. Since I liked to hit the ball the other way, and opposing teams were happy for me to do that, I had some fun with that wall out there. I didn't even have to square the ball to bounce it off that thing. The result was a whole lot of doubles. I also stroked a bunch of balls into the net for home runs. As far as homers go, Fenway, for me, was second only to County Stadium in Milwaukee among parks that I never played in as a member of the home team. But I hit more doubles there than anywhere else.

Comiskey was interesting. It was basically a pitcher's park, with deep fences, but I enjoyed all that space in the outfield. Except for RFK in Washington, where the Senators played through 1971, Comiskey was the only park I batted .300 in for my career. I didn't hit many home runs there, or drive in many runs, but as a visitor I *scored* more runs at Comiskey Park than anywhere else.

Bob Gibson

Forbes Field was a lot like that, real big in center field. It went forever. Flood could cover it, too. It was so far out there that they put the batting cage right on the field. Against Clemente one day,

Curt ran out and caught a ball smack in front of that batting cage. It had to be 450 feet away. I've got to believe that was one of the longest outs in major-league history.

Down the right-field line, though, Forbes was short, like Yankee Stadium. I just made sure lefties couldn't pull me, and I got along nicely there.

The worst park for me was old Busch. It was only 354 feet to right center, 322 to straightaway right, and 310 down the line. The screen ended at the 354 mark, so you could hit a 355-foot fly to right center for a home run. It was amazing how many balls happened to land just to the left of that screen.

For my career, I lost the exact same number of games at home or away, but I won seventeen more on the road. My ERA at Busch was a third of a run higher than it was in other ballparks.

But Stan Musial sure liked it.

Reggie Jackson

As much as I believed in not trying to pull the ball over a short porch in right field, I still found myself doing it at Yankee Stadium. When I was there, I even went to a half-inch shorter bat to give myself a quicker swing so I'd be out in front more often.

It didn't work. I homered in New York at about the same clip that I did in Oakland. And most of them were to right center and left center. I had a knack for finding the biggest part of any ballpark.

Bob Gibson

I was a natural high-ball pitcher, and that didn't change in a small ballpark. It didn't change when they lowered the mound five inches, either.

The guys most affected by that were the breaking-ball pitchers who threw from over the top. They liked to keep the ball down, and a lot of them had a hard time doing it after 1968. I didn't throw many curves anyway, but starting in 1969 I threw even fewer because they were always up in the zone.

You know, the Dodgers didn't lower their mound in '69.

Instead, they raised home plate. The infield at Dodger Stadium had a steep crown to it, so the mound always looked like—and felt like—it was sitting way up high. But because the whole middle of the diamond was already elevated, the mound itself wasn't sloped very much. If they'd leveled it another five inches, it would have been too flat. The new rules said that the mound had to be ten inches higher than the plate, instead of fifteen, so the Dodgers achieved the same result by jacking up the plate. I don't know if that accounted for the full five inches, but it was definitely different.

I wish more teams had done it that way, because three of the next four games I pitched there were shutouts.

Reggie Jackson

Whatever they did in the American League, it worked for me. I hit more home runs in 1969 than any other year.

Bob Gibson

But then, I liked playing on the West Coast in general. It was cooler. Especially San Francisco. It was *cold* in San Francisco, and the wind would be whipping, and I loved that. The hitters didn't care so much for it, though. The bat stings when you hit the ball in cold weather. If it were up to me, baseball could take a little vacation from June through August, just like school. You should have to shovel the field before you play.

Actually, the main advantage of cool weather is that you don't get so tired. In San Francisco, or in Chicago or Milwaukee in April, I'd wear long underwear and I'd put on wintergreen and hot oil and it wouldn't take long at all to break a sweat. I'd be nice and warm, and the hitters would be blowing on their hands and wishing for a walk. That's a good formula. The pitcher's mound at Candlestick Park was tilted and a little cockeyed—the rubber wasn't square with home plate—but I felt so good out there that it didn't matter. Then we'd get back to St. Louis and it was so sticky that you'd be whipped by the fifth or sixth inning.

It was difficult to pitch in St. Louis after the sixth inning. It was pretty much blood and guts at that point. You'd just be tired.

You'd lose weight. You'd cramp. You'd give anything for an ocean breeze.

Reggie Jackson

I had more cramps, hamstring pulls, and muscle tightness when I played in cool weather in Oakland. It was just harder to get loose. I did get better after I started spending time stretching before games.

But I'll take the hot weather that carries the ball and wears down the pitchers.

Bob Gibson

The best thing about hot weather was that it put me in a bad mood. I found that a bad mood was generally good for pitching.

Reggie Jackson

The mood that worked for me was being excited. The ballpark could play a part in that. I was always excited to play in Yankee Stadium because of all the history. And the crowds. I loved big crowds, loud crowds, rowdy crowds, any kind of crowd.

I got a charge out of Fenway, too, especially as a Yankee. I enjoyed the fans being right there when I was in the outfield, screaming and cussing at me. I was in my element. It was easy to get your blood running at Fenway Park.

And then that Green Monster always standing by, calling to me. Great place.

Distractions

Bob Gibson

I knew it was time to quit when I'd be out on the mound thinking about something else. Some nonsense that was going on off the field. I'd be out there rehashing something that my wife had said to me, and there's Willie Mays standing at the plate. What the hell?

You can't pitch successfully in the major leagues without the ability to block out everything else. That's essential. If you can't do that, you don't belong on the field. You cannot let your personal life interfere with the job you have to do for two and a half hours. The great players all have the ability to shut out distractions.

Reggie Jackson

When there's a lot of hubbub all around you, the game becomes your sanctuary. I'd get on the field and could finally be alone with what I wanted to do. Didn't have to worry about what somebody was saying or what was written in a newspaper. I was in my world.

I received a death threat during the 1973 World Series—something that had to do with voodoo—and went out and won the Series MVP Award. Even made some nice catches in center field. I was scared, but not distracted. There was next to nothing that could distract me during a World Series.

For that matter, there wasn't much, if anything, that could distract me during a ballgame, period. No matter what was going on in my life—in the clubhouse or away from the park—I was a happy camper when the game started. Let's play baseball.

Bob Gibson

For most of my career, I could focus no matter what. If I was angry about something going on at home, all the better. Once, on Father's Day in St. Louis, I had the biggest, nastiest argument with my wife that I'd ever had, went to the ballpark, pitched a shutout, and when I got home we took up right where we'd left off. That's the way it has to be.

Reggie Jackson

I was only married for a short time at the beginning of my career, so I didn't have many domestic distractions. But I *did* have support from people close to me, family and friends. Thank God for that.

In 1977, when I was caught up in all the drama with Billy Martin, it was the intervention of my father, my brother, George

Steinbrenner, and a friend from Arizona, Gary Walker, that enabled me to get through it. Gary called me every day from Arizona. George would call my father and my father would drive to Trenton, New Jersey, not far from where my brother lived while he was in the Air Force. We'd all meet in Jersey and talk it out. The conversations were about playing ball and forgetting Billy Martin.

But even with all that support—plus Fran Healy in the clubhouse—and even though I was playing the game I loved for the greatest franchise in the world, it was a struggle to keep my head where it needed to be. There was a stretch that year when I was so overwhelmed and distraught by all the stuff that was going on— with Billy, with my teammates, with the feeding frenzy the media created—that I sat on my terrace for five straight hours one day, just staring into Central Park. I wasn't myself. I was at the bottom emotionally and couldn't pull out of it. My girlfriend had to come tell me when it was time to leave for the ballpark. I cried all the way there.

Then the game started, I got a couple hits, and we picked up a victory.

I played my best ball down the stretch that year and had a huge World Series. I had to. It was New York. If I hadn't produced, they'd have run me out of town.

And Billy would have won.

Bob Gibson

In St. Louis, the media doesn't swallow you whole like it does in New York. The writers didn't bother me much. We had an understanding: I'd talk if I felt like it and I wouldn't if I didn't. They respected that. So I never had a problem.

The way I saw it, the only thing I owed the public—and my boss, for that matter—was a good performance. I definitely owed them that. But as far as giving over and above that, it's strictly a personal choice. I considered myself a public figure on the field only. If a guy happens to have the type of personality that's outgoing and engaging and he's comfortable doing appearances and chatting with the media, fine. But if he doesn't have that kind of personality, why should he have to bear that burden?

Reggie Jackson

I actually felt the same way about the press. A lot of people might not believe that, because I was known for engaging the writers. It's true, there were a lot of them around my locker and I filled their notebooks. I developed several friends who were newspaper writers: Dave Anderson, Dick Young, Bob Ryan, Mike Lupica, Murray Chass, Steve Jacobson, Leonard Koppett, and Jim Murray among them. However, I dealt with them on my terms.

I spoke my mind. I was honest. If there were writers I didn't want to talk to because they hadn't done their research or I didn't like their questions, I'd tell them so. If I felt someone didn't respect the game or tried to get me to comment negatively about a teammate—what did you think of the play that Nettles made, or what about what Sparky Lyle did?—I'd say, write it yourself. I would end an interview at any time.

For the most part, I wasn't really bothered by what anybody wrote. I felt that as long as I had a bat in my hands, I could rewrite the story anyway. My dad made that point to me, and it stuck.

Bob Gibson

One of the sensitive aspects of talking to the press is that it becomes a spectacle in the clubhouse. There'll always be writers and cameras at your locker after a good ballgame, and that's expected, but some players get self-conscious about having the media gathered around them on a regular basis or when there's no obvious reason for it. The other players see that, and you don't want it to get to the point that they resent it. You don't want to give the impression that you think you're the star, or that you're the story.

Reggie Jackson

There's another side to that: A lot of players are happy to have somebody take the press off their backs. I had teammates in Oakland who felt that way. It was something I had to watch in New York—especially when I was still new to the clubhouse—but the fact is that a lot of guys would rather not have to deal with the media. If I was willing to do it, it took the pressure off some of them.

Personally, I welcomed it. On the whole, I enjoyed talking to the writers, because a lot of them are very bright and bring up interesting points. I didn't fear them like a lot of players do. I treated them as people, and if they happened to be ignorant I reacted accordingly. If they were bright, I had respect for them. I don't have to apologize for the fact that I made myself accessible to the press and liked some of them.

When you play for the Yankees you're going to be all over the papers anyway, so why not take some control of that? Say what you think so there's no misunderstanding and no misrepresentation. I was still misunderstood and misrepresented from time to time, but that comes with the territory.

On the other hand, I was on the cover of *Sports Illustrated* eight times, and I've always been proud of that. I can still describe every one of them. They're a validation of who I am as a player and what I've accomplished as a player. I went out of my way to cooperate with the *SI* writers and photographers because, well, I thought it had value to me. I thought the publicity embellished my image.

In 1980, for my sixth cover, the photographer, Walter Iooss Jr., followed me around for about a week. At the end of it, we were playing a Sunday game against Kansas City. I asked him if he needed anything else and he told me, mostly kidding, that he could use another home run or two. I nodded, then hit one off Rich Gale my first time up. The next at-bat I thought I might have had the second one, but the ball was caught on the warning track. I apologized to Walter. In that issue, *SI* referred to me as "the most obliging" of all their cover subjects, ever. I appreciated that.

It got crazy for a while there in New York, but by and large I *loved* being in the spotlight. It fit me. It drove me. So why not make the best of it? The media's not going away.

CHAPTER EIGHT

ATMOSPHERE

Clubhouse

Reggie Jackson

I don't know if I understand the term they use to describe a good clubhouse. What's chemistry? A good clubhouse is good people. People of quality. When you put good people together with good people, you've got something.

Chemistry, as they call it, is important, but it isn't about everybody being chummy and agreeing with each other. It's about good people—and a lot of talented players who win. *That's* chemistry.

Bob Gibson

You never hear about some bozo being a team leader. It's always somebody who can flat-out play.

Reggie Jackson

It's somebody who shows the way by example. Since I've been around the Yankees, for almost twenty-five years, we've had great examples in the clubhouse—all the way back to Catfish Hunter, Ron Guidry, Goose Gossage, Thurman Munson, and Dick Howser. They were guys who made positive impacts.

There's not a standard profile for a team leader. Different types can affect people in different ways. Players like Derek Jeter and Henry Aaron go about their jobs in a very professional fashion. They discuss problems in private, not in the press. Andy Pettitte talks things over behind closed doors. Munson was a strong personality. Mariano Rivera exudes a quiet strength. George Steinbrenner demands excellence.

Pete Rose left everything on the field. George Brett was like that. Jorge Posada wears his heart on his sleeve. Bernie Williams went about his business. Frank Robinson would do whatever was necessary to win a ballgame. When Bob Gibson takes the mound, or if it's Catfish Hunter's turn, you know there is no dilly-dallying around today. There's a seriousness and a focus that rubs off on everybody. Michael Jordan was that kind of leader.

Bob Gibson

And if Michael Jordan hadn't been a great player, nobody'd know that.

The press tends to have its own ideas about who the leaders are and who sets the example in the clubhouse. Most good ballplayers are pretty smart guys. Most. There are some who aren't. But if somebody speaks well and knows pretty much what he's talking about and will stand there and answer questions without being snippy or rude, the press thinks, wow, what a great guy and wonderful role model. The writers automatically assume that this is the type who's a team leader. Maybe, maybe not.

It doesn't matter what the media thinks. Regardless of what writers would write about me, I'd still go about my job the only way I knew how to go about it. Regardless of what my teammates thought about me, same thing. I got along with most of them, but I was outspoken and blunt and I'm sure a lot of guys didn't like me. I didn't care. I'm sure they still don't like me, and I still don't care.

Reggie Jackson

I'll grab on to that, because I know all about teammates not liking you.

I was in a tumultuous situation with the Yankees, in terms of personalities and the sociology of the clubhouse. I found my freedom when I was on the field. I was the judge and jury as long as I took a turn in the batter's box. Those are some of the concepts I've tried to pass along to Alex Rodriguez when he's had his struggles. When you come to bat, you have control. You're not being tried in court anymore; you're judge and jury.

Anyway, there's no such thing as a perfectly harmonious clubhouse. I was in Oakland for nine years, I was in New York for five, I was in Anaheim for five, and there were fracases in each place. Guys get chippy when they're not doing well or the team's not playing well. Most of the fights start from kidding, and then they escalate. A lot depends on who's doing the kidding. It's sort of like family. If it's somebody you know well, somebody you're close to, that's one thing. But if an outsider starts up with it, he'll get filleted.

Most of my problems in New York occurred when I was the new guy. I grew up with my teammates in Oakland, and the players in New York grew up without me. It was like that for A-Rod, too, coming up with the Mariners and then signing a record-breaking contract with a team that had won 101 games without him the year before. Alex has a totally different personality than I, but the dynamics were basically the same.

For most of the 1977 season, I couldn't get into the rhythm of the clubhouse. It was so uncomfortable for a while that a couple guys even moved their lockers away from me. Ouch!

Bob Gibson

A little friction is to be expected when you get that many high-spirited people in the same room every day. You'll have conflicts. But it shouldn't reach the point where you fight about it.

Reggie Jackson

Our Oakland teams were famous for that. We were mad all the time because Charlie Finley was so cheap and we didn't have the amenities that most teams did, even though we were winning championships. We couldn't slug Charlie, so we took it out on each other. I had little tiffs with Mike Epstein and John (Blue Moon) Odom, and a bigger one with Billy North. Vida Blue and Bert Campaneris got into it one day. Blue Moon threw a Coke bottle at one of our guys.

We were young and full of testosterone. Fights were so common in that clubhouse that we'd just deal the cards and keep on playing, unless it was your turn to break it up. But everybody always made up afterwards. I don't think it ever undermined what we were trying to do on the field. If anything, we were united in our anger toward Finley.

Bob Gibson

It's far more important to respect one another than like each other. It'd be nice if everybody was everybody's pal, but for whatever reason—jealousy or what have you—that just doesn't happen.

Reggie Jackson

There's always going to be some jealousy of the superstars. That's life. The sociology of what goes on inside a baseball team is very similar to what goes on inside society. There are good people and there are bad people. There are agreeable people and disagreeable people. There are people who are admirers and people who are jealous. It's not extraordinary to have jealousy and resentment within a group of twenty-five competitive men who are all compensated differently.

That said, I *do* think it's rare to see real animosity inside a clubhouse. If there is some, you still have a job that you're paid to do. There's still a responsibility to be professional about your work.

You earn respect by the way you play. You have to play hard. That's something I thought was easy to do. I wasn't really concerned about whether you liked me or disliked me, but you were *going* to respect me. You were going to respect the way I played the game.

Bob Gibson

Too much is made of camaraderie and chemistry and all that stuff. I don't need a teammate that I love. Give me one who can *play*.

Reggie Jackson

But you know, I found that I attracted more respect toward the end of my career, when I *couldn't* play the way I could in 1969 or 1977. My second time around in Oakland, when I batted .220 with fifteen home runs, I was viewed by my teammates as a leader. I called a team meeting after a long, bad road trip, and the players responded. During the season, I broke the hamate bone in my right hand and was thinking about retiring early until the other guys stepped forward and persuaded me not to.

Bob Gibson

Your attitude toward the game, and toward your teammates, tends to evolve as you go along. I know mine did. Late in your career, when you can't do the things you could before, you're a little humbler. And the people around you pick up on that.

But in a case like Reggie's, there's something else that comes into play. It wasn't any ordinary ballplayer they were talking to. It was Mr. October. They were dealing with a guy who was headed to the Hall of Fame, who was all over the magazine covers, who they all watched hit three straight home runs to close out a World Series.

Johnnie LeMaster retired from the A's that year, too. Did they try to talk *him* out of it?

Reggie Jackson

I would have liked to go to the World Series with that team. We had a hell of a roster: Mark McGwire, Jose Canseco, Carney Lansford, Terry Steinbach, Dave Stewart, Dennis Eckersley, with Tony La Russa calling the shots . . .

Bob Gibson

Offhand, I'd guess there was a shortage of starting pitchers.

If I'm putting together a team, I don't start with leadership qualities. I start with three really good starting pitchers. The Braves didn't do so well when they had Aaron, Darrell Evans, and Davey Johnson all mashing forty home runs, but they won the division every year with Greg Maddux, Tom Glavine, and John

Smoltz in the rotation. After three pitchers, the next thing I want is a good center fielder.

It doesn't hurt to have somebody on the team who can make you laugh, but if he can't play ball I couldn't care less how funny the guy is. Aaron was no comedian. Give me *him*.

You take Uecker.

Reggie Jackson

In my era, as well as Bob's—particularly *early* in my era—camaraderie and relationships weren't even thought of. On my Birmingham team, I was the only "colored" player (that was the term of the period). Had it not been for Joe Rudi, Dave Duncan, Rollie Fingers, and others, I would have really struggled socially. John McNamara was our manager, and he looked after me, as well. He cared about my feelings. If I couldn't stay in a hotel, he wouldn't let the team stay there. If I couldn't eat in a restaurant, he had somebody bring out the food for everyone. John McNamara was ahead of the curve, but the fact remains that blacks and whites just didn't mix very much in those days. It wasn't normal. When I roomed with Rudi and Chuck Dobson on different occasions in 1968 and 1969, it was a big deal.

The bigger deal to me, though—as it was for most African-American players—was the opportunity to take care of myself and my family. Those situations didn't present themselves very often in the real world. We had a chance to make some serious money and pull our mothers and fathers out of debt. We could get something to eat and turn on the heat at night. That was my focus—not the relationships. Not the camaraderie. I can count on one hand the guys whose houses I went to for dinner.

Bob Gibson

The Cardinals were different. A group of us would go out to eat after a game on the road, and there'd be a dozen guys or so, black and white. Some of the white players—Stan Musial and Ken Boyer, to start with—were as adamant against segregation as the black players were.

The tone for all of that was set in St. Petersburg, where we trained. Bill White made some public statements about the Jim Crow customs down there—what ticked him off was that only the white players were invited for breakfast at the St. Petersburg Yacht Club—and several of the black players, including me and Curt Flood, took up the cause with him. We went to August Busch, the owner, and expressed our dissatisfaction with various discriminations and inconveniences, including the fact that we couldn't stay in the Bainbridge Hotel with the rest of the team. Right away, Busch arranged for a businessman he knew to buy a motel, and all the players moved into it. Musial and Boyer were living in beachfront bungalows, but they gave them up to come stay with the rest of us. People would drive by just to see all these black and white guys swimming and grilling steaks together.

Before long, practically the whole ball club was on guard against bigotry. The wives were our intelligence officers. If they picked up on some racial slur, they'd pass the information along to me or White and we'd confront the perpetrator and straighten it out. Of course, all of this wasn't easy, at first, for some of the Southerners on the team, but the atmosphere of mutual respect was so strong that in time just about everybody bought in. We enjoyed each other's company. We didn't all see eye-to-eye on every social issue—there were plenty of opinions represented in our clubhouse—but we agreed not to let the differences drive us apart. Boyer had some strict thoughts on interracial marriage, for example, and yet he and I could sit down calmly and exchange our views on the subject.

Reggie Jackson

When I was a kid in Philadelphia, everything about baseball seemed like it was divided between black and white. We'd go to Shibe Park and sit in left field—the "colored" section—for fifty cents. That's where all the blacks sat—not because we had to, but because it was what we could afford. Your favorite team was the Dodgers because they had Jackie Robinson. You didn't root for anybody else. You didn't even pay attention to the American

League. I didn't know anything about the Red Sox or the Washington Senators, because they didn't have black players. You didn't root for the Yankees. You rooted for the *Dodgers*.

Later, when I played, I made a point of looking for black people in the ballpark. Friendly faces. I wanted to see who was coming and who *could* come; who could come and enjoy me hitting a home run. There weren't many.

Even then, there was no mistaking that we were playing a white man's game.

Bob Gibson

Yep, you looked around for black faces, just to see. It was the same when we barnstormed in the off-season.

After my rookie year, I toured with the Willie Mays All-Stars, and we were all black. We played the all-white Harmon Killebrew All-Stars, with Mickey Mantle. That's how blatant the separation was between the races, and how taken for granted it was, just fifty years ago. The teams traveled in their own caravans and would meet up at ballparks in Oklahoma, Texas, and Mexico. It was an education just being with those guys and listening to their stories. Everybody had essentially the same story, with different names and places. Reggie has the same stories I have, except that he was too young to experience the Willie Mays All-Stars.

Barnstorming was good fun and good money, but it was a challenge just getting something to eat in those towns. Most of the time we'd have to find the black neighborhood and hope we got there before everything closed. Or we'd send somebody into the restaurant with a chauffeur's cap and have him carry out the food for us. Or Sam Jones, who was light-skinned, would pull a stocking cap down over his head, pass as white, and pretend he was a deaf-mute.

When we played against the Killebrew guys, there was no ill will. But we did beat the hell out of them.

Reggie Jackson

What I wouldn't have given to be along for that . . .

SIXTY FEET, SIX INCHES

Bob Gibson

Latin players have always been separated, somewhat, by language, but it hasn't stopped them from taking a big part in the clubhouse atmosphere. I'm thinking way back to guys like Tony Perez and Orlando Cepeda. Perez meant so much to the morale of the Big Red Machine that its demise is attributed to Cincinnati trading him. And Cepeda, in 1967, was the Cardinals' unofficial spirit captain. After every game, whether we won or lost, he'd jump up on the trunk where we kept our valuables and lead us in a round of cheers for something or other. Because of Cha-Cha, they called us El Birdos.

As cynical as I am about that sort of thing, I have to acknowledge that the camaraderie on that team made it special. The '67 Cardinals probably banded together more than any club I ever played on. We were so team-oriented, to a man, that we'd fine anybody who was caught looking at the stat sheet.

Reggie Jackson

Now, that's a *team*. That was a team that overcame a broken leg by its Hall of Fame pitcher, dominated the National League, and won the World Series.

If you didn't know better, it might make you believe in chemistry.

Managers

Reggie Jackson

A manager sets a tone. The best example of that, from what I've seen, was Joe Torre with the Yankees.

He had a calmness about himself that permeated that team. We had a lot of high-profile personnel there, with Jeter, A-Rod, Roger Clemens, Andy Pettitte, Mike Mussina, Randy Johnson, Mariano Rivera, Jason Giambi, Gary Sheffield, Jorge Posada . . . That's quite a collection of stars, and still, Joe's even temperament created a low-key atmosphere in that clubhouse—a controlled atmosphere, where no one got out of kilter, no one was too big for his britches. It was about the *team*.

Torre's personality rubbed off on that ball club, in a good way. A team reflects that calmness in qualities like confidence and poise.

Bob Gibson

A bad manager can affect a team more than a good manager. Good managers know when they have a good ball club, and they let good ballplayers play. They don't overmanage. A bad manager wants to be in control at all times. It's impossible to maintain a really good team when one man controls every thought.

There comes a time when a player has to make his mind up, when he has to make a decision without looking into the dugout to get instructions from the manager. When a manager controls the game to the point that guys are looking for him before they make a move, that's counterproductive. You can't play smart baseball that way, because players aren't thinking on their own.

Reggie Jackson

When Torre took over the Yankees, he was the same person he'd been with the Mets, Braves, or Cardinals. But he had different players—great players almost everywhere—and The Boss's wallet. That helped him become a better manager.

But that doesn't mean every manager can achieve the same results with good players. A manager must understand his personnel. He has to know when guys need days off. How to keep them out of situations where they won't succeed. How to stay out of the way when a guy is going well. He and the players have to fit.

Bob Gibson

What makes a good manager—at least one of the things—is that everybody he manages knows what his job is; everyone knows what's expected of him. It's a lousy deal to go to work and not know when you're expected to play or what you're expected to do, period. Players don't want to guess about their status. How can you perform your role to the best of your ability when you don't even know what it is? The skipper needs to tell his guys what's up, and tell 'em in advance. That's really important. You may not like it when you hear that you're not playing and some other guy is, but at least you know where you stand.

Evidently, another thing that makes a good manager is being a fan. *All* fans are great managers. Just listen to the call-in shows and you can tell that.

Reggie Jackson

I don't know that there have ever been two managers more different than Joe Torre and Billy Martin. And I can't believe I just said that, because I didn't think I'd ever put Joe Torre and Billy Martin in the same sentence.

You really can't compare Billy to anybody. When he didn't drink he was a much different person than he was when he was drinking; it's just that he drank a lot. He'd come to the ballpark sometimes and have to sleep on the couch. He wouldn't even go out for batting practice.

I didn't drink much, but I suppose Billy and I were alike in some ways—probably *too* alike. We were both proud. We were both proud to be *Yankees*. And we both liked to be in the thick of things. For me, that applied to the ballfield. I wanted to do something *in the game* to be in the middle of the action, the center of attention. In his case, I didn't quite get it. It's kind of hard for a manager to bring the crowd to its feet.

Bob Gibson

When a player and a manager find themselves in competition with each other, the player suffers; and when the player suffers, the ball club suffers; and when the ball club suffers, the manager suffers. It stinks for everybody.

Reggie Jackson

It eventually got me suspended in 1978, and it eventually cost Billy his job—for a while, anyway. The suspension was over me bunting after they'd taken off the bunt sign. It was pride and stubbornness on my part; I didn't like being told to bunt in the first place. Billy was so mad that I thought he might come after me in the dugout, like he'd done the year before in Boston. My suspension was five games, and the Yankees won them all. When I came back, Billy talked to the press in the airport lounge in Chicago and said that I should shut up because they were winning without me. That was when he made the comment about me and Steinbrenner: "One's a born liar and the other's convicted." The next day, he resigned.

We were ten games behind Boston at the time. After Bob Lemon took over we caught the Red Sox, beat them in the one-game playoff, and took care of the Dodgers in the World Series. Billy came back halfway through the 1979 season. I thought I'd die when they announced that! We didn't win the division that year. Then Dick Howser managed in 1980, and we *did*.

Dick Howser gave me a pretty good idea of what it would have been like to play for Torre. Howser was a manager I could talk to. He was a manager who let his players play. Under Dick, there was a lot less turmoil on the ball club. Guys were free to go about their business without all the baggage on their backs. That didn't get us into the World Series, but we did win 103 games during the regular season, which was more than we ever won under Martin. It's probably no coincidence that my one season playing for Howser was the only time I hit forty homers (forty-one, actually) for the Yankees. It was also the only time in my career that I batted .300. I could have used a few more seasons under Dick Howser.

It's just good business when a boss handles his personnel with respect and consideration.

Bob Gibson

Joe's the only manager who ever hired me as a coach. He did it three times. With the Mets, he gave me the title of "attitude coach," which was interesting. There had never been one of those before, so I kind of made it up as I went along. Then, with the Braves and Cardinals, he hired me to work with the pitchers.

So obviously he's a smart guy.

Reggie Jackson

It helps to be smart, but managing is more an art than a science. Strategic moves are important, but the great majority of them are predictable and don't vary much from manager to manager.

Fans, writers, and broadcasters love to second-guess managers on their batting orders, when they take pitchers out, whether they bunt or swing away—all the stuff that's easy to see and criticize. They judge the manager by what's in the book. But there's a lot more to it than that. You could sit there with the book in your lap to tell you what the percentages call for. That doesn't take much skill. A good manager knows the book, but he relies on his head and his gut.

Needless to say, that's not enough unless he has a load of talent. Talented players make managers smart and great.

Bob Gibson

If you're looking for something to criticize a manager for, you can always find it. Always. There's a lot of failure in baseball.

Reggie Jackson

A manager's value is in the intangibles. Does he create an environment in which everybody can do his job at peak capacity? What kind of comfort level does he bring to the club? How does he maintain morale and confidence? How does he communicate? Does he understand his opponents? Does he understand his personnel? Does he motivate his personnel? Does he teach? Does he treat everybody fairly? Does he command respect? Does he surround himself with good coaches? How does he handle the front office, ownership, and the media? It all plays a part.

Bob Gibson

The position is about managing people. A manager can't come barging in with a bunch of rules and expect them to work for every team and every player and every situation. Everybody can't be treated the same way. One set of rules just doesn't do the trick.

This isn't the Army. It would be an ideal situation if everything was that black and white, but it's not. If a veteran player has been getting the job done for seven years and he has to tend to a personal matter and miss two days of spring training, he's probably earned that privilege. You know what you're going to get from that guy, and a couple days of spring training won't make a difference. But a young player coming out of Triple-A, trying to make the ball club—he can't afford to miss those two days. He's in a position where he has to prove not only his talent but his work ethic and makeup. It's a different situation.

Managing isn't about bed checks or putting on the hit-and-run. It's about understanding twenty-five personalities and twenty-five skill sets and turning them all in the same direction.

Reggie Jackson

As far as actually managing the game on the field, the most intricate part of it is handling the pitching staff. A manager needs to know who can pitch back-to-back, who can't, who gets this guy out, who gets that guy out. The right people for the right job.

There's a lot more to it than meets the eye. People watching at home don't know that you can't get Mariano Rivera warmed up unless he's going to pitch. If Mariano gets up, he's coming in. You can't use this other guy tonight because he warmed up twice last night. This guy pitches really well two days in a row, but this other guy can't pitch two days in a row. It may look like there's a spot for a certain left-hander tonight, but the skipper knows that the guy would run the risk of getting hurt if he pitched again, because his arm probably wouldn't stand it.

If the manager doesn't have a good sense of his ball club, the players feel it. Something's not right. Guys lose their rhythm. Jobs don't get done. People start to fail and get fired.

Bob Gibson

Fans complain about a manager taking a pitcher out after seven innings of shutout ball. Well, maybe the catcher told him— or the pitcher himself—that the slider's not biting or the fastball's not sailing like it was. Or maybe he can see something that nobody else sees. He might recognize a subtle change in the pitcher's motion, and that tells him the guy's getting tired. He might notice that the foot's not landing in the same spot or the arm angle has dropped a couple ticks. If you let the guy go another inning, it could lead to bad habits. It could lead to an injury. It could blow his confidence.

Reggie Jackson

There's not a fan or journalist out there who knows what Dick Williams knows when he's running a team or running a ballgame, or what Tony La Russa knows. I had the privilege of playing for both of those guys, and both of them will be in the Hall of Fame when Tony gets in. They were completely different as personalities, but completely the same in their devotion to winning and their grasp of the game.

Dick was combative and feisty, a colorful character—not unlike Billy Martin in that respect—and our A's took on that personality. La Russa's just as strong, but in a subtler, more cerebral way. Neither one of them would ever be undermined or outmanaged.

People view Tony as cold and calculating, but he showed me plenty of emotion when I was grinding through my final season, my Oakland encore. He once said that I was the only player he ever managed who brought tears to his eyes. (I hope he wasn't talking about the way I ran after fly balls.)

On the other hand, I doubt that anybody ever brought tears to Dick Williams's eyes. He could be fearsome, he could be intimidating, and he could be too heavy-handed for my taste—we clashed over that—but he was a great manager who earned my loyalty and the whole team's. First off, we understood that managing for Charlie Finley couldn't be easy. We respected Williams for standing up to Finley. I played for a manager who didn't do that. We won a World Series under Alvin Dark, but Charlie put some dents in his authority.

Dick Williams was another matter. As bizarre as Finley was, and as domineering as he tried to be, Dick was strong enough to keep everybody on track and focused on winning. He ran a unique team. Took it to two straight world championships. Unfortunately, after the second one, in 1973, he'd had enough. That was the Series in which Mike Andrews, a utility infielder who'd come to us late in the season, made a couple errors in the twelfth inning of Game Two. Finley then forced him to sign a statement saying he was injured, which enabled Charlie to drop him off the roster. At least, that was his scheme. The players and Williams both made a fuss about it, and Bowie Kuhn, the commissioner, intervened to put Andrews back on the active list. After we'd beaten the Mets in seven games, Williams up and quit.

Personally, I know that Dick Williams made me a better player. I can't say that about Billy Martin.

Gene Mauch, who managed the Angels when I went to Anaheim after New York, was somebody I loved playing for. Mauch was as good and dedicated a baseball man as there ever was. He and Dick Williams were each as old-school and hard-boiled as the other. But I was more impressionable when I played for Dick. In terms of developing my fundamentals and team mentality, he took over what Bobby Winkles had started at Arizona State and Frank Robinson continued when he managed me one winter in Puerto Rico.

I was young and a long way from home when I arrived in Oakland, and Dick, as gruff as he was, was sort of a father figure to me. His toughness was what I needed.

Bob Gibson

I don't know if I'd call any of my managers a father figure, but Johnny Keane—who, in fact, had studied to be a priest—certainly nurtured me as a pitcher. He was actually my first minor-league manager in Omaha. In my professional debut, I had a terrible time getting the ball over the plate and was letting up to throw strikes. Of course, that led to getting pounded. I remember Keane coming out to the mound and taking the ball and saying, "That's pretty good for the first time. We'll get back to you later."

My first three years in St. Louis, the manager was Solly Hemus, and I'm pretty sure I'd have been traded if the Cardinals hadn't fired him halfway through the 1961 season. Keane took over, with Howard Pollet as his pitching coach, and it was a different world. That was the year when Sandy Koufax broke through and became an all-star. Keane pointed out to me that Koufax had started out just like I had—wild and depending too much on the fastball. My manager was building up my belief in myself. And the next year, *I* was an all-star.

Johnny Keane telling me that, and putting his faith in me, meant more than a hundred successful hit-and-runs.

Owners

Bob Gibson

There are always exceptions—the Yankees, obviously—but on most teams, players aren't that familiar with the owner of the ball club. We don't see them much and don't hear from them much and they don't have much to do with the identity of the team. If you've got good ballplayers, the owner can do his thing, whatever it is, and it won't make much of a difference.

Of course, he has to do his part in *getting* those good ballplayers. The owner has to give the general manager the latitude—the *money*, basically—to go out and put together a championship team. If he's willing to do that, it shows the players that the organization is serious about winning and will come up with whatever it takes, at least to a reasonable extent.

George Steinbrenner messed with that Yankee clubhouse all the time, but he always signed the best ballplayers available. He did it to a *more* than reasonable extent. Nothing else matters as much as that.

Reggie Jackson

I played for the exceptions. Steinbrenner and Finley had a hell of a lot to do with the personalities of their teams. It all started with them.

Both of them were controversial, critical, loud, stubborn, and very successful. And so were we. Their tough-mindedness was reflected in their ball clubs.

In my opinion, they both deserve Hall of Fame recognition. Both were ahead of the times. Finley, in addition to putting championship teams on the field, was a tremendous innovator—he pushed for the night World Series, the night All-Star Game, and the designated hitter—and a master promoter (among other things, he was the first to hire ball girls). George should get credit for raising the value of major-league franchises. Under him, the Yankees became the big draw for every team they played on the road, not to mention the TV networks.

Bob Gibson

Gussie Busch didn't have a lot in common with those guys except success. And certainly stubbornness. He was rigid in his defense of the reserve clause and his opposition to collective bargaining for the players.

As far as putting a team on the field, I never really understood whether or not he cared if we won. I know that Bill DeWitt does. The Cardinals have great ownership these days. When they're short on something, he makes sure they have the means to get it. With Busch, I never had that sense one way or the other.

But he deserves some credit. He shelled out the money to pick up a big hitter from time to time—Cepeda, Dick Allen, and Torre. And he made an effort to accommodate the players. The motel situation in St. Petersburg was the most dramatic example, but it says something that we had four Hall of Famers during my time, and only one of them—Steve Carlton—ever left the Cardinals. Musial and I spent our entire careers in St. Louis, and Lou Brock was there for his last sixteen seasons. If you add it up for the three of us, the total is fifty-five straight seasons in the organization. On top of that, guys like Red Schoendienst, George Kissell, and Bing Devine were fixtures in the dugout and front office. That's a lot of continuity and stability.

Reggie Jackson

I won't attempt to associate those words with Charlie Finley.

We heard more of Charlie than we saw of him. He was usually back home in Indiana, but he listened to the games over the phone line and thought he always knew exactly what we needed. Of course, he wasn't interested in paying much for it. Once, he was about to send Phil Garner to the minors so he wouldn't have to give him a major-league contract. I had to get him on the phone to explain that all Garner wanted was $800 a month. When he heard it laid out that way, Charlie okayed the contract.

I could talk to Finley, but most of the talking seemed to be about money. After I hit forty-seven home runs in 1969, I had to fight him tooth and nail to get $50,000 for 1970. Charlie was so furious about the contract that he ordered me to the bench. A couple weeks later, I came through with a pinch-hit grand slam and raised my fist toward his box when I crossed home plate. He called me to his office and told me I'd be sent to the minors unless I signed a public apology. He was a proud man and I'd openly challenged his authority. Well, *I'm* a proud man, too, and he'd openly humiliated me. I never did sign that apology.

Charlie O was so stingy he wouldn't even supply stamps for the fan mail we answered. We wore the same uniforms for two years. We were given two hats to last us the season. We also had a limited number of bats, and if we broke them all we didn't get new ones. We borrowed from other players.

Maybe the most generous thing Charlie ever did was offer all the players $300 to grow mustaches for Mustache Day. I already had one, and Rollie Fingers and Darold Knowles had started to grow their own just to make me shave mine. That gave Finley the idea for a cheap promotion. Naturally, a bunch of us took it further and grew out our hair and beards. It gave us the look of a rebellious, free-spirited team, and frankly, we *were*.

Mostly, we rebelled against Charlie.

Of course, he could also be a sweetheart. He showed me a lot of compassion when I tore my hamstring in the 1972 playoffs and couldn't play in the World Series.

All things considered, Finley was great practice for The Boss.

Bob Gibson

Whatever opinion people might have of Steinbrenner, he was good for the Yankees and good for New York and probably good for baseball, because he raised the bar.

A lot of owners *talk* about winning, but it'd be hard to find another one who ever went after it like Steinbrenner.

Reggie Jackson

That's the bottom line. George never spared any expense when it came to putting a team on the field. A lot of people have complained about other teams having to compete with the salaries he paid, but that's on *baseball*. He was just playing by the rules of the game, and playing hard. Losing was a disgrace to him, and that set the tone for the franchise. He created an atmosphere that was all about winning, no matter the cost. He wanted to win *every game*.

As a player, I had my share of problems with Steinbrenner. Okay, more than my share. We had our shouting matches and our times when we didn't talk to each other. I thought he blamed me for every little incident—like the fight with Nettles. I also thought he should have kept Billy Martin off my back a little more than he did. At the same time, though, Billy was upset because he thought I had George's ear. And I suppose I did. George and I were friends. We respected each other. He gave me the biggest contract in baseball history, and that put the two of us in it together. We discussed things. We met for dinner every once in a while. He got to know my family. He thought I should be hitting cleanup and told Billy. But it certainly wasn't all peaches and cream between us. I don't think it was all peaches and cream between George and *anybody*—at least, until the last ten years or so.

People thought I was the reason that George and Billy had problems and George was the reason that Billy and I had problems and Billy was the reason that George and I had problems. Maybe. That's a lot of ego for one building. In general, though, the biggest problems I had with Steinbrenner came when I wasn't playing well.

Most of the 1981 season falls under that category. I was hurt for part of the year and struggled through the rest of it. At one point, George ordered me to get a physical. I didn't care for that. I wasn't crazy about it when he failed to re-sign me after the season, either. (His advisors convinced him he should rebuild the team around speed. George has since said that it was the biggest mistake he ever made as an owner.)

I led the league in home runs the next year, with California, and number one came against Ron Guidry in New York. It was my first game against the Yankees since I'd left. I hit it well, and the fans chanted abuse at George as I jogged around the bases. He deserved better than that. He had given them a hell of a ball club. (Of course, I won't mention that after the Yankees let me go they weren't in the playoffs again for another fifteen years . . . I had to get that in.)

George sent me a silver Cartier plate in 1984, when I was with the Angels and hit my five hundredth home run. He also hired me as a special advisor. In the big picture, George Steinbrenner was great for me. We will always be family, a pair of friends and proud Yankees.

Bob Gibson

A player wants an owner who will *compete*. Steinbrenner was the epitome of that. Under him, the Yankees became the team to beat.

They became the team that everybody *loved* to beat, if they could. Nothing wrong with that.

Reggie Jackson

George was about winning.

Bob Gibson

And he won. He won championships.

Reggie Jackson

Amen!

My feelings now about The Boss are that we're bound to-gether as part of the history of the "Steinbrenner Yankees." The same way that it's Bill Russell and Red Auerbach, Roger Staubach and Tom Landry, Bart Starr and Vince Lombardi, I feel it should always be Reggie Jax and George Steinbrenner.

CHAPTER NINE

TOWERING FIGURES

Greatness

Reggie Jackson

I've always been fascinated by greatness. Mays, Aaron, Clemente, Mantle, Koufax, Frank Robinson, Montana, Unitas, Russell, Jerry West, Michael Jordan, Jim Brown, Arnold Palmer, Jack Nicklaus, Tiger Woods, Muhammad Ali . . .

Maybe, early on, it was my desire to be looked at and revered the way the great ballplayers were, to be the guy whom everybody stops to watch when he walks by or steps up to the plate. Maybe it was pure admiration. I grew up in a generation when black players were rising to the top level of major-league baseball, even dominating it, and those guys were heroes to me. For as long as I can remember, I've had a deep reverence for the stars of that era. They're just fifteen or so years older than I, and I was captivated by what they did in the way of paving the road for minorities. But it wasn't just the black players who intrigued me. It was the *great* players.

My favorites at the time were Willie Mays and Duke Snider. I didn't say much about Snider because, if you were black, your favorite Dodger had to be Jackie Robinson. He was an icon in the black community, and so were the athletes who picked up where he left off—Aaron, Mays, Frank Robinson, Gibson, Ali, Marion

Motley, Calvin Peete . . . They made us walk taller. I'd check the newspaper every morning, and if Gibson had pitched a shutout or Mays had hit a home run, I had a good day at school. It sounds like an exaggeration, I know, but that's the truth.

Bob Gibson

The difference for me was that I grew up around the game but not around the *players*. There was nothing to see in Omaha, other than A-ball, which later became Triple-A. I never even made it to the ballpark. By the time I might have been interested in going, I was out of Creighton and playing for the Cardinals and Globetrotters. In my neighborhood, the only professional athletes we paid much attention to were Jackie Robinson and Joe Louis.

So I never gave a thought to being like Satchel Paige or Don Newcombe, or like Monte Irvin if I'd become an outfielder. I was mainly concerned with making a good living—which is why I stayed with the Globetrotters until the Cardinals said they'd make up the difference in salary if I quit—and with winning. We all have different ideals.

Reggie Jackson

I wanted not only to play like the great ones and live like the great ones; I wanted to *look* like them. There was a certain way that Mays and Mickey Mantle wore their uniforms. They had their stirrups—their baseball socks—at a certain height. Mays left the top button unbuttoned, and if you were a superstar that was okay. He introduced tailored uniforms and tight pants, stuff like that. I thought it was cool. I wanted to wear my pants the way the stars did. I wanted to drive free cars like they did. I wanted everything about me to be just like them.

When I made it to the big leagues with the A's, we trained in Arizona, where the Cubs and Giants also had their camps. That provided me with the opportunity to hang out with Ernie Banks, Fergie Jenkins, Billy Williams, and Willie McCovey. Mays didn't run around with us, but that was okay because Willie was magical to me. I didn't want to lose that feeling.

As it was, I was surrounded by my idols. I was a kid and they were who I wanted to grow up to be. Besides that, three of us were left-handed. I was in my glory.

Bob Gibson

You can learn a whole lot just by hanging out with guys like that. You can see for yourself what the best players eat, how they manage their schedules, how they respond to certain situations on the field and off it. You can start to see what it takes to be at that level.

But I didn't make a study of greatness like Reggie did. To me, greatness meant that I shouldn't give that guy anything good to hit.

I didn't pal around with superstars, but I wasn't oblivious to them either. It certainly made an impression on me in spring training of 1960 when I pitched against Ted Williams. I remembered distinctly—or thought I did—that I got two strikes on him with fastballs and then he ripped a curveball up the middle for a single. Years and years later, at an old-timers game, I brought that up with Williams and he said, no, that wasn't quite how it was. He said he took a fastball for a strike and hit the curve on the second pitch. It's understandable that I would remember pitching to him, because he was Ted Williams, but how in the hell could he remember batting against *me*? At that point, I was nobody. Except that I was a pitcher, and that was enough for Ted Williams. That, to me, is a study in greatness.

Reggie Jackson

Bob was one of the guys I studied. His intensity and his determination—that spread-eagle with his legs stretched out and that flying follow-through—expressed a fierceness that I admired. I watched the way he instilled fear in the batter. Gibson was the most feared of all the pitchers. It was his combination of extraordinary ability and intense will.

To me, he was the pitching equivalent of Frank Robinson,

who had the ferocity of a fighter and the reputation to go with it. In the heat of a big ballgame, I tried to summon the intensity of Gibson and Frank Robinson.

Bob Gibson

That intensity is something all great players have in common. They just show it differently. People thought Hank Aaron kind of glided along without much fire in him, but that's not possible. That man had to be seriously driven to accomplish what he did for as long as he did and put up with what he put up with.

Reggie Jackson

There might be great players who don't bring it every day, but I don't remember playing against any. I can say from experience that the great pitchers I saw were never off when I saw them. When I faced Roger Clemens, he had it that day. When I faced Tom Seaver, he had it *that* day. At least it seemed that way to me. Jim Palmer, Dave McNally, Mickey Lolich . . . I never went back to the dugout and said, "Man, he's not throwing that good today." And if a teammate said to me that he's not, I'd say, "Well, take my jersey and put on my glasses and go up and stand on the left side of the plate with number forty-four on your back. You'll see. He's not throwing me that chicken salad that you're gettin'!"

I didn't need coffee or bennies or amphetamines or whatever to get amped for Nolan Ryan or Ferguson Jenkins. Against those gentlemen, you'd better be on your game from the moment you get up. Otherwise, you're going to beat a path between home plate and the dugout. Because *they're* going to be on it. If you don't get them in the first three innings, you'll be in for a painfully long day.

I didn't ever go to Baltimore and Frank Robinson had the flu, or a stiff neck. He wasn't in a slump. He wasn't swinging bad. He wasn't limping. My gosh, we'd go to play the Orioles and they'd have four twenty-game winners lined up for us. We got *all* of them. It wasn't like, hey, McNally went to see the doctor today, he had a sore elbow. He didn't have a sore elbow for *us*. When we went to see Mickey Lolich in Detroit, he had a big ol' belly, he threw in the low nineties, he had a slider and a curveball to go with it, and he was going to be there for nine innings. That guy pitched 376 innings one year. He was going to be there until he either won or lost. When it was 1–0, either way, he was there, baby. When it was 5–5, he was *still* there. You had to be ready when you got out of bed.

That's how it is with the great ones.

Aaron

Reggie Jackson

When we went to Shibe Park we'd go stand around where the players came out, but we weren't allowed to speak to them. As a black kid, you weren't supposed to be noticed. That's how it was in those days. And that was okay. It was enough for me just to *see* those guys.

We'd watch Jackie Robinson walk by and get on the bus with Duke Snider, Clem Labine, Carl Erskine, Don Newcombe, Junior Gilliam, and Roy Campanella. But my most vivid memory is the Braves coming out one night. I'll never forget seeing Hank Aaron wearing black slacks, a black turtleneck, and a houndstooth black and white sport coat. I'm sure Mathews, Spahn, Adcock, and all those guys were there. Lew Burdette, Bob Buhl, Del Crandall, Johnny Logan. But all I remember is Hank Aaron and Billy Bruton, a center fielder who was about my complexion.

I was just amazed. Right there, Hammerin' Hank Aaron. He was the first major-league baseball player I'd ever seen up close.

Bob Gibson

I have to say I was never quite that enthused about seeing Hank Aaron. In fact, there was probably no player in the National League who enthused me less.

That man did not miss a fastball.

Reggie Jackson

In Oakland I wore number nine, but when I came over to the Yankees that number was already taken by Graig Nettles. So I chose forty-four because of my admiration for Willie McCovey and Hank Aaron. I was also aware that Jim Brown and Ernie Davis had worn forty-four at Syracuse. Great number.

Bob Gibson

Aaron hit more home runs against me than anybody but Billy Williams, and McCovey was only one behind him. Reggie chose well.

But they were different types of hitters. McCovey was a fly-ball hitter and Aaron wasn't. When he got to Atlanta, where the ball carried so well, Aaron began to lift and pull it more, but I thought he was a better hitter as a young player in Milwaukee, when he was swinging downward and smoking line drives all over the park. You know, he was a two-time batting champion in Milwaukee, and he might have made a run at four thousand hits if he'd stayed there. Either way, he was such a great fastball hitter that I threw him a lot of breaking balls, a lot of sliders.

The worst pitch in baseball is the changeup slider, but I'd throw Aaron that changeup slider and he'd be out on that front foot and hit rockets, two hops to the shortstop. All of our short-stops took balls in the chest off the bat of Aaron. They'd go, "Goddamn, Gibby!"

I'd say, "Hey, this is the way I get him out. He's gonna knock you over, so be ready for it."

Reggie Jackson

Nobody had quicker hands than Aaron. He was a unique hit-ter and a unique player. Hank was so low-key and unassuming that he had about six hundred home runs before most people real-ized what he was all about. I'm *still* not sure they understand.

Frank Robinson was a guy who would drive himself, slide hard, take pitches on the elbow, and fight the third baseman for tagging him out. Aaron wasn't like that on the outside.

The inside was another story. Henry Aaron had the calmness of a cobra. Don't mess with him! He'll fool you, for sure.

That man was quiet death with a bat at home plate.

McCovey

Bob Gibson

I think I've made it pretty clear how I felt about opponents hitting home runs. I wanted no part of it. That's why, to me, Willie McCovey was the scariest hitter in baseball.

He hit seven against me, and that was more than enough to make me wary of him, but don't forget that for every game I pitched there were four more that I watched. And I always made it a point to pay attention when McCovey took his turn, just in case some other pitcher figured out something that I hadn't thought of. That didn't mean you could do the same thing, but it was worth taking a peek.

I was watching in St. Louis one night when McCovey hit a shot against Al Jackson that I'll never forget. It was a hanging breaking ball. Usually his home runs stayed up in the air because of that long, arcing swing of his, but this one was a line drive to the upper deck and over the scoreboard. It hit a façade out there and bounced back onto the field. I'd never seen anything like it. We were sitting in the dugout talking, keeping an eye on Stretch—that's what everybody called him—and all of a sudden there was stone silence. Then we all stood up to see. The only other ball I ever saw hit that even resembled that one was a home run Duke Snider hit in the old ballpark in St. Louis. That one hit off the clock on top of the stands in right field. It had to be five hundred feet. But the one McCovey hit had to be five-fifty, maybe six hundred. They didn't measure them in those days, and Mickey Mantle always got credit for the longest home run at 565 feet, but I have to believe that this one was right there with it.

Reggie Jackson

I was playing center field in 1969 when McCovey hit two home runs in the All-Star Game in Washington, D.C. One of them smashed against that cement block wall in center field where the clock was. They interviewed Stretch after the game and asked him if it was the hardest ball he ever hit. He had that thick, Mobile, Alabama, accent—he and Aaron were both from Mobile—and he said, "I don't know . . . But I hit it pretty good."

Stretch was a little calmer than Willie Mays and didn't attract attention in the same way, but it was a mistake to underestimate him. Ask any pitcher from that era—Seaver, Jenkins, Gibson, Perry, whoever—and he'll tell you the most feared hitter in the game wasn't Mays or Clemente or Aaron; it was Willie "Stretch" McCovey.

If you didn't pitch him accordingly, you'd be getting a new baseball from the umpire.

Bob Gibson

That was not a mistake I was likely to make. To me, McCovey was the ultimate power hitter. The trouble was, the Giants had a ridiculous batting order with him and Mays and Cepeda and Jim Ray Hart and Felipe Alou. Even their catcher, Tom Haller, had four home runs off of me. It wasn't a lineup that allowed you to pitch around somebody very easily.

But none of the others put the fear in me that McCovey did. Not even Mays. He was right-handed.

Reggie Jackson

Since McCovey and I were never in the same league, except for a few weeks he spent with Oakland in 1976, his impact on me was mostly social. The time I spent in Arizona with him, Fergie, and Billy Williams—another great player from Mobile—meant the world to me. As a young, ambitious, wide-eyed African-American, that experience just embraced me in a way that made me feel like I was part of something special.

Each guy took his turn buying dinner. At the time, I was making about twenty grand and those guys were all making a hundred, so I didn't have to pay very often. But that wasn't the best part. The best part was what I picked up by just being there. It brought about a comfort level with who I was. Before long, I became known as one of the first black guys who really spoke frankly about what he thought and experienced. A lot of that came from the poise and confidence I'd gained by being with those guys.

They were men who had already done what I was earnestly setting out to do. They sensed that about me, and they provided me with an understanding of the dynamics, politics, and challenges of big-time baseball. They made me better able to manage myself—my angst, in particular. They'd gotten through it, and they showed me *how* they got through it. They helped me understand the signage when I traveled down the road. Thank you, my friends!

They talked about being careful not to stay out too late, how one hour after one o'clock is worth two hours before. I soon figured out that it meant you should go to bed at eleven. And if you're not with somebody before twelve, you're probably not going to be with her *after* twelve.

You can't drink, smoke, and chase women. You can do one and get by. Two will shorten your career. Three will end it.

That's what I learned from those men. My guys!

Bob Gibson

My mentor with the Cardinals was George Crowe, a part-time first baseman who once hit thirty-one homers for the Reds. He was older, wiser, had been around the league, and he kind of took me under his arm. He also let me use his Jeep. In fact, we called him Jeep. He was more like a dad and a teacher than a teammate, and most of what he counseled me on had nothing to do with playing the game.

George didn't make it to the major leagues until he was twenty-nine, and by the time I started to have some success he was finished. But he helped me make it through those first couple years when Solly Hemus was our manager. Thank God for Jeep.

Reggie Jackson

One night, in 1974, it was my turn to drive and I picked up McCovey for dinner. We were going to a place in Phoenix called the Fig Tree to meet Billy and Fergie. Well, I'd won the MVP Award in 1973 and a guy had given me a T-top Pontiac. It was raining when I picked up Stretch, and the Pontiac was leaking—leaking on *his* side. After a little while of that, Stretch turned and said to me, real slow, "Man, Reggie, this thing is no *star's* car."

You don't think *that* made an impression? To this day, I laugh when I think about it.

I love Stretch.

Mays

Reggie Jackson

My teammates, and only my teammates, called me Buck. They knew how I felt about Willie Mays, and that's what Willie's teammates called *him.* Chuck Dobson, a pitcher for the A's and a good friend, pinned that on me. I appreciated it.

More than anybody else, Willie Mays is the guy who got me jacked up about playing baseball when I was a kid. I was a fan who became a player, and a player who wanted to be Willie Mays. My goodness, what a player. Willie was one of the greatest hitters in the history of the game, and he could go oh-for-four and still beat you.

Bob Gibson

If I had to pick one position where I'd want my best glove, it would be center field. Curt Flood was my man out there. And maybe the best compliment I can give Curt is to say that he could play center field almost as well as Willie Mays.

Aaron may have been a better hitter, but in the outfield nobody was quite like Willie. A guy like Jim Edmonds is really good, but with Willie you knew what you were getting every day—except that, on some days, he would make plays you couldn't believe.

Reggie Jackson

One of the best things about the Cactus League was that we played the Giants and I got to see Willie Mays. It was like watching Michael Jordan. I'd stop following the game sometimes and just study Willie.

He could put on a show just by arriving. For a one-o'clock road game in Mesa, Willie would drive in about quarter to one. He had a big Imperial that Chrysler gave him, and he'd pull up by the right-field line, jog out onto the grass, and get loosened up a little. He'd warm up throwing underhanded in that signature style of his. I couldn't take my eyes off him. We'd start, he'd bat twice, hit two line drives, then he'd be gone. The game wouldn't be the same after that. Time to go get popcorn.

Bob Gibson

Mays didn't hurt me as much as Aaron did, as long as I didn't make a mistake or throw him a breaking ball. He had a skittish left leg. I'd come in on him and he'd spin out and go flying, and the ball would just miss the plate a few inches. He'd act like I was trying to kill him. So after doing that a time or two, I'd just throw him fastballs down and away.

Where Willie hurt me was in the field. Since the Cardinals didn't hit many home runs, we expected to at least put some balls in the gaps. With Willie out there, that was asking a lot. There was plenty of substance along with that style.

Reggie Jackson

There's no style without substance.

There was also a lot of substance to Willie's personality. With Mays, Henry, and Stretch, there's a sensitivity that's still in them. Ernie Banks was a different type. Ernie would make light of

216

things to the extent that you'd never hear him talk seriously. A lot of people looked at him as insincere, a glad-hander; but I think that was simply Ernie's way of masking his disappointment or anger, his way of handling the second-class-citizen sociology that came with being a minority. I know it bothered him. It affected him. His way of coping was just different than my way or Gibson's way or McCovey's or Aaron's or Robinson's or Mays's.

They all had their own styles. Mays's style was just a little flashier than the others'. Willie made you look.

He was everything a young black kid could hope to be one day.

Robinson

Reggie Jackson

If Willie Mays was the Michael Jordan of baseball, Frank Robinson was the Bill Russell. Fierce. Intimidating. Intelligent. A ballplayer's ballplayer. A winner through and through. It was like having Gibson on the field seven days a week.

Frank became a mentor to me when I played for him in Santurce, Puerto Rico, in 1970. I'd had a bad year with the A's, only twenty-three home runs and sixty-six RBIs. It affected me. I was disgusted with myself, and showed my frustration in ways that were counterproductive. I had temper issues. I threw things. I broke things. Frank watched a little of that, then put his hand on my shoulder and said, "Take it easy for a second, would you? Get your mind in the game. What, don't you think you're going to strike out now and then? You don't think you're going to make outs? You don't think you're ever going to look foolish at the plate? Don't forget, you only need one strike to hit. But you can't hit when you're angry. If you try to, you're wasting your time up there. Be in control of your at-bat. Give your talent a chance. Don't get in your own way!"

He said, "You should be a leader, Reggie. You can't lead the way you're acting. You're a star, you get a lot of attention, and guys are going to want to follow you. If they follow you the way you're acting, it'll be all wrong. You'll be taking them down the wrong path."

When Frank Robinson spoke to me, I listened. He changed my thought process. He helped me mature and get rid of the young, dumb behavior that I was prone to. He made me understand that I wasn't perfect and couldn't be. He worked with me to develop some patience in my approach to the game. He coached me on how to control my temper and channel my emotion into something valuable. How to manage myself on the field. How to hustle without overhustling. How to be a professional. How to go about *winning*.

It might not have meant as much if I'd heard the same things from Mickey Mantle or Al Kaline or even my old hero, Duke Snider. I respected those guys, too, but their experience and history didn't resonate with me as much as Frank's did, or Gibby's, or Stretch's. The black stars had dealt with a special kind of anger and angst. They understood oppression. They were relevant to me. I listened to them with a sense of veneration.

Bob Gibson

Frank Robinson might have been the best I ever saw at turning his anger into runs. He challenged you physically as soon as he stepped into the batter's box, with half his body hanging over home plate.

His fearlessness played a tremendous part in making him the hitter he was. He practically dared you to clip him or knock him down, and when you did, he'd use it as intensity. He seemed to gain strength from it. If you couldn't drive him off the plate—and you couldn't—then you couldn't take away his outside corner. Frank Robinson refused to be bullied when he batted. *He* was the bully.

As a rule, I'm reluctant to express admiration for hitters; but I make an exception for Frank Robinson.

Reggie Jackson

A lot of people remember the home run I hit into the light tower at Tiger Stadium in the 1971 All-Star Game. I was pinch-hitting for Vida Blue in the third inning, with a runner on, and we were down 3–0 at the time. Dock Ellis was pitching—this was five years prior to when he hit me in the face—and he served me a high slider on a three-one count. Al Kaline, who played his whole career in Detroit, called it the longest home run he'd ever seen. As Willie McCovey would say, "I hit it pretty good."

But that alone was not what made the occasion special for me. What topped it off was that Frank Robinson was hitting cleanup for the American League and later in the same inning he hit a two-run homer that put us ahead for good. That made him the MVP of the game. Afterwards, when all the writers were asking me about the home run, I was able to dedicate it to Frank. This was the season right after he'd managed me in Puerto Rico, and it meant everything to be able to share the moment with the player I most respected. We also shared the awards. Plymouth gave me a four-speed Barracuda 440.

I'm indebted to Frank Robinson. Following the 1973 season, when baseball's arbitration process was initiated, I was involved in heavy salary negotiations with Charlie Finley. I'd just won the American League MVP Award, which certainly worked in my favor, but Charlie despised parting with his nickels. It wasn't a pleasant experience. The tipping point might well have been a telegram from Frank that called me the best player in the league. I came away with a $60,000 raise that nearly doubled my salary.

Talk about owing a guy.

Allen

Reggie Jackson

When Dick Allen—he was Richie then—was playing with the Phillies, people seemed to think it was a terrible thing that he wore a mustache. Well, my *father* wore a mustache. I thought Richie Allen was pretty cool

And he was. He never lost that cool over anything. He'd show up twenty minutes before a ballgame, no problem, stroll to the plate with that big forty-two-ounce club of his, and just whale on the ball. He'd smoke in the dugout. He'd skip spring training. That kind of stuff wouldn't work for most guys, but it worked for Dick Allen. He had so much ability that you had to admire him.

He was my favorite Phillie. And he was a great guy, to boot.

Bob Gibson

He was a good teammate. Especially on the Cardinals. I'd never played with a guy who could hit home runs and deliver on command like Dick Allen.

It'd be 1–0 or 2–1 and we'd get to the sixth or seventh inning and Dick, who didn't say much, would come over and tell me real quietly, "Don't worry about it. I'll get him." Then, often as not, he'd go up there and, bop, home run. We only had him in 1970, but in that season alone he must have handed me five ballgames. It started on Opening Day against Montreal, when he hit a homer to tie the game in the eighth inning and we won it in the ninth. In May, I was scuffling and really needed a victory, and he beat his old team with two home runs against Jim Bunning. In August— I don't know if I should thank him for this one or not—he homered to tie a game against San Diego in the eighth inning and I had to pitch all the way through the fourteenth before we finally pulled it out. I wish we'd have had three or four Dick Allens.

Reggie Jackson

No, he didn't say much. And he let me know that, in his opinion, I said way *too* much. Dick told me to speak with my bat, not my mouth. Actually, he just pointed to his mouth and told me not to use that. Then he pointed to my bat and told me to use *that*. He was practicing what he preached, I guess.

He told me not to promote myself so much, and also not to complain about a called strike. He said, "I don't ever want to see you arguing with an umpire. If you need more than one strike to hit, I don't want to know you."

At one point, Dick said something to a *Sports Illustrated* writer that I took exception to at the time. He said, "I look in the record book and I see Reggie has never hit .300. And I wonder how he can do all that talking." But it was consistent with what he always told me to my face.

He also enlightened me quite a bit about the art of hitting. We had long, rambling discussions about hitting. That was a subject he knew a whole lot about.

Bob Gibson

He could hit a ball so incredibly hard that it was easy to look at Dick as just a raw, natural talent at the plate, and a lot of people did. But I can assure you that the man was a thinker up there. He certainly outfoxed me a time or two. It was always a duel with Dick, because he'd remember something you threw him three months before. Of course, I remembered, too. That's what made it interesting.

Reggie Jackson

Dick Allen was a special mix of talent, brains, and style. That's why he appealed to me so much. He was the kind of player you just found yourself watching.

I borrowed part of my home-run routine from Dick. People claimed that I started the business of admiring your home runs and styling around the bases, but that's not true. I actually got my inspiration from Harmon Killebrew. Harmon couldn't run a bit, but I liked the way he stood at the plate for just a brief moment, taking in what he'd done. He always knew when the ball was gone. He'd wait for it to come down and then take one or two walking steps out of the batter's box. He also had a nifty little flip of the bat that made it turn over once and land real nicely on the ground. His trot was slow and easy.

I didn't do *all* of that. I copied the parts where he watched the ball for a second and flipped the bat, but then I *ran* the bases. I ran fast. And when I got home, that last part is what I took from Dick Allen. He walked the last four or five steps. I wasn't quite that showy. I walked the last two or three. Then I touched the corner of the plate and peeled off.

I also grew a mustache.

Koufax

Bob Gibson

I prided myself on being a workhorse, but nobody pulled a load like Sandy Koufax in his prime. That could be why his prime only lasted about four years and he had to retire at the age of thirty after going 27–9 with a 1.73 earned run average. In his last year, 1966, he led the National League with 323 innings. The year before, he led the league with 335. No wonder he couldn't lift his arm to brush his teeth.

His teammate, Don Drysdale, put in almost as many innings, because the Dodgers used their starting pitchers on a four-day rotation. The Cardinals went with five days. The way it worked out, I usually ended up facing one or the other. Marichal would usually get shifted to another day when we played the Giants, so I stopped seeing him, but it seemed like I always lined up against Jenkins and Seaver, too. Red Schoendienst was our manager, and I could never figure out why he would do that. I asked him, "Red, why don't you manipulate it so I don't have to pitch against those guys and we'd make sure we win that ballgame?"

He said, "Oh no. You beat them, and we could sweep the series."

I said, "I lose, and we could *lose* the series."

Koufax was the worst guy to pitch against. It seemed like he could have shut us out *right*-handed. Whenever it was his turn, our guys would sit in the clubhouse before the game going, "Man, this is going to be a tough day." We were intimidated before he even stepped on the mound.

Part of it was his reputation. Part was his fastball. And part was his curveball.

Reggie Jackson

My first year in the major leagues was his first year out of the game, but I heard plenty about him from the guys I hung out with in spring training. Koufax was a guy whose name always came up.

In 1971, Vida Blue became a sensation for us at the age of twenty-one, a left-hander with electric stuff. He pitched twenty-four complete games that year and struck out over three hundred batters. There was a game against the Angels in Oakland when he went eleven innings and struck out seventeen. Meanwhile, Rudy May went twelve innings for the Angels and struck out thirteen. In all that time, neither team scored. We finally won, 1–0, in twenty innings. Anyway, Vida struck out one of their outfielders, Billy Cowan, five straight times. Cowan had played in the National League for several years, and it so happened that a few weeks earlier somebody had asked him to compare Vida Blue with Sandy Koufax. He had said, "He ain't no Sandy Koufax."

Vida must have remembered that.

Bob Gibson

Vida Blue actually threw harder than Sandy. Koufax had a light fastball that would, whoosh, sail up on you. But his curve was just devastating.

We only had two guys who could touch him, and they were two of the unlikeliest—Gene Oliver and Bob Uecker. Most of Uecker's hits against him came in one season, but even so, it was astonishing enough to stick in my memory. Oliver just wore him out, and none of us could understand why or how. Gene was a big catcher who hit just about every batting-practice pitch out of the park—a great BP hitter—and that was about it. Except when Sandy Koufax was out there.

Otherwise, we were helpless against Koufax—until Brock figured out in 1965 that he could bunt on him. Once he was on first base he could run on him, too, because Sandy didn't have a pick-off move; he had to either pitch to the plate or step off and throw to first. One game, Brock bunted twice for hits and both times stole second and third. Koufax was a gentleman, and it wasn't easy to get him riled. Drysdale and Stan Williams were the ones who did most of the dirty work for the Dodgers. But leave it to Brock. The next time he came to bat, Sandy hit him in the back of the shoulder and cracked it.

Fortunately, I wasn't pitching that day. If I'd been pitching, I'd have had to wait for Koufax to come up and he'd have gotten it. Usually, when Brock made somebody mad enough to hit him, I'd just knock down the first guy I saw, because you couldn't be sure that the pitcher would still be around by the time his next turn at bat came up. But *that* particular pitcher would have been around.

It would have been my chance to do what nobody else on the club seemed to be able to—hit Sandy Koufax.

Other Notables

Bob Gibson

I did, however, put a ball in the back of his first baseman, Ron Fairly. He was the guy on the Dodgers who killed me. My goodness, that man must have had six thousand hits off of me. Actually, it was forty-eight, but that was even more than Billy Williams. He'd punch the ball over the shortstop's head and you couldn't strike him out. I tried to pitch him in, like I did a lot of left-handed hitters, and I didn't have any luck with that. I'd pitch him away, make a good pitch, and he'd dump it over the shortstop's head.

One day he had already poked a ball or two over the shortstop's head and I got a base hit, and when I was standing at first he said to me, "Goddamn, Gibby, you've got such good stuff, I don't know how anybody could ever hit you." I didn't say a word. Fairly was a schmoozer and he'd probably be a great guy at a party just to sit and talk to, but I sure didn't feel like shooting the breeze with him at first base after he had dumped another ball over the shortstop's head. I didn't want to hear it. Get your base hits and shut up. Joe Torre was catching for us, and when Fairly came up to the plate the next time he turned to Joe and said, "I'm not going to like this at-bat, am I?" Smoked him right in the middle of the back. Get your damn hits and leave me alone. I couldn't get him out and he says he doesn't know how anybody ever hits me. Hit *this*.

Reggie Jackson

My Ron Fairly was Dave Stieb, with that slider boring in on my hands. By the time he came into the league I was a veteran, and I'd learned to lay off the inside pitch from just about everybody but him. He was a right-handed power pitcher, which should have been right up my alley; but I went to bat fifty-five times against Dave Stieb and never had an RBI. He walked me a lot, probably because he wasn't giving me anything to hit. Not a thing.

The other guy who tore me up was Tommy John, whom you might expect because he was left-handed and could put the ball wherever he wanted it. He approached me differently than Stieb; he seldom walked me. But his control was so good in the strike zone that I just couldn't square the ball against him. I batted sixty-nine times against Tommy—in the regular season, that is—and never had an extra-base hit.

With that bias, I'd like to see Tommy in the Hall of Fame. He won 288 games and lasted twenty-six years in spite of revolutionary elbow surgery smack in the middle of his career. He actually had two careers—one before the surgery and another after. My other bias on his behalf comes from having played behind him in New York and California. You could learn about the game just by watching Tommy John pitch. He has more wins than any eligible pitcher who's not in the Hall, and more than a lot who *are*.

For that matter, Bert Blyleven has only one fewer. As I see it, Blyleven's numbers should put him in Cooperstown. He had enough stuff, wins, and strikeouts that I call him a Hall of Famer. That said, I don't think he was quite the pitcher that Jack Morris was. Morris was one of the great pitchers of his era, and he was a winner, as well. During the time I played against him, he was very close to being the best pitcher in the American League.

Bob Gibson

Jim Kaat ought to be in there, too. He doesn't have any elbow surgery named for him, but his career was a lot like Tommy John's. Twenty-five years, 283 victories.

Reggie Jackson

Kaat had something else in common with Tommy, and I'm not talking about being a crafty left-hander. He was two different pitchers. When he was young, he threw hard. After he hurt his arm a couple times, he became a magician. He stood funny on the mound, had an awkward motion, and he turned the element of surprise into an art. He'd quick-pitch, he'd sink the ball, he'd throw slop, he'd change speeds—anything to trick a batter and goad him into a mistake. He was also one of the best-fielding pitchers of all time.

Bob Gibson

Tony Oliva could be in the Hall of Fame very easily. Curt Flood could be in there, and not because of his contribution to the players' union. He was nearly a .300 hitter and second only to Mays in center field. I'm prejudiced, no doubt, because Flood was one of my favorite people in baseball and he saved a lot of games for me, but I saw day after day what a great player he was.

Ron Santo is another guy who deserves to be in. He's like a lot of good ballplayers who don't get elected because they never made it to the World Series. I appreciate the fact that a lot of the reputation I enjoy came from the World Series. Same with Reggie.

Santo was like Mays in the way that he was kind of skittish on balls that came in too close. That's why I didn't have much trouble with him, although he didn't remember it that way. I'd been doing some radio interviews at Randy Hundley's fantasy camp, and somebody had evidently heard me say that Santo could never hit me. Santo got wind of it, and later that day he ran up to me and said, "Hey, I heard about that comment you made on the radio. I used to hit you pretty good!"

I said, "Really? I want you to check, and the next time I see you I want you to let me know what you found out."

A few days after that, he got up to make a speech and he said, "You know, it's nice to be here, seeing guys that I used to play against—guys like Gibson. You know, I didn't hit him very well." Evidently, he checked.

Not that my memory is infallible. Torre told me that he'd hit a home run against me and I told him he was full of it. So he found an old newspaper clip and sent it to me. He actually hit two. Joe could hit. He couldn't *run,* but he could hit. He was with us in 1971 when he led the league in hitting at .363, with 230 hits. To hit .363 with his speed is an amazing accomplishment.

Reggie Jackson

Joe's close to a Hall of Famer as a player, but surely he'll get in as a manager. I just hope he doesn't keep hurting his image, which could have an effect with the voters.

Bob Gibson

Pete Rose, on the other hand, will *not* get in as a manager, and it's looking like he won't get in at all—at least in the foreseeable future. Good ballplayer? Yeah. Whole bunch of hits? Yeah. Do I care whether he gets into the Hall of Fame? No. He violated a sacred rule.

But I'll admit it's a tough call on where to draw the line. Between gambling and steroids and spitballs and the policies of the game and the laws of the nation, there are a lot of gray areas. I don't pretend to have all the answers.

What I *do* know is that Rose was basically a singles hitter. I didn't lose much sleep over singles hitters.

CHAPTER TEN

MAKEUP

Pride

Bob Gibson

When I was growing up, my brother Josh would rent a big van and carry our little neighborhood team to small towns in Nebraska and Iowa, where the people would make fun of us. Bear in mind, this was the late 1940s. I'm sure we were a sight to those country folks, all these skinny black kids crowded into that van just having a ball.

I was always on my best behavior in those places, because I didn't want anybody laughing at me. One particular time—I must have been twelve or thirteen—we pulled up to this town square somewhere in Iowa and they had watermelon for everybody. I'm sure they got a big kick out of seeing us tear into that watermelon, and I wanted some in the worst way. But I wouldn't eat it, because we had to sit there on the curb before we went to the ballgame and I refused to have people riding by laughing at me. I guess my pride just took over.

When you're going along in your career, trying to make your mark, trying to win ballgames and take care of business, you don't think a lot about what it is that drives you. You don't do a lot of self-analysis. At least I didn't. But when I look back at times like that, I can see that the pride was there from the beginning. I'm sure that that pride had a lot to do with the makeup I took to the big leagues. Inside, I was the same person at a hundred and ninety-five pounds in St. Louis that I was at ninety-five in Omaha.

Reggie Jackson

A reporter once asked me what sets apart the great player, the Hall of Famer, from everybody else. I said it was pride. Pride is what makes a man believe that he's the best at what he does. It's what makes him confident, makes him intense; what makes him great.

Pride is the *will* to succeed. That's what sets the great player apart.

Bob Gibson

Well, you can have all the pride in the world, but if you don't have the talent to go with it, it doesn't matter much. Just the pride itself is not going to make you successful.

Reggie Jackson

But it's what you start with. You can be a great ballplayer without a rifle arm or blazing speed, but you can't be a great player without a tremendous amount of will.

Think about Robinson, Aaron, Gibson, Palmer, Seaver, Mays, Banks, Rose, Munson, Ripken, Brett, Gwynn, Clemens, Maddux, Jeter, A-Rod, Pujols, Bonds . . . Those guys are the embodiments of determination, which grows out of pride. You can sense the greatness when they walk onto the field. You can see the pride. The will to succeed oozes out of them.

Think about *Jackie* Robinson. About the legacy of pride that he left behind.

Bob Gibson

In our day, if you succeeded as a black player there was a certain pride that went along with it, because, first off, you needed it just to endure; but also because you knew you had to be *better* to get there. Sometimes even that wasn't good enough.

When I was a senior at Omaha Tech High School, our coach started five black players in the state semifinal basketball game. The other team was small and scrappy and had to stall to keep the game close. Somehow, four of our starters fouled out in the first half, and I followed them a few minutes into the second half. And this was in a slowdown game! We lost by a point, and afterwards I cried. It affected me. It taught me something about our society. It hardened me.

When I got to college, it became clear to me that I could not get where I wanted to go by being average. I was the first black player on Creighton's baseball *and* basketball teams, and I understood that, if I wanted to win a position and be treated as an equal, I had to be better than the other guys.

All the black players from my generation came to feel the same way, no matter where they were from.

Reggie Jackson

I was *told* by my father that I needed to clearly outdistance the field. Don't let it be a photo finish. You're black, so you're not going to have the same opportunities. You must clearly be better than whites. Let there be no dispute on that point.

My dad also told me, "If you don't make the first team, son, you can't sit on the bench; you've got to come home and work. You've got to help around the house. There'll be no sitting on the bench. There's nothing going on there. You need to be on the first team." That wasn't pressure; that was life. My father, whose heritage was Latin American, white, black, and who knows what else—and I'm proud of all of it!—ran his own tailoring and laundry business. He worked all day and bought groceries on the way home. There was nothing in the refrigerator. I'd go over to my white friends' houses and they'd have milk waiting for them on the porch in the morning, delivered right to the front step. You'd go in the garage and they'd have a case of Coke sitting out there in a wooden box with "Coca-Cola" written on the side. Man, that was living!

The part that made me angry was that my father worked so much harder than my friends' fathers and had so much less to show for it. It made me hungry to reap the rewards of my labors. My dad propelled me toward *doing* something with my life, trying to excel, making something of myself. He'd been a ballplayer—he played some with the Newark Eagles of the old Negro Leagues— and he saw sports, either football or baseball, as my opportunity.

If I had to play ball better than the white boys, I accepted that part of it. I could handle that. There was plenty of other stuff to be angry about.

Bob Gibson

I wasn't on a mission to prove anything on behalf of the black player. I was on a mission for *me*. I had to prove that *I* was better.

In some ways—if you could get through the doors—the realities worked to the benefit of the black players. It wasn't hard to motivate yourself for what you had to do. I was at Creighton because Indiana University told me they'd already met their quota. They had to have one black guy on the team. I watched them play and just shook my head. I knew they had the wrong one, and I had some interest in proving that.

Reggie Jackson

Out of high school, I had more football offers than baseball. I might have been one of the few black players at Oklahoma, but the deal was that I had to be in by ten o'clock at night. If you were black, they wanted you off the streets for the sake of safety. I could have gone to Duke or a few other Southern schools, but I was afraid to take that step.

In 1967, before I came up with the A's, I was playing in Birmingham, and Bear Bryant's son was the general manager there. Bear was a close friend of Charlie Finley, and he came to a lot of our games. One night he walked into the clubhouse and was talking to his son and a writer named Alf Van Hoose and a few other people. I had my shirt off. I weighed about 205 pounds and could run like a deer in those days. Bear Bryant put his arm around me and said, "You know, this is just the kind of nigger boy we need down here. If not, we're not going to be able to continue to compete, because Southern California and the teams out west are going to go by us." When he said "nigger boy," it somehow sounded like a compliment. Understanding where I was, I really wasn't offended. It was awkward, but what was I to do? I was barely twenty-one years old. I was in Birmingham, Alabama. Bear Bryant, in his own way, was complimenting me.

Bob Gibson

That wouldn't have worked with me.

Reggie Jackson

It hurt when I heard it, but I knew he didn't mean it as a slight. It was just the way it was in 1967. Sad!

Even in baseball, even back east, blacks weren't yet on equal footing. In 1965, after my freshman year at Arizona State, I tried out for Walter Youse's famous amateur team in Baltimore. Walter was a legend in amateur baseball. He also scouted for the Orioles, and ultimately rated me higher than any other prospect he ever looked at. But when I tried out for Leone's, he'd never had a black player on the team. A long time after that, Walter told me, kiddingly, that the more he saw of me that day of the tryout, the whiter I got.

When I was eligible for the draft in 1966, there was a lot of talk that I would be the first player chosen in the country. Then, when the draft was close, our coach at ASU, Bobby Winkles, called me into his office to tell me that it wasn't going to happen that way, even though it *should*. I didn't understand. He said it was because the Mets, who had the first pick, found out I was dating a white girl—actually, she was Mexican—and thought it might cause problems in baseball and society. So they drafted

Steve Chilcott with the first pick. Charlie Finley's A's took me next and sent me to Lewiston, Idaho.

While I was in Lewiston, I got beaned. The local hospital refused to admit me. The next day I was in Modesto, California, and the next year it was Birmingham, where I slept on couches. Dave Duncan, Joe Rudi, and Rollie Fingers were all married, and I rotated between their apartments. Those guys really stuck up for me.

You deal with those things, and you get over them, but you don't forget them. It all becomes part of your makeup. I'll remember Duncan, Rudi, and Fingers for the rest of my life, and not just as ballplayers.

Bob Gibson

Over the years, a lot of black athletes have been characterized as playing with a chip on their shoulder. Well, a chip is usually put there by somebody else. It's put there by the way you're treated.

Reggie Jackson

My chip on the shoulder, which some people might have viewed as being terse or having an attitude, came from how you approached me, or my interpretation of how society was treating me. When I was young, it came out as anger. I was from a broken home. My father was a man I greatly admired, and he was incarcerated when I was a junior in high school for driving on a suspended license. My mother was living in Baltimore. I was at home with my brother, James. My upbringing was odd.

I missed my father and I was angry that he couldn't be with us, couldn't provide for us. I got suspended twice from school. I was mean. It made me a tough and nasty football player, but it didn't help me in anything else. I once threw a guy up against a wall and threatened to kill him for eating a couple of my pretzels. I had a '55 Chevy and would sit in a church parking lot with my buddies, who also had '55 Chevies, and we'd drink a beer, then go crash a party, strong-arm the rich kids, and take their coats. Then wear the coats to school. The rich kids didn't say anything, because we'd beat them up if they did. My girlfriend was white, and they used to tease her about how crazy I was. Her father didn't like me because I was black, so I'd send a friend over to pick her up.

Bob Gibson

And people say *I* was mean. Damn.

Reggie Jackson

Everybody's a product of their experience. I was bitter about mine. When I was little, I was playing ball one day with some friends in a place called Glenside. It was about two miles from our house in Wyncote, and I needed to be home on time for dinner, so my buddy loaned me his bicycle. His mother had married a fireman who was a big fat guy, and as I was riding home he drove up in his '57 yellow Chevrolet convertible with a Continental spare and twin antennas. I was about halfway home at the time. He stopped, made me get off the bicycle and *walk* it back to his house. He said, "I don't want you riding my son's bicycle." Things like that stick with you.

When I was in Little League, maybe eleven years old, I was on an all-star team from Pennsylvania and we were playing a series against an all-star team from Florida, which was kind of a big deal. I was the youngest kid on the team and the best player, but the only black player. I could not play in that series. The reasoning was, if I slid hard into second base or whatever, there might be a fight. So I sat on the bench for the whole five-game series except to pinch-hit at the very end. I never moved the bat off my shoulder. Afterwards, I walked home in my number eighteen Glenside jersey and my shower shoes, with my spikes hanging over my shoulder, crying all the way. I'd go from telephone pole to telephone pole, walking to one and then running to the next one. I don't know why I did that, but I remember it, and I vividly remember what I was saying to myself the whole time. I just repeated, over and over, "I'm gonna be a big-leaguer, I'm gonna be a big-leaguer," for as long as it took me to get home.

Bob Gibson

We all have these stories about things that happened when we were kids, and when we were in school, and when we were in the minor leagues, but it didn't stop there. Reggie makes a good point about pride, because if you didn't have it as a black player, you wouldn't *get* to the big leagues in the first place; and if somehow you did, you wouldn't *last*. You'd be run off by guys like Solly Hemus.

When I came up with the Cardinals in 1959, Hemus let me know, right away, that I wasn't smart enough to be much of a pitcher. In meetings, he'd tell me I didn't have to worry about the scouting reports, that I should just throw the ball over the plate. At one point, he recommended that I quit and go play basketball. Of course, he was also the guy who had Stan Musial playing hit-and-run.

Reggie Jackson

Solly Hemus couldn't play, could he?

Bob Gibson

No. Couldn't manage, couldn't play. And he was a racist.

Reggie Jackson

That's probably what it was.

Bob Gibson

I *know* that's what it was. I was in the dugout, almost standing next to him, when we were playing the Pirates and he was calling their pitcher, Bennie Daniels, a black bastard. It was all I could do to restrain myself. But what can you do? You hit him, and you're out of baseball. So I had to take it. I had to swallow it. I was twenty-three years old. If he'd called *me* that, I probably *would* have been out of baseball. I see Hemus from time to time, and after fifty years he has never told me he was sorry about that incident or any other.

Reggie Jackson

When I got to New York in 1977, Billy Martin would *not* hit me cleanup. For the record, I ultimately batted fourth for *nine* different division champions; but it didn't happen in New York until Munson and Lou Piniella went to Billy in August of 1977 and said, "You need to put that man at cleanup."

Bob Gibson

What was his reason for that?

Reggie Jackson

I can only say what I believe it to be. He came from the days of Mickey Mantle and Yogi Berra, and he didn't want to give me the honor of hitting cleanup for the New York Yankees. The Yankees were Ruth, Gehrig, DiMaggio, and his friends Mickey and Whitey Ford.

After Munson and Piniella went to him in August, when we were struggling, I started hitting cleanup and we won thirty-nine of the next forty-nine games. Within two weeks, we had overtaken the Orioles and Red Sox and were on our way to winning the American League East. And ultimately, the World Series.

Bob Gibson

When you start putting money in their pockets like that, people tend to change their opinions of you.

Reggie Jackson

That was the hardest year of my life, and it wasn't just Billy Martin's doing. For a long period, I had a tough time fitting in with my teammates. I had signed for a lot of money, had called a lot of attention to myself, and they considered me an uppity you-know-what. I was an outsider on my own team, and it sent me into a horrible funk. I was miserable. I wasn't the kind of guy who could not care what anybody thought. I cared a lot.

In the end, it was pride and support from friends and family that pulled me out of it—along with my prayerful thoughts of God.

Bob Gibson

That's all well and good, but if you'd have put that pride inside of Mickey Rivers, the result would not have been four straight home runs in the World Series.

Confidence

Bob Gibson

Ted Simmons, who was one of my catchers, said once that the best thing I had going for me as a pitcher was the force of my personality—the will to win, I guess—and that you can't separate the physical from the emotional. That's probably right.

To get to the top in baseball, and most other things, you've got to have that tenacity, that win-at-all-costs mentality, to go along with the ability. They go hand in hand. In my case, I think that was just my makeup. Tell me I can't do it, I'm gonna do it.

Reggie would call it pride. Yeah, there's a lot of that. But for me, it all comes back to confidence. Confidence gives you courage, and courage gives you encouragement.

I had the courage to work a corner because I was confident I wouldn't miss it by too much in the wrong direction. I was encouraged to challenge a good hitter with a high fastball because I was confident that my fastball was better than his bat.

To be a fierce competitor, you need to be fiercely confident.

Reggie Jackson

A lot of people thought I was *too* confident. Another word for that is cocky.

I came up alongside a lot of the players on the A's, and they just shrugged it off when I'd go into a hot-dog mode. They knew they could count on me as a teammate. They knew I was harmless and respectful of them. But I was also respectful of myself.

I wrote an autobiography when I was still with the A's. The first line was "My name is Reggie Jackson and I am the best in baseball." I used to tell my teammates that if I played in New York they'd name a candy bar after me—which they did. (When the Reggie bar came out, Catfish Hunter said that when you unwrap it, it tells you how good it is. I've got to admit—that's a great line.)

In Oakland, we were all free spirits and strong individuals. Maybe more than any other team in baseball history, our A's teams of the seventies proved that players can have their differences socially—they can all express their own personal styles—as long as they have a collective pride in their jobs and are willing to come together every night for nine innings. The A's weren't bothered by my razzmatazz. At the least, they appreciated the fact that I got the reporters out of their faces.

When I arrived in New York, though, the Yankees were already established as the American League champions. It didn't go over so well when I was quoted in *Sport* magazine—rather, misquoted—calling myself "the straw that stirs the drink." I didn't say that. But on the other hand, I didn't hesitate to tell anybody who asked, or anybody who didn't, that I was a star before I got there.

Was that a lie? We had won three World Series in Oakland. Some of my new teammates might not have appreciated me saying it, but I *was* a star before I got to New York. That's why George Steinbrenner gave me the big contract (although $600,000 a year is ashtray change for a good ballplayer nowadays). With free agency, we had finally reached the age when players could go to the highest bidder, and it was in my best interest to market myself. I was out in front with that—and Steinbrenner was smarter than I was to understand that if I marketed myself in New York, I'd be marketing the Yankees at the same time.

So I was confident—cocky, if you must. I was likened to Muhammad Ali in that respect. Ali was cocky because he *knew* how good he was, and he knew that knowing it only made him better. His talent made him confident. I could relate to that.

Cockiness is just confidence worn on the outside. And winking about it.

Bob Gibson

Solly Hemus did all he could to alienate me and destroy my confidence. Fortunately, his replacement, Johnny Keane, did all he could to embrace me and *restore* my confidence. When he took over as manager, Keane called me into his office and said, "Bob, I've think you've got good enough stuff to be one of the best pitchers in baseball. You're going to be out there every five days for me. I don't want you to have to worry about whether you're going to pitch or not going to pitch." Those good vibes turned everything around for me.

Reggie Jackson

Some of the best teammates are the ones who, in their own way, restore your confidence when you're down. I was never down as low as I was that first year with the Yankees, and I had Fran Healy to thank for being an ally. He tried his best to keep my spirits up. That's what being a teammate is all about; and being a friend.

Bob Gibson

Well, Dick Allen didn't give me any pep talks, but I thought he was a pretty good teammate when he drove in 101 runs. I thought Curt Flood was a pretty good teammate when he was tracking down every fly ball hit in the direction of center field. I thought *I* was a pretty good teammate in 1968, when I had that 1.12 earned run average and threw forty-seven straight scoreless innings.

In 1968, I felt I could throw the ball anywhere I wanted anytime I wanted to. If I wanted to be up and in, that's where it was gonna be. The thing I had that year was control, and *confidence* in my control, which led to better control. Confidence feeds the beast. When you're confident as a pitcher, you feel like you can put a ball on a corner without even looking. Bam! There it is. If you want to miss by just a little, you miss by just a little. It's like magic.

Of course, there are other times when you can't get the ball where you want it to save your soul. I don't know that there's an explanation for that. I'm sure that mechanics have something to do with it, but why are your mechanics different from one day to the next, or one inning to the next, or one pitch to the next? The days you've got it going, they describe it as being in a zone. I don't really know what that is.

Maybe it's just a heightened state of confidence.

Reggie Jackson

As important as confidence is, you'd think that players—and managers, for that matter—would work on it more. A lot of it was just my makeup, but I was constantly exercising the confidence muscle.

Writers were surprised when they'd ask me if I'd intended to hit that home run that won the game and I'd say yeah, sure I had. I guess I was supposed to tell them that I was just trying to make good contact and was fortunate that the ball came in where I was looking for it; but I saw no reason to cover up my confidence. When I was in Oakland, I told at least one writer that I was *going* to be great and *wanted* to be the greatest ever. I told another that after Jackie Robinson, I was the most important black player in baseball history.

I guess that was over-the-top, but let me explain what I meant. There were black players before me who spoke their minds when asked, but there weren't many. There weren't any who did it as freely and frankly as I did. I had a reputation for seeking out the media, and it was attributed to self-publicity, but it was more than that. I truly felt that I was raising the profile of the black ballplayer. That's how I got the reputation for speaking out so much.

Bob Gibson

Troublemaker.

Reggie Jackson

Yes, I was sometimes labeled a troublemaker. When a white player would speak out, he'd be described as a coach on the field, or on the floor. When a black player spoke out, he was a troublemaker.

Bob Gibson

I was a troublemaker all my life. I read in the paper just the other day that I was outspoken. You don't say?

A guy like Hank Aaron spoke his mind, ultimately—when he was chasing Babe Ruth's home-run record and had a platform— but for most of his career, Hank was very quiet. It was just his nature. He felt strongly about certain things, particularly when it came to discrimination or racial matters, but he wouldn't make a fuss about it. I was more like Fred Sanford: Hey, man, don't step out of line with me or else we might have to fight. That was my way of dealing with it. I didn't know any other way.

Reggie Jackson

Especially when I got to New York and we were all over the papers every day, I felt very much like a . . . well, I'm reluctant to say celebrity, but a highly visible public figure. That was difficult, and it was crazy, but it was also good in a lot of ways. It was good for the Yankees, it was good for me financially, and for the most part it was good for my ego. What was good for my ego was good for my confidence and good for my game.

I reveled in the attention. I know it sounds a little over-the-top again, but I was proud to be a superstar—a superduperstar, as *Sports Illustrated* once called me.

And then, every so often, I'd be brought back down to earth. A company I worked with in Arizona, headed by my friend Gary Walker, did a lot with the Hopi Indians. I went to their reserva-

tion one year, late in my career—it was way out in the desert—
and spoke to some of the Hopi kids about staying away from
drugs and drink. Alcoholism was a problem there, and I thought
I had a good, strong message for the young people. Then I called
for questions and one of the parents raised his hand. I said, "Yes?"

"Some of the children," he said, "would like to know who you
are."

Hmmm . . . That'll check you! I guess a little humility never
hurt anybody.

Hustle

Reggie Jackson

It's rare that a star player doesn't run out a ball or give his best
effort on the field. They don't know any other way. Think of
Derek Jeter. Think of Albert Pujols. Okay, don't think of Manny
Ramirez, but even Manny can win a game with a hustle play.

How do you say this without a double negative? Great players
do not *not* play hard. They *do not* take it easy, ever. It's the same
thing whether it's Charles Barkley, Jack Nicklaus, Jimmy Brown,
Frank Robinson, or Joe Montana.

I didn't have to *make sure* I played hard. I just did.

Bob Gibson

It's not a plan. It's natural.

Reggie Jackson

In terms of style and stuff, there's a huge difference between
Randy Johnson on the mound and Greg Maddux on the mound.
But the thing they have in common is that you're going to get
everything they have. Just because one of them is only throwing
eighty-eight miles an hour, that doesn't mean he's not pouring it
all out there. Greg Maddux is giving you not only all of his arm,
but all of his legs, all of his heart, and all of his brain. When they
say a guy "leaves it all out there," that's the definition.

Bob Gibson

There were some days when I wasn't very good, even to the point where I got booed. But that didn't mean I gave less than everything I had on that particular day. I don't know that there was ever, *ever,* a day that I went out there and didn't give it every single thing I had.

When you play hard every time out, you don't have a problem gaining the respect of the guys in the clubhouse or the writers who follow the team. I made sure I covered that base. Nobody could ever leave the park saying that I jaked it. They could say I was horse spit, and I might have been, but that was the worst of it.

Reggie Jackson

I credit Bobby Winkles for instilling the hustle ethic in me. Winkles wanted the game played *his* way, and he got what he wanted.

I tried out for the Arizona State team during the spring of my freshman year. Did it for a five-dollar bet with a guy in my dorm. There had been only one fair-skinned black player on the ASU baseball team, and Joe Paulsen bet me I couldn't make it. My plan was to make the team, collect my five dollars, and not play. So one day after spring football practice, I ran over to the baseball field with all my gear still on. Winkles agreed to watch me bat. I took off my helmet and shoulder pads, stepped up to the plate, and swung and missed a pitch or two. Fouled a few off. Then I hit a couple out of the park.

I made the team and didn't quit. You couldn't quit on Bobby Winkles. He was a tremendous teacher and motivator who demanded that you gave maximum effort at all times. Before long, he had me running back to the dugout after a strikeout—which was a lot of running, actually. After playing for Winkles, I never thought about taking it easy on a baseball field.

That's why I was so upset in 1977 when Billy Martin yanked me out of a game in Boston, in the middle of an inning, on national television. It was after I'd allowed a batter to get a double out of a bloop hit that fell in front of me. He sent Paul Blair out to right field to take my place, right on the spot. I might have been tentative on the play, and it might have looked bad, but I would never loaf after a ball. My manager should have known that. My teammates did—even the ones I wasn't getting along with.

Bob Gibson

I always ran hard to first base, which a lot of pitchers don't do. A reporter asked me one time, "Why do you run so hard on a ground ball?"

I said, "You know, I run three times a game from home to first, less than twice a week. Why *can't* I run hard?"

Reggie Jackson

It takes no ability to run hard. It takes ability to run *fast.* If you can run hard *and* fast, that's what you should do, every time.

Bob Gibson

Somebody might drop the ball. Strange things happen when you hustle. Everything you do, do it hard.

Now, with all that said, if there was a guy who could hit like Reggie and didn't run hard all the time, I'd still like to have him on my side.

Reggie Jackson

I would, too. But that would never be the case with me.

I saw Jimmy Leyland a while back and he introduced me to his family as a guy who played the game the way it should be played. I pride myself on comments like that—more than I do the long home runs I hit, or the three home runs in a World Series game. I even ran hard to first when I hit a ground ball back to the pitcher. Every time.

Hustle should be a habit. It should be a reflex, like shielding your eyes when you're looking into the sun. Hustle doesn't absolve you of your sins, but it helps. When I was in slumps, they didn't look so bad because I played hard, every play.

Sometimes, though, it can be prudent for a player to hold back a bit. I can understand a guy like Ken Griffey Jr. not running all-out on an easy ground ball, because he had three or four years when he just walked onto the field and got hurt. He'd swing and miss and break his toe. He'd jog to first on a base on balls and blow a hamstring. That guy would've had a shot at eight hundred home runs if his body hadn't broken down. I mean, he tore a hamstring *off the bone*. After a while, you're going to check yourself. You don't want to end your career on a tap back to the pitcher. But if you watch Griffey closely, you'll notice that he never goes half-speed after a fly ball or when he's trying to take an extra base. He hustles. It's just that, after the problems he's had with injuries, he hustles *smart*.

That's what a manager wants. I had hamstring issues, and I never let up because of them; but there are times when the good of the ball club has to outweigh your own personal pride. Dick Howser talked to me about that when he was managing the Yankees. I ran into a wall one day and he said, "Look, I want that shillelagh of yours to get to the plate." A shillelagh is like a wooden club, an Irish thing.

Bob Gibson

You've got to wear a kilt to swing one of those, don't you? I'd like to see that.

--- **Heart** ---

Reggie Jackson

We played hurt all the time. That was one of the first lessons I learned from Frank Robinson and Billy Williams. They both told me, "You don't get hurt. You realize that, right? You play every day." Hank Aaron used to tell his younger teammates that they needed to play 150 games a year.

When he advised me to be careful out there, Howser also said that if he had to mention something to the press about me not diving after a ball or some such, he'd be happy to do so. I appreciated that, but I couldn't change my style of play. I was going to slide, dive, fall, get hit by pitches, and I was *not* going to get hurt. My hamstrings didn't always understand that, but my heart did.

I owed that much to myself, the team, the owner, the fans, my family, and God. I was given the talent. It was my job to use it every day.

Bob Gibson

Of course, that was back then. There are still guys who play hurt and crash into fences and dive on their faces, but it's going out of style. With the agents and big investments and guaranteed contracts and medical staffs they have today, players are generally less inclined to put their bodies on the line.

And that's not all bad. It's less likely that you'll have somebody pitching on a broken leg, which is what I did until it popped in half. It was when Roberto Clemente hit me right above the ankle with a line drive. Of course, I didn't know it was broken at first. Our trainer, Bob Bauman, sprayed it with ethyl chloride and I told him he was spraying the wrong spot because that wasn't where it hurt. He told me to take a look, and there was a dent in my skin the shape of a baseball. Then he put a little tape on it and I threw a couple soft pitches and thought, all right, it's okay, let's go. I walked Willie Stargell, got Bill Mazeroski to pop up, and on a three-two pitch to Donn Clendenon I was trying to open up on a fastball and, pow, the fibula bone snapped in two. Today, I wouldn't have been out there after the line drive hit me. I'd have been taken somewhere for an X-ray. You don't even have to limp around; they just take you.

Anyway, for a few years afterwards, every young pitcher who came to the Cardinals heard that story. We didn't have many guys missing games with stiff necks or blisters on their feet.

Reggie Jackson

There are times when your body just can't handle it; but there's no question that players have different levels of tolerance. If a guy always has an excuse why he can't play, he probably doesn't have the heart to be great. He's too easily defeated. Give me the guy who will do whatever it takes to succeed, whatever the circumstances. Jeter comes to mind. When he's hurt, he won't tell anyone.

That was how my dad taught me. When he gave me a job, he didn't want to hear why I couldn't get it done. He was awfully proud when I became a big-league all-star, but I don't know if that made him any prouder than he was the day he sent me to the store for some Neapolitan ice cream.

We lived about half a block from an intersection with two grocery stores, a gas station and Fleischer's Drug Store, where you could get a cherry Coke or chocolate soda at the soda fountain. One evening my father sent me out for a pint of Neapolitan ice cream, which was about twenty-five cents at the time. I had a quarter, but Fleischer's didn't have any Neapolitan that day, so I went across the street to Kelso's Market and borrowed another quarter from Bob Kelso. Then I went to Bob Bradshaw, who owned the Mobil gas station—the big, red, flying Pegasus—and borrowed a quarter from him. With seventy-five cents now, I walked back across the street to Fleischer's and bought a pint of chocolate, a pint of vanilla, and a pint of strawberry. Then I ran back home and told my father, "Dad, they didn't have a pint of Neapolitan, but I got one of each. You owe Uncle Bob Kelso a quarter and you owe Mr. Bradshaw a quarter, too, because I had to borrow money from them."

He looked at me and said, "Good job, son. You did what you had to do."

That was the mentality that pervaded our household. I have an older brother who, now that we're grown up, is about half my size. But when I was ten or twelve and he was twenty, he'd whup my butt if I didn't get in the kitchen and do the dishes or take out the trash or whatever chores I was supposed to do.

Bob Gibson
Sometimes a little cuff behind the head really helps you focus.

Reggie Jackson

If he caught me not doing my job, my dad would instruct my oldest brother or my sister to get the strap and tell Reggie—or he called me Boone; that was a nickname I got from a guy who worked for him—to get on up the stairs and take his clothes off, get ready for "a lickin'." I'd be up in my bed, waiting, sniffling and crying. About two hours later he might have forgotten, but I'd still be crying in the bed, waiting for him.

It was the same way with playing ball. I had a job to do and I had to figure out how to get it done. I couldn't let anything stand in my way. My dad always said, "I don't want to hear any air-ay-boo."

Bob Gibson

What's *that*?

Reggie Jackson

That meant no stammering around, no making excuses. Old-school for "BS."

Bob Gibson

Sounds a lot like my brother bloodying my face and sending me back out there with a Band-Aid.

Reggie Jackson

Same thing. It's why a guy named Bob Gibson pitches to three batters on a broken leg! It's why I played through I don't know how many hamstring pulls. It's the culture we grew up with.

Now, a guy gets a hamstring and he's out two months. We were out a week or ten days, they'd wrap it, and there you go. I'd say that, by July, most players in the big leagues have something wrong with them. More than half your lineup has a ding somewhere that they're playing with, or sometimes—particularly these days, it seems—*not* playing with.

Today, technology finds more that's wrong with you. There are more ways of treating your aches, tweaks, and injuries, and more understanding of how much time you should take off. The technology we had was a guy who was someone's buddy who gave you a rubdown with analgesic balm, they called it, slapped a hot pack on you, and gave you some aspirin, or something like that. "All right, go get 'em!" We had a team doctor who came by a couple days a week, and that was pretty much it. Now the Yankees have a hand specialist, a shoulder specialist, a knee specialist, a general practitioner, a special-meds doctor, an eye doctor, a dentist . . . It's the Mayo Clinic. You name it, we've got it.

Bob Gibson

When I was a bullpen coach, the kids would complain about their sore arms and I'd say, "You know, I can tell you what causes that."

They'd say, "Yeah? Tell me, what is it?"

And I'd say, "*Pitching.* If you don't pitch, you don't have that."

I didn't worry about a little soreness when I played. It would go away after two or three days. Today you get a sore arm and they call it tendonitis. I guess I pitched with tendonitis. I don't know. All I can tell you is that I've been retired for more than thirty years and my arm still hurts.

One year, seventeen times in a row, I had my knee drained before I pitched that day. It would fill up with fluid, they'd drain it, I'd pitch, and after the game it would fill up again. But I wouldn't have it drained until the next time I pitched. You think they'd do that today?

Reggie Jackson

That would probably be an operation.

Bob Gibson

I did need one. It was cartilage, and I finally snapped it. I had the operation and pitched two more years on a knee without any cartilage to speak of.

But I'm not saying we were heroes or tough guys or anything like that. That's just the way it was. After a game I pitched—that night—everything was sore. I'd drag my right foot through that hole that you always dig out in front of the rubber, and it would be bloody by the time I got back to the clubhouse. I've still got a knot in the joint between my big toe and my foot. My knee was sore from bone crunching on bone. After I got into the season, my legs didn't bother me much—at least not when my knees were young. Arm-wise, I had more trouble with my elbow than my shoulder. My shoulder was always sore, but my elbow was sorer. Invariably, there'd be some guy who'd meet you and want to show you how strong he was by shaking your hand and grabbing you by the elbow. Man, that would hurt. It got to the point where guys would come to shake my hand and I'd put out my left and give them kind of a backhand shake. I'm sure my elbow wasn't as bad as Sandy Koufax's, but there were a lot of times when it was so sore I didn't want to brush my teeth. I should have learned to do it with my left.

The point is, playing through pain was a big part of the game. Don't get me wrong, though. If I were pitching today, I'm sure I'd welcome all the precautions they take.

Reggie Jackson

But even today, it's important for a superstar to suck it up and play through minor injuries, because all the young players take their cue from him. Leadership is more about what you *do* than what you say: the Jeter way.

In thirteen seasons, Derek Jeter has only once played fewer than 149 games. You see Albert Pujols limping around out there and playing Gold Glove first base with a messed-up arm, and he's never been in fewer than 143 games. And that's not to mention Cal Ripken.

With Ripken, you could always say never. He was never too sick, never too sore, never too tired, never had an excuse, never had a day off . . .

Bob Gibson

Leadership is wonderful and everything, but it's hard to demonstrate it from the disabled list.

When I was near the end of my career and Barney Schultz was our pitching coach, he wanted me to go out to the outfield and run with the rest of the guys. He said it would set a good example. I told him I'm sure it would, but I'm not helping the ball club if I'm out there pounding what's left of my knees to the extent that they won't get me through the next game. I'm thirty-nine years old and you want me out there running when my legs hurt? No, I'm not going to do that. It's the same thing that a player like Ken Griffey Jr. has gone through. No matter how much of a gamer a guy is, you need to make some concessions at that age.

But then there's this: Sometimes when a black player doesn't answer the bell he's considered a malingerer, as if he isn't actually hurt or can't deal with little aches and pains. There has always been an undercurrent to that effect, and at times it's been joked about. White guys, kiddingly, have said, "Come on, man, you're black, you know you can't be hurt."

It may be intended as humor, and even sympathetic, but there's something there beneath the surface. There's something they're *referring* to. It's the underlying notion that white guys play with more heart and character; black guys get by on natural ability.

I only wish I'd have realized that when I was a kid back in Omaha. I'd have mentioned it to Josh when he was bouncing ground balls off my face.

Grace (Under Pressure)

Bob Gibson

It's hard for me to explain how I was able to thrive under pressure. It was just in my makeup. It just happened.

It wasn't only in baseball; it was in basketball or anything I played or did. The bigger the game or moment, the more I was on top of it. When there was a pressure situation, I just always seemed to excel. It's like it was expected of me. At least, *I* expected it of me.

Reggie Jackson

When there's pressure, usually, there's also an unusual amount of attention from the outside. Everybody in the park—and sometimes, everybody in the country—is watching. That was a good scenario for me. I liked that. I *needed* that. It helped me focus.

I called those Reggie Moments.

Bob Gibson

We're both known for what we did in the World Series, and you'd think, because of that, that there must be something similar in our makeup. I'm sure there is, in terms of concentration and confidence and all that. But I don't think my feeling *about* those situations was much like Reggie's.

He thrived when all eyes were on him. I've heard people say that he's the best hitter there ever was when everybody was watching. That worked for him. I had success in the same types of situations, but for me that part of it was only incidental. It wasn't where I was coming from.

For me, the World Series was all on the field, and in the dugout with my teammates. It was us against them, for everything. It was the height of competition. *That's* what brought out the best in me.

Reggie Jackson

The World Series put you on a stage, and that was where I liked to be. I wanted to bring the crowd to its feet. I wanted to bring the *country* to its feet. Sometimes I did, sometimes I didn't. But I never ran from it. I ran *to* it.

There were moments like that during the regular season, too, when the game would heighten, grow to a crescendo, would come *get* me, but . . . I'm not proud to say it, but during the season I got bored sometimes. In the *post*season, I understood what it meant to win the game. I always yearned to somehow, some way, be a part of the victory. The postseason was do or die. I died sometimes, but I *did* a lot, too, because everything around me—all the trappings, all the intensity—forced me to focus and get my faculties gathered up for the moment.

Bob Gibson

Everybody reacts differently to pressure. I saw plenty of players who absolutely couldn't perform under it.

The Cardinals had an outfielder who, when he found out he was going to start Game Five of the 1968 World Series, went and sat in his locker facing the inside, scared to death. Everybody saw it. We all thought, what the hell is wrong with this guy? He had the chance of a lifetime to start in a World Series game. The World Series is the time to show what you can do, the greatest opportunity a ballplayer can have, it's where we've always hoped to be someday—our Carnegie Hall—and his ship comes in and he's *scared*. I couldn't understand that. To me, it just didn't compute.

I was nervous, too, in situations like that, but never scared. Hell no. And as soon as the game started, the nervousness left me. I might have played with more adrenaline than usual, but that's different than being nervous. A lot different.

Reggie Jackson

I didn't get nervous. I got intense. My sensitivities were enhanced. I had the ability to take the adrenaline, the focus, the intensity, and let it drive me.

All those feelings and emotions can hurt you if you don't get them in check. That's why I sometimes felt that I *survived* pressure situations more than I thrived in them. Once you acknowledge the pressure, it's something you have to deal with. I thrived in the spotlight, but I survived the pressure.

Bob Gibson

Pressure sort of felt right to me. I got accustomed to it by playing for Josh when I was a kid. I grew up under it. It wasn't World Series pressure, but I'm not sure it was any easier, either.

Josh absolutely wouldn't accept any kind of failure on my

part, or anything less than mental toughness. He imposed that toughness. He demanded it; and when my big brother demanded something of me, I did everything in my power to come through. It wasn't that he would beat me or criticize me if I didn't. He was just somebody I wanted badly to please, and when he told me to get the job done, I made damn sure I got the job done.

And the main job was being better than everyone else. Winning, in other words.

CHAPTER ELEVEN

FORTY YEARS OF CHANGE

Changes

Reggie Jackson

Baseball began to really change right around the time I got into it. I'm not saying that the events are related, just that I happened to be part of a very significant period in the game.

My first full year was 1968, and after the season they lowered the mound and shrunk the strike zone . . .

Bob Gibson

To me, the biggest effect of all that was the change in the environment. There had been a mutual ill will between pitchers and hitters, and when they started giving out warnings every time a pitch came inside off the plate, that element was taken away.

Reggie Jackson

I was Oakland's alternate player rep when Marvin Miller got us thinking about a labor strike in 1972 . . .

Bob Gibson

And then Gussie Busch sealed the deal with his remark about the players union: "We're not going to give them another god-damned cent. If they want to strike—let 'em."

Reggie Jackson

I was with the A's in 1973 when the American League introduced the designated hitter, which was pushed hard by Charlie Finley . . .

Bob Gibson

That went hand in hand with the umpire warnings. The upshot of the DH is that, since the pitcher doesn't come to bat, the only retaliation against him is to charge the mound. It changed the whole culture.

Reggie Jackson

I was Catfish Hunter's teammate when he took his contract with Finley to arbitration and became the first free agent . . .

Bob Gibson

Curt Flood should have been the first free agent. He was the martyr in the fight against the reserve clause.

Reggie Jackson

And after the 1976 season, I was in the first class of players eligible for the reentry draft. I was the first guy drafted, and ended up signing the largest contract.

Bob Gibson

At that point, there was no stopping Steinbrenner.

Steroids

Bob Gibson

I honestly don't know what I would have done if I'd been in the game when players were using steroids. You get pressured into that sort of thing if it becomes a matter of keeping up. If other players had been getting ahead of me by taking steroids, would I have done it? Maybe. Maybe.

Reggie Jackson

In spring training a year or so ago I was talking to Jason Lane, who was hoping to hang on as a part-time outfielder. He was telling me how difficult it was for him, being an extra player and having to compete for a roster spot against guys who were taking steroids. He blamed it on major-league baseball. His point was that the commissioner's office didn't monitor the situation closely enough, and it cost him a job. He believed that guys were outperforming him because they had taken steroids.

Probably true, and very sad.

Bob Gibson

I can sympathize with that. I can see where guys might feel penalized for staying clean. I can also see where some players might be compelled to do what they felt they had to do.

Steroids wouldn't have been a temptation for me in 1968 or 1970, when I was at my peak, but if I'd felt that my skills were slacking and there was something I could take to keep me around longer, that might have been a different matter. I would have been more tempted in 1974 or 1975, when my knees were shot and my legs were gone. But I don't know that drugs could have helped me at that point.

I have a harder time with players putting up career years and breaking records on steroids, if that's the case. But then, there's so incredibly much money at stake these days, and a whole lot of it goes to guys who hit home runs. The ballparks are smaller than they used to be, the strike zones are smaller, the highlights are on ESPN every night—everything is screaming for people to hit the ball out of the park. I'm sure, to a lot of players, the reward seems greater than the risk.

Reggie Jackson

I really believe that if Barry Bonds hadn't been shut out of the game—and they pitched to him—he'd still be winning home-run titles, steroids or not. He was unbelievable there for a while. He overmatched the league.

Bob Gibson

With his skills, it's hard to say where and how much steroids came into play. I remember when Bonds wasn't nearly as big and strong as he became later; but the thing is, he just doesn't miss the ball very much. He's got such a short stroke. He doesn't have that long, wild swing that most home-run hitters do. Has a great eye, besides.

Reggie Jackson

But when all is said and done, I can't overlook the fact that, with the advent of steroids in baseball, there were guys who didn't have power who suddenly got power. There were guys who didn't throw hard who suddenly threw hard. Then, after testing, they lose eight or nine miles an hour in one year.

So can you acquire performance? You certainly can acquire power. You can acquire a fastball. You can acquire strength. Steroids!

Bob Gibson

For pitchers, a big advantage would be that, with steroids, you might be able to last longer in a game. Instead of getting tired in the sixth inning, you're able to pitch eight or nine.

On the other hand, it's been a while since pitchers went eight or nine innings on a regular basis.

Reggie Jackson

If my father ever thought I'd used steroids, he'd have raised holy hell with me.

He was in the car with me during spring training in Fort Lauderdale one year when I was playing for the Yankees. I stopped at a little store to get three packs of Redman for Catfish Hunter, three packs of Levi Garrett for Ron Guidry, and a couple bags of sunflower seeds for myself. When I got back to the car, my dad was holding an empty beer can that had been under the seat. From there on, I couldn't get to the ballpark fast enough. He went on and on for two weeks about how you're going to embarrass your family name, people will think I haven't raised you properly, your brothers and sisters will all be ashamed if the police pull you over and you get arrested for drinking in the car . . . This was in the seventies, in the South. If they stopped a black man with an open beer can in the car, he was going to jail, pure and simple. Dad was right, as usual.

My father was crippled, so he had a beach chair that he sat in between the dugout and where I played in right field. He was friends with Steinbrenner, and George came to the game that day and walked down the foul line to talk to my dad. They talked for about three innings. I was scared to death that my dad was going to tell Steinbrenner that I had an open beer can in my car. I came out of the game and was running in the outfield and George still wouldn't leave. He just kept talking to my father. I was worried sick.

Anyway, I wouldn't have done steroids. Suppose I'd taken them and they had affected my God-given talent? Suppose the steroids, having been bought off the street, had changed me in a negative way?

No, thanks. God gave me a good body, and my side of the deal was to make the most of it. And be grateful for what I had.

Bob Gibson

It's not all that clear to me.

People in baseball have been cheating for years. Gaylord Perry threw spitballs. Don Sutton, same thing. That was illegal. So if they're in the Hall of Fame after throwing spitballs, how can you be punished for taking steroids when baseball didn't have any rules against it? They finally made it illegal, and that's fine, but I don't see how players can be penalized for what they did before the rules were in place.

Reggie Jackson

That's a good point, except that the use of steroids is against the law of the land, unless they're prescribed by a doctor. So why would it be legal in baseball? Why does baseball need a special rule that says you can't use steroids? Do I need a law that says, as a baseball player, I can't drive over the speed limit? If you're pulled over for speeding, you can't say I'm a ballplayer and I'm on my way to the game. That's how I view it.

But of the baseball guys who have apparently used steroids, none of them has been disciplined by the legal authorities. The courts of the land haven't punished Bonds, but the public court has. He's been judged guilty by the fans and media. He can't play anywhere.

Bob Gibson

Baseball is always talking about the integrity of the game. That term just might be a little bit of bull. The integrity of the game seems to be defined by how many people still come to the ballparks and watch on TV.

If a team signed Barry Bonds, it would have a major headache on its hands. Who'd want to deal with all the heat from the press and the public? It would jeopardize the integrity of the bottom line.

Reggie Jackson

The same arguments are going to come up when Bonds, Clemens, Rafael Palmeiro—any of the players publicly connected to performance-enhancing drugs—are eligible for election to the Hall of Fame. It'll be interesting to see how that plays out. I think we caught a little preview when Mark McGwire hit the ballot and fell so short of the votes he needed.

Bob Gibson

If I had a vote, I really don't know what I'd do. If performance-enhancing drugs are going to keep you out of the Hall of Fame, so be it. But then they have to keep out everybody who used them. Baseball didn't test during the time when most of these guys are implicated, so how do you determine who was using and who wasn't? What do you go by?

But then, how do you ban Pete Rose for gambling and give a pass to guys who used steroids? Gambling really has nothing to do with the outcome of a game unless you're throwing games yourself. Of course, the chance that you *can* throw a game is there, and the whole situation casts suspicion and erodes the public confidence in the sport. On top of that, baseball has always made it clear that gambling is strictly forbidden. It didn't do that for steroids. It opened the door to temptation.

Thankfully, I was out of there by that time.

Money

Reggie Jackson

More than anything else, money is what changed the whole dynamic of the game.

It impacts almost everything. The players have become so valuable that it has distorted the sport. There's an extraordinary amount of concern about the cost involved if they miss some time. As a result, hitters are overprotected and pitchers are overprotected. We've lost some of the spirit of the game.

Bob Gibson

We've lost a lot of what we've been talking about this whole time—that one-on-one battle from sixty feet and a half. The preoccupation with money has taken the edge off the competition.

I thrived on that competitive element to the game. I think it's what set me apart. With all the coddling today, I don't know that I'd be the same pitcher that I was forty years ago.

But I'd be a richer pitcher.

Reggie Jackson

I'm sure not going to sit here, though, and complain about free agency. It paid for my classic-car collection.

It's just that I've seen the Players Association evolve in a way that we didn't really intend it to. Back in 1972, we were fighting the owners for a piece of the pie. It was a genuine labor struggle. We didn't have a contract until 1968, and even then it didn't give us any rights to put ourselves in the open marketplace. The players were essentially owned. We were rebelling against being treated as property.

I believed vehemently in the cause. At the time, Marvin Miller was conducting meetings to familiarize us with what our options were, and he was surprised by how strongly a lot of us felt. I was radical about taking a stand. So were guys like Bob Boone, Tim McCarver, and Brooks Robinson.

Bob Gibson

Ray Sadecki was involved, too. I suspect that McCarver and Sadecki might have been influenced by having played on the Cardinals with Curt Flood. Flood was the one who paid the price by challenging the reserve clause in the Supreme Court, unsuccessfully—for *him*.

For that matter, they might have been influenced by having played under August Busch. It's interesting that Busch and Finley, maybe more than any of the others, were the owners who made the players feel the way we did.

Reggie Jackson

In Oakland, we certainly didn't feel as though we were treated fairly. That came to a head after the 1974 season, when Charlie O reneged on a deal he'd made with Catfish about deferring salary payments into an insurance account. Charlie found out he would lose a tax deduction if he did that, and refused. Hunter had been burned by Finley before, when Charlie changed his mind about a loan he'd given Catfish to buy a farm back in North Carolina. This time, Catfish wasn't giving any ground. He charged Charlie with breach of contract. When the arbitrator, Peter Seitz, determined that his agreement with the A's was no longer binding, Catfish essentially became a free agent. He signed with the Yankees for five years and more than $3 million.

The reserve clause wasn't really struck down for another year, when Seitz ruled in favor of the grievance filed by Andy Messersmith and Dave McNally. But I think Finley deserves some thanks, nevertheless. And Curt Flood, of course.

Bob Gibson

If I'd been about six or eight years younger . . .

Reggie Jackson

The mechanism for free agency was finally in place by the fall of 1976, and that's when my contract with the Orioles expired. (I'd spent one season in Baltimore after being traded by the A's.) Steinbrenner trotted me around New York, hustled me in Chicago, and signed me for five years and $2.9 million.

These days, that wouldn't pay for a backup catcher.

Bob Gibson

At that point, things weren't out of whack yet. They were just getting *in* whack.

Reggie Jackson

My salary never reached a million a year in New York. That happened when I was with the Angels.

I bought more antique cars and a house in the same neighborhood as Clint Eastwood, my favorite cowboy and cop.

Pitch Counts

Bob Gibson

If I were a pitching coach today, I'd probably have my starters on a pitch count. Because the manager would tell me to. Because the general manager would tell *him* to. You can't just go off and be a maverick these days. You can't buck the system that the whole game has bought into. There's too much money involved.

That aside, the pitch count is about the most ridiculous thing I can imagine.

I know they've got studies to show that certain pitchers are less effective from the hundredth pitch on, or the hundred and tenth, or whatever, and their risk of injury increases after such and such a point. I respect all that. I also realize that kids today don't throw as much as we did before everybody started spending their summers in air-conditioning, and their arms don't build up endurance like mine did, or Warren Spahn's; and that, as far as their workloads go, pitchers are brought along slowly in the minor leagues because teams are tired of losing their future starters before they even get to the majors; and that the moment a young guy goes down with an elbow or shoulder injury, people are waving statistics in the manager's face and calling for his scalp. I get all that.

But I'm thinking about playing, I don't know, the Giants, and it's 1–1 going into the eighth inning with Mays, McCovey, and Jim Ray Hart coming up, and Red Schoendienst plops down next to me in the dugout and says, "Nice job, Hoot. We'll let Hoerner take it from here."

You'll *what*?

I just can't imagine it.

Reggie Jackson

They design the staff now with just that in mind. There's not a Gibson in the rotation, where the manager can figure that this guy's going to give him thirty to thirty-five starts, with twenty to twenty-five complete games . . .

The staff then was ten pitchers, not twelve. They didn't need to save a slot or two for the sixth and seventh innings. Now they have middle relievers making two, three, four million a year just to get to the guy who's making four or five or six million to get to the closer, who's making eight or ten or fifteen million. Who would have thought?

Bob Gibson

Those dollars dictate a lot of it. When they're paying a guy millions of bucks to pitch the seventh inning, by golly, he's *going* to pitch the seventh inning.

Reggie Jackson

Nobody throws nine innings anymore on a regular basis, except Roy Halladay, C. C. Sabathia, and maybe a couple other rare pitchers. Even for those guys, the inning totals are not close to what Gibson, Koufax, Drysdale, and a lot of pitchers used to put up year after year. Go figure.

Bob Gibson

These days, if a guy reaches 105 pitches or whatever, they're looking to get him out of the game. The other team knows that. Some organizations instruct their hitters to take pitches, run up the count, and get the starter out of there.

That's not much of a ballgame to me. And you're sure not going to chase me by keeping the bat on your shoulder. You'll be seeing a lot of strikes.

I just have a hard time believing that you're going to save a guy's career by putting him on a strict pitch count. They can cite all the studies they want, and I'll cite Tom Seaver, who pitched over 250 innings eleven times and stayed healthy enough to win 311 games. I'll cite Juan Marichal, who pitched 326 innings one year and came back the next year to win twenty-one games. I'll cite Jim Palmer, who pitched more than 315 innings three years in a row and won twenty-one the year after *that*. I'll cite Steve Carlton, who pitched 346 innings the year he won twenty-seven for the Phillies. I'll cite Gaylord Perry, who pitched over three hundred innings six times in a period of seven years, and kept going until he was forty-four. I'll cite Ferguson Jenkins, who over a nine-year stretch never pitched fewer than 270 innings. Nobody *this century* has pitched 270 innings in a season.

The surprising thing about it is that training and conditioning methods have advanced tremendously. It's a science now. Teams spend enormous amounts of money to target all the right body parts and get everybody in prime shape so they don't get hurt. A lot of players take it further by hiring high-priced personal trainers.

And pitchers can't make it to the eighth inning. Or the teams won't let them.

Reggie Jackson

I remember a game when Spahn and Marichal hooked up for sixteen innings. It was 1963, when Spahn was forty-two years old. He pitched 259 innings that year and won twenty-three games. But not that one. Mays beat him with a home run in the bottom of the sixteenth.

They were talking about it one time in Cooperstown. Spahn and Marichal must have been fifty feet away from each other having this conversation, and we were all listening in awe. Marichal told him, "I didn't want to keep going out there."

Spahn said, "Well, why didn't you stop?"

And Marichal said, "You were forty-two years old and I was twenty-five. I wasn't going to let some old man outpitch me!"

Then Willie stood up and said, in that high-pitched voice of his, "You remember how that game ended?"

And Spahn said, "Well, you were one-for-six!"

Bob Gibson

I never pitched sixteen innings, but we didn't give a second thought to going ten or twelve. The most I threw was fourteen one night in 1970. That was 197 pitches.

Reggie Jackson

I saw Nolan Ryan throw 212 pitches in eleven innings one day at Yankee Stadium. It messed him up so bad that he had to retire sixteen years later, when he was forty-six.

Didn't miss a start. They moved him back a day, maybe.

Bob Gibson

Why would he miss a start? He's a big, strong fellow.

I'd normally throw about 130 pitches. We counted them. But we weren't ruled by the number.

In 1965, I already had twelve complete games, including the two previous starts, when I pitched thirteen innings against the Giants in St. Louis and Tom Haller, their catcher, beat me with a two-run homer.

In 1968, I had twelve straight complete games at one point and went into extra innings five times over the course of the season. I started thirty-four times that year and never pitched less than seven innings. From my third start on, I averaged just *over* nine innings a start.

In 1969, I finished the season with a stretch of nine, nine, ten, nine and two-thirds, ten and a third, nine, and twelve innings.

In 1970, I had another streak of a dozen complete games, *then* went fourteen innings.

But we were on a five-day rotation. A lot of teams back then had their starters going every fourth day. I used to complain about it—especially late in the season if we were trying to win a pennant. I didn't want to wait five days to get back out there. Sometimes they'd listen.

Reggie Jackson

Catfish had forty starts a couple times. In a span of two years—his last season in Oakland and his first in New York—he had eighty starts, pitched almost 650 innings, and won forty-eight games.

Think about what he did in 1975, when Bill Virdon and Billy Martin managed the Yankees. He pitched 328 innings in thirty-nine starts that year. That's over eight innings a start. In the games he started, there were only *sixteen innings all year* that he didn't pitch. Five of those were from a game at Detroit in April, when he was knocked out after three innings.

The next season, Billy pitched him nearly three hundred innings again.

And people wonder why Catfish's career didn't last longer than it did. He only pitched another four years, and never again won twenty games. As great as he was, Catfish won only two games after the age of thirty-two. It's pretty obvious why.

Bob Gibson

But he was a workhorse for a period of ten years. Over those ten years, he *averaged* 277 innings a season. Do you know the last guy to pitch at least 277 innings in a season? Charlie Hough in 1987. Knuckleballer.

And please don't tell me that pitchers today have more strain on their arms. Hey, I threw sliders, too. Catfish threw sliders. Neither one of us was in the habit of letting up.

Don't get me wrong; I'm not claiming that we were better men than the pitchers today. I'm sure there are guys out there now who would go three hundred innings if their managers allowed them to. I'm sure there are guys who would *love* to do that.

But that's not how they play the game anymore.

Evolution

Reggie Jackson

We didn't have the advantage of breaking down our swings on digital video. It's amazing what players can watch now on their computers. With a keystroke, they can pull up all their good at-bats, all their bad at-bats, or all their at-bats against A. J. Burnett on weeknights in May with a forty percent chance of thunderstorms. If the Red Sox bring in Jonathan Papelbon for the ninth inning, Derek Jeter can duck into the clubhouse and quickly run through the last two or three or seventeen times he hit against him. As you watch the tape—I still call it that—you can pause it, slow it down, or set it to a Simon & Garfunkel song. You can even run two at-bats side by side, frame by frame, to examine the differences. If you ground out to shortstop, you can jog straight from first base, through the dugout, to wherever the laptop is set up, and see for yourself what just happened. Teams have full-time video coordinators who gather all this together for the players—whatever they want.

I think it helps. Tony Gwynn could add ten points to his batting average every time there was a technological advance in the study of hitting. I've looked at video, and even an old-timer like me is able to read it fairly well.

But every time I watch myself, I wonder how the heck I ever hit the ball.

Bob Gibson

To me, video is more useful for scouting *yourself* than your opponent. If I'm having a good day, I don't care how many or what kind of tapes you've been watching; I think I can still get you out.

Reggie Jackson

I'd agree with that. I'd use it for adjusting myself more than studying the pitcher. You're not worried about the pitcher's mechanics; you just want to know where the ball is coming from and what kind of movement it has—the things you pick up by actually batting against the guy.

But if it's somebody you haven't seen before, it sure can't hurt to watch some tape on him. The best scout in the game is the video camera. You no longer have to depend on what somebody thinks he saw. Video gets it right. It enables you to actually visualize yourself standing in the batter's box against Josh Beckett.

Now, with MLB's live satellite feed, you can sit at home in an overstuffed chair, or in the clubhouse eating Raisin Bran, and watch virtually any game that's being played. Each one of them comes with a former player or manager or expert of some sort who breaks down practically every pitcher and hitter. It's all right there for you.

This is not your father's scouting report.

Bob Gibson

It beats word of mouth and a few scribbles on a piece of paper. I'm glad the Yankees didn't have digital technology before the '64 World Series, or the Red Sox in '67 or the Tigers in '68.

Reggie Jackson

Still, the biggest difference to me is not the electronics involved. It's the fact that hitting is now viewed as a science.

Guys like Ted Williams and Rogers Hornsby may have looked at it that way, but there wasn't much hitting instruction when I was a young player. The dynamics of how, technically, to swing the bat, or how to hit a particular pitcher, just weren't thought about like they are now. A lot of players read Williams's book (*The Science of Hitting*) after it came out in 1971, but in general we didn't yet have the knowledge of how to dissect and decipher the mechanics of the game. It was more a case of whether you could hit or not.

Bob Gibson

On top of that, there's all the analysis now by numbers. The statistics available for every player these days are mind-boggling. You can just flip around on your computer a little bit and come up with something like a guy's batting average for the balls he actually puts in play, or the percentage of line drives he hits. I'm not sure what all that tells you, but it's right there on your screen. You can get a pitcher's ERA adjusted for the ballpark he pitches in. You can find out what your won-loss record would have been if some of the stuff you couldn't control—like run support, relief pitching, that sort of thing—had turned out exactly average. I saw somewhere that, in 1968, I should have been 28–4 instead of 22–9.

But there were no instructions on how to apply for the back pay.

Reggie Jackson

It's ironic: Now that we can *see* more baseball than we ever could, it seems like fewer and fewer people—outsiders, anyway—are actually using their eyes to evaluate players.

Bob Gibson

There's another effect of all the games on TV. A lot more players these days have started thinking of themselves as stars.

In my day, guys didn't do that much strutting or showboating. They knew better. Really, the only one was Willie Montañez. He'd hit a home run and he'd veer all the way over in front of the other dugout when he was circling the bases.

Reggie took being a star to a different level—he was known for that famous quote, "the magnitude of me"—and he sort of refined the home-run trot; but that was just *Reggie.* He was an original. The guys today are poor imitations. Every other second baseman has his own trot.

And the hell of it is, if you try to spot a fastball to put a guy in his place, he wants to fight you and the umpire wants to throw you out.

Reggie Jackson

Plus, the batter's standing in there wearing armor up and down his body.

Bob Gibson

That doesn't bother me. I think I could break some of it.

Reggie Jackson

I just don't like the look of it. I think the game should be played the way it was meant to be played.

When I watched Mantle, when I watched Aaron and Mays, the dream was to wear the major-league uniform and look like one of the great players. They weren't up there with battle armor and two gloves on. I wouldn't do it if I played today. If they made me wear an ear flap, I'd get used to the rules and wear it; but I really don't like all the gingerbread that goes with the armor and the gloves.

Bob Gibson

The extra padding, to me, is just another little thing that chips away at the basic nature of baseball. But I'm not concerned that it gives the hitter an advantage. If a pitcher makes good pitches, he'll get most guys out. The protection might make a batter feel a little more comfortable at the plate, which goes against my grain, but it doesn't matter that much. There are bigger issues than that.

Reggie Jackson

I just never like it when they mess with what I consider to be the natural order of the game—the war between the batter and the pitcher. Retaliation is a part of that. When you allow a guy to go up to the plate in a suit of armor, you're interfering with the natural process of retaliation.

Bob Gibson

We old guys tend to think that the natural order of the game is the way it was when *we* played it. Maybe we shouldn't get too caught up in thinking that our time is the standard for everything.

I could grumble, for example, that they've messed with the baseball itself. I was playing in a fantasy camp in Arizona once, and a guy gave me a sixty-mile-an-hour fastball that I hit over a twenty-foot-high fence more than four hundred feet away in dead center field. I was in my fifties. I couldn't hit a ball that far in my *twenties*. I was using an aluminum bat, and I'm sure that accounted for some of it, but there was no doubt in my mind that the ball was a whole lot livelier than the one we played with.

Who's to say, though, that ours was superior to the one they use today?

Reggie Jackson

Better the ball be juiced than the players.

Bob Gibson

There are two separate areas in all of this. There's the spirit of the game and there's the integrity of the game. If you sit on the back porch of the Otesaga Hotel in Cooperstown, shooting the bull with Hall of Famers, you'll hear some guys who are concerned about one and some guys who are concerned about the other and some guys who are concerned about both. You won't hear many old-timers who aren't concerned about either.

Steroids undermine the integrity of the game. I'd just as soon leave that one for other people to negotiate, because integrity, to me, is a briar patch.

It's the *spirit* of the game that I'm worried about.

Reggie Jackson

Put me down for both.

ACKNOWLEDGMENTS

The authors would like to acknowledge David Black, for pulling it all together; Bill Thomas, for his vision; Reggie's associate, Frank Perry; Reggie's boss, The Boss, George Steinbrenner; and Dennis Tuttle, Lonnie's sounding board. Reggie would also like to thank the individual who recruited him for this project, "arguably the greatest right-handed pitcher of all time, and the one I most admire." All agree that it has been an honor.